101 Infallible Reasons Why We Desperately Need Religion

Micah

Novelty-Land Books
ISBN: 9781089182764
Title: *101 Infallible Reasons Why We Desperately Need Religion*
Author: Micah
Digital distribution | 2019
Paperback Edition | 2019

Dedication:

I'd like to start off by thanking every Religious person who is wholeheartedly against LGBT rights because of the Bible and the Koran. I'd like to thank each religion, from the Jews, the chosen people who Genocided the Canaanites in name of their faith, to the Christians and their Crusades, to the radical Islam movement we see today, yet oddly enough, each religious person of a faith claims that their faith is the most persecuted. I'd like to thank the three major religions in this world for claiming they are correct, even though Hinduism and the Chinese have been around longer. I would especially like to give thanks to whatever new Global religion will be the most popular in 1000 years from now, we have set the trend for you. Yet despite all of this, I found myself driven to compile this list of 101 reasons why we absolutely MUST keep religion if we are to move towards an age of peace.

Chapter 1: Why keeping our strong belief in our Religions will end us up in Peace eventually.

It fucking won't. It fucking won't. It fucking won't.
It fucking won't. It fucking won't. It fucking won't.
It fucking won't. It fucking won't. It fucking won't.
It fucking won't. It fucking won't. It fucking won't.
It fucking won't. It fucking won't. It fucking won't.
It fucking won't. It fucking won't. It fucking won't.
It fucking won't. It fucking won't. It fucking won't.
It fucking won't. It fucking won't. It fucking won't.
It fucking won't. It fucking won't. It fucking won't.
It fucking won't. It fucking won't. It fucking won't.
It fucking won't. It fucking won't. It fucking won't.
It fucking won't. It fucking won't. It fucking won't.
It fucking won't. It fucking won't. It fucking won't.
It fucking won't. It fucking won't. It fucking won't.
It fucking won't. It fucking won't. It fucking won't.
It fucking won't. It fucking won't. It fucking won't.
It fucking won't. It fucking won't. It fucking won't.
It fucking won't. It fucking won't. It fucking won't.
It fucking won't. It fucking won't. It fucking won't.
It fucking won't. It fucking won't. It fucking won't.
It fucking won't. It fucking won't. It fucking won't.
It fucking won't. It fucking won't. It fucking won't.
It fucking won't. It fucking won't. It fucking   It
fucking won't. It fucking won't. It fucking won't. It
fucking won't. It fucking won't. It fucking won't. It
fucking won't. It fucking won't. It fucking won't. It
fucking won't. It fucking won't. It fucking won't. It
fucking won't. It fucking won't. It fucking It fucking
won't. It fucking won't. It fucking won't. It fucking
won't. It fucking won't. It fucking won't. It fucking
won't. It fucking won't. It fucking won't.

won't. It fucking won't. It fucking won't. It fucking
won't. It fucking won't. It fucking won't. It fucking
won't. It fucking won't. It fucking won't. It fucking
won't. It fucking won't. It fucking won't. It fucking
won't. It fucking won't. It fucking won't. It fucking
won't. It fucking won't. It fucking won't. It fucking
won't. It fucking won't. It fucking won't. It fucking
won't. It fucking won't. It fucking won't. It fucking
won't. It fucking won't. It fucking won't. It fucking
won't. It fucking won't. It fucking won't. It fucking
won't. It fucking won't. It fucking won't. It fucking
won't. It fucking won't. It fucking won't. It fucking
won't. It fucking won't. It fucking won't. It fucking
won't. It fucking won't. It fucking won't. It fucking
won't. It fucking won't. It fucking won't. It fucking
won't. It fucking won't. It fucking won't. It fucking
won't. It fucking won't. It fucking won't. It fucking
won't. It fucking won't. It fucking won't. It fucking
won't. It fucking won't. It fucking won't. It fucking
won't. It fucking won't. It fucking won't. It fucking
won't. It fucking won't. It fucking won't. It fucking
won't. It fucking won't. It fucking won't. It fucking
won't. It fucking won't. It fucking won't. It fucking
won't. It fucking won't. It fucking won't. It fucking
won't. It fucking won't. It fucking won't. It fucking
won't. It fucking won't. It fucking won't. It fucking
won't. It fucking won't. It fucking won't. It fucking
won't. It fucking won't. It fucking won't. It fucking
won't. It fucking won't. It fucking won't. It fucking
won't. It fucking won't. It fucking won't. It fucking

won't. It fucking won't. It fucking won't. It fucking
won't. It fucking won't. It fucking won't. It fucking
won't. It fucking won't. It fucking won't. It fucking
won't. It fucking won't. It fucking won't. It fucking
won't. It fucking won't. It fucking won't. It fucking
won't. It fucking won't. It fucking won't. It fucking
won't. It fucking won't. It fucking won't. It fucking
won't. It fucking won't. It fucking won't. It fucking
won't. It fucking won't. It fucking won't. It fucking
won't. It fucking won't. It fucking won't. It fucking
won't. It fucking won't. It fucking won't. It fucking
won't. It fucking won't. It fucking won't. It fucking
won't. It fucking won't. It fucking won't. It fucking
won't. It fucking won't. It fucking won't. It fucking
won't. It fucking won't. It fucking won't. It fucking
won't. It fucking won't. It fucking won't. It fucking
won't. It fucking won't. It fucking won't. It fucking
won't. It fucking won't. It fucking won't. It fucking
won't. It fucking won't. It fucking won't. It fucking
won't. It fucking won't. It fucking won't. It fucking
won't. It fucking won't. It fucking won't. It fucking
won't. It fucking won't. It fucking won't. It fucking
won't. It fucking won't. It fucking won't. It fucking
won't. It fucking won't. It fucking won't. It fucking
won't. It fucking won't. It fucking won't. It fucking
won't. It fucking won't. It fucking won't. It fucking
won't. It fucking won't. It fucking won't. It fucking
won't. It fucking won't. It fucking won't. It fucking
won't. It fucking won't. It fucking won't. It fucking
won't. It fucking won't. It fucking won't. It fucking

won't. It fucking won't. It fucking won't. It fucking
won't. It fucking won't. It fucking won't. It fucking
won't. It fucking won't. It fucking won't. It fucking
won't. It fucking won't. It fucking won't. It fucking
won't. It fucking won't. It fucking won't. It fucking
won't. It fucking won't. It fucking won't. It fucking
won't. It fucking won't. It fucking won't. It fucking
won't. It fucking won't. It fucking won't. It fucking
won't. It fucking won't. It fucking won't. It fucking
won't. It fucking won't. It fucking won't. It fucking
won't. It fucking won't. It fucking won't. It fucking
won't. It fucking won't. It fucking won't. It fucking
won't. It fucking won't. It fucking won't. It fucking
won't. It fucking won't. It fucking won't. It fucking
won't. It fucking won't. It fucking won't. It fucking
won't. It fucking won't. It fucking won't. It fucking
won't. It fucking won't. It fucking won't. It fucking
won't. It fucking won't. It fucking won't. It fucking
won't. It fucking won't. It fucking won't. It fucking
won't. It fucking won't. It fucking won't. It fucking
won't. It fucking won't. It fucking won't. It fucking
won't. It fucking won't. It fucking won't. It fucking
won't. It fucking won't. It fucking won't. It fucking
won't. It fucking won't. It fucking won't. It fucking
won't. It fucking won't. It fucking won't. It fucking
won't. It fucking won't. It fucking won't. It fucking
won't. It fucking won't. It fucking won't. It fucking
won't. It fucking won't. It fucking won't. It fucking
won't. It fucking won't. It fucking won't. It fucking
won't. It fucking won't. It fucking won't. It fucking
won't. It fucking won't. It fucking won't. It fucking

won't. It fucking won't. It fucking won't. It fucking
won't. It fucking won't. It fucking won't. It fucking
won't. It fucking won't. It fucking won't. It fucking
won't. It fucking won't. It fucking won't. It fucking
won't. It fucking won't. It fucking won't. It fucking
won't. It fucking won't. It fucking won't. It fucking
won't. It fucking won't. It fucking won't. It fucking
won't. It fucking won't. It fucking won't. It fucking
won't. It fucking won't. It fucking won't. It fucking
won't. It fucking won't. It fucking won't. It fucking
won't. It fucking won't. It fucking won't. It fucking
won't. It fucking won't. It fucking won't. It fucking
won't. It fucking won't. It fucking won't. It fucking
won't. It fucking won't. It fucking won't. It fucking
won't. It fucking won't. It fucking won't. It fucking
won't. It fucking won't. It fucking won't. It fucking
won't. It fucking won't. It fucking won't. It fucking
won't. It fucking won't. It fucking won't. It fucking
won't. It fucking won't. It fucking won't. It fucking
won't. It fucking won't. It fucking won't. It fucking
won't. It fucking won't. It fucking won't. It fucking
won't. It fucking won't. It fucking won't. It fucking
won't. It fucking won't. It fucking won't. It fucking
won't. It fucking won't. It fucking won't. It fucking
won't. It fucking won't. It fucking won't. It fucking
won't. It fucking won't. It fucking won't. It fucking
won't. It fucking won't. It fucking won't. It fucking
won't. It fucking won't. It fucking won't. It fucking
won't. It fucking won't. It fucking won't. It fucking
won't. It fucking won't. It fucking won't. It fucking

won't. It fucking won't. It fucking won't. It fucking
won't. It fucking won't. It fucking won't. It fucking
won't. It fucking won't. It fucking won't. It fucking
won't. It fucking won't. It fucking won't. It fucking
won't. It fucking won't. It fucking won't. It fucking
won't. It fucking won't. It fucking won't. It fucking
won't. It fucking won't. It fucking won't. It fucking
won't. It fucking won't. It fucking won't. It fucking
won't. It fucking won't. It fucking won't. It fucking
won't. It fucking won't. It fucking won't. It fucking
won't. It fucking won't. It fucking won't. It fucking
won't. It fucking won't. It fucking won't. It fucking
won't. It fucking won't. It fucking won't. It fucking
won't. It fucking won't. It fucking won't. It fucking
won't. It fucking won't. It fucking won't. It fucking
won't. It fucking won't. It fucking won't. It fucking
won't. It fucking won't. It fucking won't. It fucking
won't. It fucking won't. It fucking won't. It fucking
won't. It fucking won't. It fucking won't. It fucking
won't. It fucking won't. It fucking won't. It fucking
won't. It fucking won't. It fucking won't. It fucking
won't. It fucking won't. It fucking won't. It fucking
won't. It fucking won't. It fucking won't. It fucking
won't. It fucking won't. It fucking won't. It fucking
won't. It fucking won't. It fucking won't. It fucking
won't. It fucking won't. It fucking won't. It fucking
won't. It fucking won't. It fucking won't. It fucking
won't. It fucking won't. It fucking won't. It fucking
won't. It fucking won't. It fucking won't. It fucking
won't. It fucking won't. It fucking won't. It fucking
won't. It fucking won't. It fucking won't. It fucking

won't. It fucking won't. It fucking won't. It fucking
won't. It fucking won't. It fucking won't. It fucking
won't. It fucking won't. It fucking won't. It fucking
won't. It fucking won't. It fucking won't. It fucking
won't. It fucking won't. It fucking won't. It fucking
won't. It fucking won't. It fucking won't. It fucking
won't. It fucking won't. It fucking won't. It fucking
won't. It fucking won't. It fucking won't. It fucking
won't. It fucking won't. It fucking won't. It fucking
won't. It fucking won't. It fucking won't. It fucking
won't. It fucking won't. It fucking won't. It fucking
won't. It fucking won't. It fucking won't. It fucking
won't. It fucking won't. It fucking won't. It fucking
won't. It fucking won't. It fucking won't. It fucking
won't. It fucking won't. It fucking won't. It fucking
won't. It fucking won't. It fucking won't. It fucking
won't. It fucking won't. It fucking won't. It fucking
won't. It fucking won't. It fucking won't. It fucking
won't. It fucking won't. It fucking won't. It fucking
won't. It fucking won't. It fucking won't. It fucking
won't. It fucking won't. It fucking won't. It fucking
won't. It fucking won't. It fucking won't. It fucking
won't. It fucking won't. It fucking won't. It fucking
won't. It fucking won't. It fucking won't. It fucking
won't. It fucking won't. It fucking won't. It fucking
won't. It fucking won't. It fucking won't. It fucking
won't. It fucking won't. It fucking won't. It fucking
won't. It fucking won't. It fucking won't. It fucking
won't. It fucking won't. It fucking won't. It fucking
won't. It fucking won't. It fucking won't. It fucking

won't. It fucking won't. It fucking won't. It fucking
won't. It fucking won't. It fucking won't. It fucking
won't. It fucking won't. It fucking won't. It fucking
won't. It fucking won't. It fucking won't. It fucking
won't. It fucking won't. It fucking won't. It fucking
won't. It fucking won't. It fucking won't. It fucking
won't. It fucking won't. It fucking won't. It fucking
won't. It fucking won't. It fucking won't. It fucking
won't. It fucking won't. It fucking won't. It fucking
won't. It fucking won't. It fucking won't. It fucking
won't. It fucking won't. It fucking won't. It fucking
won't. It fucking won't. It fucking won't. It fucking
won't. It fucking won't. It fucking won't. It fucking
won't. It fucking won't. It fucking won't. It fucking
won't. It fucking won't. It fucking won't. It fucking
won't. It fucking won't. It fucking won't. It fucking
won't. It fucking won't. It fucking won't. It fucking
won't. It fucking won't. It fucking won't. It fucking
won't. It fucking won't. It fucking won't. It fucking
won't. It fucking won't. It fucking won't. It fucking
won't. It fucking won't. It fucking won't. It fucking
won't. It fucking won't. It fucking won't. It fucking
won't. It fucking won't. It fucking won't. It fucking
won't. It fucking won't. It fucking won't. It fucking
won't. It fucking won't. It fucking won't. It fucking
won't. It fucking won't. It fucking won't. It fucking
won't. It fucking won't. It fucking won't. It fucking
won't. It fucking won't. It fucking won't. It fucking
won't. It fucking won't. It fucking won't. It fucking
won't. It fucking won't. It fucking won't. It fucking

won't. It fucking won't. It fucking won't. It fucking
won't. It fucking won't. It fucking won't. It fucking
won't. It fucking won't. It fucking won't. It fucking
won't. It fucking won't. It fucking won't. It fucking
won't. It fucking won't. It fucking won't. It fucking
won't. It fucking won't. It fucking won't. It fucking
won't. It fucking won't. It fucking won't. It fucking
won't. It fucking won't. It fucking won't. It fucking
won't. It fucking won't. It fucking won't. It fucking
won't. It fucking won't. It fucking won't. It fucking
won't. It fucking won't. It fucking won't. It fucking
won't. It fucking won't. It fucking won't. It fucking
won't. It fucking won't. It fucking won't. It fucking
won't. It fucking won't. It fucking won't. It fucking
won't. It fucking won't. It fucking won't. It fucking
won't. It fucking won't. It fucking won't. It fucking
won't. It fucking won't. It fucking won't. It fucking
won't. It fucking won't. It fucking won't. It fucking
won't. It fucking won't. It fucking won't. It fucking
won't. It fucking won't. It fucking won't. It fucking
won't. It fucking won't. It fucking won't. It fucking
won't. It fucking won't. It fucking won't. It fucking
won't. It fucking won't. It fucking won't. It fucking
won't. It fucking won't. It fucking won't. It fucking
won't. It fucking won't. It fucking won't. It fucking
won't. It fucking won't. It fucking won't. It fucking
won't. It fucking won't. It fucking won't. It fucking
won't. It fucking won't. It fucking won't. It fucking
won't. It fucking won't. It fucking won't. It fucking
won't. It fucking won't. It fucking won't. It fucking

won't. It fucking won't. It fucking won't. It fucking
won't. It fucking won't. It fucking won't. It fucking
won't. It fucking won't. It fucking won't. It fucking
won't. It fucking won't. It fucking won't. It fucking
won't. It fucking won't. It fucking won't. It fucking
won't. It fucking won't. It fucking won't. It fucking
won't. It fucking won't. It fucking won't. It fucking
won't. It fucking won't. It fucking won't. It fucking
won't. It fucking won't. It fucking won't. It fucking
won't. It fucking won't. It fucking won't. It fucking
won't. It fucking won't. It fucking won't. It fucking
won't. It fucking won't. It fucking won't. It fucking
won't. It fucking won't. It fucking won't. It fucking
won't. It fucking won't. It fucking won't. It fucking
won't. It fucking won't. It fucking won't. It fucking
won't. It fucking won't. It fucking won't. It fucking
won't. It fucking won't. It fucking won't. It fucking
won't. It fucking won't. It fucking won't. It fucking
won't. It fucking won't. It fucking won't. It fucking
won't. It fucking won't. It fucking won't. It fucking
won't. It fucking won't. It fucking won't. It fucking
won't. It fucking won't. It fucking won't. It fucking
won't. It fucking won't. It fucking won't. It fucking
won't. It fucking won't. It fucking won't. It fucking
won't. It fucking won't. It fucking won't. It fucking
won't. It fucking won't. It fucking won't. It fucking
won't. It fucking won't. It fucking won't. It fucking
won't. It fucking won't. It fucking won't. It fucking
won't. It fucking won't. It fucking won't. It fucking
won't. It fucking won't. It fucking won't. It fucking

won't. It fucking won't. It fucking won't. It fucking
won't. It fucking won't. It fucking won't. It fucking
won't. It fucking won't. It fucking won't. It fucking
won't. It fucking won't. It fucking won't. It fucking
won't. It fucking won't. It fucking won't. It fucking
won't. It fucking won't. It fucking won't. It fucking
won't. It fucking won't. It fucking won't. It fucking
won't. It fucking won't. It fucking won't. It fucking
won't. It fucking won't. It fucking won't. It fucking
won't. It fucking won't. It fucking won't. It fucking
won't. It fucking won't. It fucking won't. It fucking
won't. It fucking won't. It fucking won't. It fucking
won't. It fucking won't. It fucking won't. It fucking
won't. It fucking won't. It fucking won't. It fucking
won't. It fucking won't. It fucking won't. It fucking
won't. It fucking won't. It fucking won't. It fucking
won't. It fucking won't. It fucking won't. It fucking
won't. It fucking won't. It fucking won't. It fucking
won't. It fucking won't. It fucking won't. It fucking
won't. It fucking won't. It fucking won't. It fucking
won't. It fucking won't. It fucking won't. It fucking
won't. It fucking won't. It fucking won't. It fucking
won't. It fucking won't. It fucking won't. It fucking
won't. It fucking won't. It fucking won't. It fucking
won't. It fucking won't. It fucking won't. It fucking
won't. It fucking won't. It fucking won't. It fucking
won't. It fucking won't. It fucking won't. It fucking
won't. It fucking won't. It fucking won't. It fucking
won't. It fucking won't. It fucking won't. It fucking
won't. It fucking won't. It fucking won't. It fucking

won't. It fucking won't. It fucking won't. It fucking
won't. It fucking won't. It fucking won't. It fucking
won't. It fucking won't. It fucking won't. It fucking
won't. It fucking won't. It fucking won't. It fucking
won't. It fucking won't. It fucking won't. It fucking
won't. It fucking won't. It fucking won't. It fucking
won't. It fucking won't. It fucking won't. It fucking
won't. It fucking won't. It fucking won't. It fucking
won't. It fucking won't. It fucking won't. It fucking
won't. It fucking won't. It fucking won't. It fucking
won't. It fucking won't. It fucking won't. It fucking
won't. It fucking won't. It fucking won't. It fucking
won't. It fucking won't. It fucking won't. It fucking
won't. It fucking won't. It fucking won't. It fucking
won't. It fucking won't. It fucking won't. It fucking
won't. It fucking won't. It fucking won't. It fucking
won't. It fucking won't. It fucking won't. It fucking
won't. It fucking won't. It fucking won't. It fucking
won't. It fucking won't. It fucking won't. It fucking
won't. It fucking won't. It fucking won't. It fucking
won't. It fucking won't. It fucking won't. It fucking
won't. It fucking won't. It fucking won't. It fucking
won't. It fucking won't. It fucking won't. It fucking
won't. It fucking won't. It fucking won't. It fucking
won't. It fucking won't. It fucking won't. It fucking
won't. It fucking won't. It fucking won't. It fucking
won't. It fucking won't. It fucking won't. It fucking
won't. It fucking won't. It fucking won't. It fucking
won't. It fucking won't. It fucking won't. It fucking
won't. It fucking won't. It fucking won't. It fucking

won't. It fucking won't. It fucking won't. It fucking
won't. It fucking won't. It fucking won't. It fucking
won't. It fucking won't. It fucking won't. It fucking
won't. It fucking won't. It fucking won't. It fucking
won't. It fucking won't. It fucking won't. It fucking
won't. It fucking won't. It fucking won't. It fucking
won't. It fucking won't. It fucking won't. It fucking
won't. It fucking won't. It fucking won't. It fucking
won't. It fucking won't. It fucking won't. It fucking
won't. It fucking won't. It fucking won't. It fucking
won't. It fucking won't. It fucking won't. It fucking
won't. It fucking won't. It fucking won't. It fucking
won't. It fucking won't. It fucking won't. It fucking
won't. It fucking won't. It fucking won't. It fucking
won't. It fucking won't. It fucking won't. It fucking
won't. It fucking won't. It fucking won't. It fucking
won't. It fucking won't. It fucking won't. It fucking
won't. It fucking won't. It fucking won't. It fucking
won't. It fucking won't. It fucking won't. It fucking
won't. It fucking won't. It fucking won't. It fucking
won't. It fucking won't. It fucking won't. It fucking
won't. It fucking won't. It fucking won't. It fucking
won't. It fucking won't. It fucking won't. It fucking
won't. It fucking won't. It fucking won't. It fucking
won't. It fucking won't. It fucking won't. It fucking
won't. It fucking won't. It fucking won't. It fucking
won't. It fucking won't. It fucking won't. It fucking
won't. It fucking won't. It fucking won't. It fucking
won't. It fucking won't. It fucking won't. It fucking
won't. It fucking won't. It fucking won't. It fucking

won't. It fucking won't. It fucking won't. It fucking
won't. It fucking won't. It fucking won't. It fucking
won't. It fucking won't. It fucking won't. It fucking
won't. It fucking won't. It fucking won't. It fucking
won't. It fucking won't. It fucking won't. It fucking
won't. It fucking won't. It fucking won't. It fucking
won't. It fucking won't. It fucking won't. It fucking
won't. It fucking won't. It fucking won't. It fucking
won't. It fucking won't. It fucking won't. It fucking
won't. It fucking won't. It fucking won't. It fucking
won't. It fucking won't. It fucking won't. It fucking
won't. It fucking won't. It fucking won't. It fucking
won't. It fucking won't. It fucking won't. It fucking
won't. It fucking won't. It fucking won't. It fucking
won't. It fucking won't. It fucking won't. It fucking
won't. It fucking won't. It fucking won't. It fucking
won't. It fucking won't. It fucking won't. It fucking
won't. It fucking won't. It fucking won't. It fucking
won't. It fucking won't. It fucking won't. It fucking
won't. It fucking won't. It fucking won't. It fucking
won't. It fucking won't. It fucking won't. It fucking
won't. It fucking won't. It fucking won't. It fucking
won't. It fucking won't. It fucking won't. It fucking
won't. It fucking won't. It fucking won't. It fucking
won't. It fucking won't. It fucking won't. It fucking
won't. It fucking won't. It fucking won't. It fucking
won't. It fucking won't. It fucking won't. It fucking
won't. It fucking won't. It fucking won't. It fucking
won't. It fucking won't. It fucking won't. It fucking
won't. It fucking won't. It fucking won't. It fucking

won't. It fucking won't. It fucking won't. It fucking
won't. It fucking won't. It fucking won't. It fucking
won't. It fucking won't. It fucking won't. It fucking
won't. It fucking won't. It fucking won't. It fucking
won't. It fucking won't. It fucking won't. It fucking
won't. It fucking won't. It fucking won't. It fucking
won't. It fucking won't. It fucking won't. It fucking
won't. It fucking won't. It fucking won't. It fucking
won't. It fucking won't. It fucking won't. It fucking
won't. It fucking won't. It fucking won't. It fucking
won't. It fucking won't. It fucking won't. It fucking
won't. It fucking won't. It fucking won't. It fucking
won't. It fucking won't. It fucking won't. It fucking
won't. It fucking won't. It fucking won't. It fucking
won't. It fucking won't. It fucking won't. It fucking
won't. It fucking won't. It fucking won't. It fucking
won't. It fucking won't. It fucking won't. It fucking
won't. It fucking won't. It fucking won't. It fucking
won't. It fucking won't. It fucking won't. It fucking
won't. It fucking won't. It fucking won't. It fucking
won't. It fucking won't. It fucking won't. It fucking
won't. It fucking won't. It fucking won't. It fucking
won't. It fucking won't. It fucking won't. It fucking
won't. It fucking won't. It fucking won't. It fucking
won't. It fucking won't. It fucking won't. It fucking
won't. It fucking won't. It fucking won't. It fucking
won't. It fucking won't. It fucking won't. It fucking
won't. It fucking won't. It fucking won't. It fucking
won't. It fucking won't. It fucking won't. It fucking
won't. It fucking won't. It fucking won't. It fucking

won't. It fucking won't. It fucking won't. It fucking
won't. It fucking won't. It fucking won't. It fucking
won't. It fucking won't. It fucking won't. It fucking
won't. It fucking won't. It fucking won't. It fucking
won't. It fucking won't. It fucking won't. It fucking
won't. It fucking won't. It fucking won't. It fucking
won't. It fucking won't. It fucking won't. It fucking
won't. It fucking won't. It fucking won't. It fucking
won't. It fucking won't. It fucking won't. It fucking
won't. It fucking won't. It fucking won't.

It fucking won't. It fucking won't. It fucking
won't. It fucking won't. It fucking won't. It fucking
won't. It fucking won't. It fucking won't. It fucking
won't. It fucking won't. It fucking won't. It fucking
won't. It fucking won't. It fucking won't. It fucking
won't. It fucking won't. It fucking won't. It fucking
won't. It fucking won't. It fucking won't. It fucking
won't. It fucking won't. It fucking won't. It fucking
won't. It fucking won't. It fucking won't. It fucking
won't. It fucking won't. It fucking won't. It fucking
won't. It fucking won't. It fucking won't. It fucking
won't. It fucking won't. It fucking won't. It fucking
won't. It fucking won't. It fucking won't. It fucking
won't. It fucking won't. It fucking won't. It fucking
won't. It fucking won't. It fucking won't. It fucking
won't. It fucking won't. It fucking won't. It fucking
won't. It fucking won't. It fucking won't. It fucking
won't. It fucking won't. It fucking won't. It fucking
won't. It fucking won't. It fucking won't. It fucking

won't. It fucking won't. It fucking won't. It fucking
won't. It fucking won't. It fucking won't. It fucking
won't. It fucking won't. It fucking won't. It fucking
won't. It fucking won't. It fucking won't. It fucking
won't. It fucking won't. It fucking won't. It fucking
won't. It fucking won't. It fucking won't. It fucking
won't. It fucking won't. It fucking won't. It fucking
won't. It fucking won't. It fucking won't. It fucking
won't. It fucking won't. It fucking won't. It fucking
won't. It fucking won't. It fucking won't. It fucking
won't. It fucking won't. It fucking won't. It fucking
won't. It fucking won't. It fucking won't. It fucking
won't. It fucking won't. It fucking won't. It fucking
won't. It fucking won't. It fucking won't. It fucking
won't. It fucking won't. It fucking won't. It fucking
won't. It fucking won't. It fucking won't. It fucking
won't. It fucking won't. It fucking won't. It fucking
won't. It fucking won't. It fucking won't. It fucking
won't. It fucking won't. It fucking won't. It fucking
won't. It fucking won't. It fucking won't. It fucking
won't. It fucking won't. It fucking won't. It fucking
won't. It fucking won't. It fucking won't. It fucking
won't. It fucking won't. It fucking won't. It fucking
won't. It fucking won't. It fucking won't. It fucking
won't. It fucking won't. It fucking won't. It fucking
won't. It fucking won't. It fucking won't. It fucking
won't. It fucking won't. It fucking won't. It fucking
won't. It fucking won't. It fucking won't. It fucking
won't. It fucking won't. It fucking won't. It fucking
won't. It fucking won't. It fucking won't. It fucking

won't. It fucking won't. It fucking won't. It fucking
won't. It fucking won't. It fucking won't. It fucking
won't. It fucking won't. It fucking won't. It fucking
won't. It fucking won't. It fucking won't. It fucking
won't. It fucking won't. It fucking won't. It fucking
won't. It fucking won't. It fucking won't. It fucking
won't. It fucking won't. It fucking won't. It fucking
won't. It fucking won't. It fucking won't. It fucking
won't. It fucking won't. It fucking won't. It fucking
won't. It fucking won't. It fucking won't. It fucking
won't. It fucking won't. It fucking won't. It fucking
won't. It fucking won't. It fucking won't. It fucking
won't. It fucking won't. It fucking won't. It fucking
won't. It fucking won't. It fucking won't. It fucking
won't. It fucking won't. It fucking won't. It fucking
won't. It fucking won't. It fucking won't. It fucking
won't. It fucking won't. It fucking won't. It fucking
won't. It fucking won't. It fucking won't. It fucking
won't. It fucking won't. It fucking won't. It fucking
won't. It fucking won't. It fucking won't. It fucking
won't. It fucking won't. It fucking won't. It fucking
won't. It fucking won't. It fucking won't. It fucking
won't. It fucking won't. It fucking won't. It fucking
won't. It fucking won't. It fucking won't. It fucking
won't. It fucking won't. It fucking won't. It fucking
won't. It fucking won't. It fucking won't. It fucking
won't. It fucking won't. It fucking won't. It fucking
won't. It fucking won't. It fucking won't. It fucking
won't. It fucking won't. It fucking won't. It fucking
won't. It fucking won't. It fucking won't. It fucking
won't. It fucking won't. It fucking won't. It fucking

won't. It fucking won't. It fucking won't. It fucking
won't. It fucking won't. It fucking won't. It fucking
won't. It fucking won't. It fucking won't. It fucking
won't. It fucking won't. It fucking won't. It fucking
won't. It fucking won't. It fucking won't. It fucking
won't. It fucking won't. It fucking won't. It fucking
won't. It fucking won't. It fucking won't. It fucking
won't. It fucking won't. It fucking won't. It fucking
won't. It fucking won't. It fucking won't. It fucking
won't. It fucking won't. It fucking won't. It fucking
won't. It fucking won't. It fucking won't. It fucking
won't. It fucking won't. It fucking won't. It fucking
won't. It fucking won't. It fucking won't. It fucking
won't. It fucking won't. It fucking won't. It fucking
won't. It fucking won't. It fucking won't. It fucking
won't. It fucking won't. It fucking won't. It fucking
won't. It fucking won't. It fucking won't. It fucking
won't. It fucking won't. It fucking won't. It fucking
won't. It fucking won't. It fucking won't. It fucking
won't. It fucking won't. It fucking won't. It fucking
won't. It fucking won't. It fucking won't. It fucking
won't. It fucking won't. It fucking won't. It fucking
won't. It fucking won't. It fucking won't. It fucking
won't. It fucking won't. It fucking won't. It fucking
won't. It fucking won't. It fucking won't. It fucking
won't. It fucking won't. It fucking won't. It fucking
won't. It fucking won't. It fucking won't. It fucking
won't. It fucking won't. It fucking won't. It fucking
won't. It fucking won't. It fucking won't. It fucking
won't. It fucking won't. It fucking won't. It fucking

won't. It fucking won't. It fucking won't. It fucking
won't. It fucking won't. It fucking won't. It fucking
won't. It fucking won't. It fucking won't. It fucking
won't. It fucking won't. It fucking won't. It fucking
won't. It fucking won't. It fucking won't. It fucking
won't. It fucking won't. It fucking won't. It fucking
won't. It fucking won't. It fucking won't. It fucking
won't. It fucking won't. It fucking won't. It fucking
won't. It fucking won't. It fucking won't. It fucking
won't. It fucking won't. It fucking won't. It fucking
won't. It fucking won't. It fucking won't. It fucking
won't. It fucking won't. It fucking won't. It fucking
won't. It fucking won't. It fucking won't. It fucking
won't. It fucking won't. It fucking won't. It fucking
won't. It fucking won't. It fucking won't. It fucking
won't. It fucking won't. It fucking won't. It fucking
won't. It fucking won't. It fucking won't. It fucking
won't. It fucking won't. It fucking won't. It fucking
won't. It fucking won't. It fucking won't. It fucking
won't. It fucking won't. It fucking won't. It fucking
won't. It fucking won't. It fucking won't. It fucking
won't. It fucking won't. It fucking won't. It fucking
won't. It fucking won't. It fucking won't. It fucking
won't. It fucking won't. It fucking won't. It fucking
won't. It fucking won't. It fucking won't. It fucking
won't. It fucking won't. It fucking won't. It fucking
won't. It fucking won't. It fucking won't. It fucking
won't. It fucking won't. It fucking won't. It fucking
won't. It fucking won't. It fucking won't. It fucking
won't. It fucking won't. It fucking won't. It fucking

won't. It fucking won't. It fucking won't. It fucking
won't. It fucking won't. It fucking won't. It fucking
won't. It fucking won't. It fucking won't. It fucking
won't. It fucking won't. It fucking won't. It fucking
won't. It fucking won't. It fucking won't. It fucking
won't. It fucking won't. It fucking won't. It fucking
won't. It fucking won't. It fucking won't. It fucking
won't. It fucking won't. It fucking won't. It fucking
won't. It fucking won't. It fucking won't. It fucking
won't. It fucking won't. It fucking won't. It fucking
won't. It fucking won't. It fucking won't. It fucking
won't. It fucking won't. It fucking won't. It fucking
won't. It fucking won't. It fucking won't. It fucking
won't. It fucking won't. It fucking won't. It fucking
won't. It fucking won't. It fucking won't. It fucking
won't. It fucking won't. It fucking won't. It fucking
won't. It fucking won't. It fucking won't. It fucking
won't. It fucking won't. It fucking won't. It fucking
won't. It fucking won't. It fucking won't. It fucking
won't. It fucking won't. It fucking won't. It fucking
won't. It fucking won't. It fucking won't. It fucking
won't. It fucking won't. It fucking won't. It fu It
fucking won't. It fucking won't. It fucking won't. It
fucking won't. It fucking won't. It fucking won't. It
fucking won't. It fucking won't. It fucking won't. It
fucking won't. It fucking won't. It fucking won't. It
fucking won't. It fucking won't. It fucking won't. It
fucking won't. It fucking won't. It fucking won't. It
fucking won't. It fucking won't. It fucking won't. It
fucking won't. It fucking won't. It fucking won't. It
fucking won't. It fucking won't. It fucking won't. It

fucking won't. It fucking won't. It fucking won't. It
fucking won't. It fucking won't. It fucking won't. It
fucking won't. It fucking won't. It fucking won't. It
fucking won't. It fucking won't. It fucking won't. It
fucking won't. It fucking won't. It fucking won't. It
fucking won't. It fucking won't. It fucking won't. It
fucking won't. It fucking won't. It fucking won't. It
fucking won't. It fucking won't. It fucking won't. It
fucking won't. It fucking won't. It fucking won't. It
fucking won't. It fucking won't. It fucking won't. It
fucking won't. It fucking won't. It fucking won't. It
fucking won't. It fucking won't. It fucking won't. It
fucking won't. It fucking won't. It fucking won't. It
fucking won't. It fucking won't. It fucking won't. It
fucking won't. It fucking won't. It fucking won't. It
fucking won't. It fucking won't. It fucking won't. It
fucking won't. It fucking won't. It fucking won't. It
fucking won't. It fucking won't. It fucking won't. It
fucking won't. It fucking won't. It fucking won't. It
fucking won't. It fucking won't. It fucking won't. It
fucking won't. It fucking won't. It fucking won't. It
fucking won't. It fucking won't. It fucking won't. It
fucking won't. It fucking won't. It fucking won't. It
fucking won't. It fucking won't. It fucking won't. It
fucking won't. It fucking won't. It fucking won't. It
fucking won't. It fucking won't. It fucking won't. It
fucking won't. It fucking won't. It fucking won't. It
fucking won't. It fucking won't. It fucking won't. It
fucking won't. It fucking won't. It fucking won't. It
fucking won't. It fucking won't. It fucking won't. It
fucking won't. It fucking won't. It fucking won't. It

fucking won't. It fucking won't. It fucking won't. It
fucking won't. It fucking won't. It fucking won't. It
fucking won't. It fucking won't. It fucking won't. It
fucking won't. It fucking won't. It fucking won't. It
fucking won't. It fucking won't. It fucking won't. It
fucking won't. It fucking won't. It fucking won't. It
fucking won't. It fucking won't. It fucking won't. It
fucking won't. It fucking won't. It fucking won't. It
fucking won't. It fucking won't. It fucking won't. It
fucking won't. It fucking won't. It fucking won't. It
fucking won't. It fucking won't. It fucking won't. It
fucking won't. It fucking won't. It fucking won't. It
fucking won't. It fucking won't. It fucking won't. It
fucking won't. It fucking won't. It fucking won't. It
fucking won't. It fucking won't. It fucking won't. It
fucking won't. It fucking won't. It fucking won't. It
fucking won't. It fucking won't. It fucking won't. It
fucking won't. It fucking won't. It fucking won't. It
fucking won't. It fucking won't. It fucking won't. It
fucking won't. It fucking won't. It fucking won't. It
fucking won't. It fucking won't. It fucking won't. It
fucking won't.

It fucking won't. It fucking won't. It fucking
won't. It fucking won't. It fucking won't. It fucking
won't. It fucking won't. It fucking won't. It fucking
won't. It fucking won't. It fucking won't. It fucking
won't. It fucking won't. It fucking won't. It fucking
won't. It fucking won't. It fucking won't. It fucking
won't. It fucking won't. It fucking won't. It fucking
won't. It fucking won't. It fucking won't. It fucking

won't. It fucking won't. It fucking won't. It fucking
won't. It fucking won't. It fucking won't. It fucking
won't. It fucking won't. It fucking won't. It fucking
won't. It fucking won't. It fucking won't. It fucking
won't. It fucking won't. It fucking won't. It fucking
won't. It fucking won't. It fucking won't. It fucking
won't. It fucking won't. It fucking won't. It fucking
won't. It fucking won't. It fucking won't. It fucking
won't. It fucking won't. It fucking won't. It fucking
won't. It fucking won't. It fucking won't. It fucking
won't. It fucking won't. It fucking won't. It fucking
won't. It fucking won't. It fucking won't. It fucking
won't. It fucking won't. It fucking won't. It fucking
won't. It fucking won't. It fucking won't. It fucking
won't. It fucking won't. It fucking won't. It fucking
won't. It fucking won't. It fucking won't. It fucking
won't. It fucking won't. It fucking won't. It fucking
won't. It fucking won't. It fucking won't. It fucking
won't. It fucking won't. It fucking won't. It fucking
won't. It fucking won't. It fucking won't. It fucking
won't. It fucking won't. It fucking won't. It fucking
won't. It fucking won't. It fucking won't. It fucking
won't. It fucking won't. It fucking won't. It fucking
won't. It fucking won't. It fucking won't. It fucking
won't. It fucking won't. It fucking won't. It fucking
won't. It fucking won't. It fucking won't. It fucking
won't. It fucking won't. It fucking won't. It fucking
won't. It fucking won't. It fucking won't. It fucking
won't. It fucking won't. It fucking won't. It fucking
won't. It fucking won't. It fucking won't. It fucking
won't. It fucking won't. It fucking won't. It fucking

won't. It fucking won't. It fucking won't. It fucking
won't. It fucking won't. It fucking won't. It fucking
won't. It fucking won't. It fucking won't. It fucking
won't. It fucking won't. It fucking won't. It fucking
won't. It fucking won't. It fucking won't. It fucking
won't. It fucking won't. It fucking won't. It fucking
won't. It fucking won't. It fucking won't. It fucking
won't. It fucking won't. It fucking won't. It fucking
won't. It fucking won't. It fucking won't. It fucking
won't. It fucking won't. It fucking won't. It fucking
won't. It fucking won't. It fucking won't. It fucking
won't. It fucking won't. It fucking won't. It fucking
won't. It fucking won't. It fucking won't. It fucking
won't. It fucking won't. It fucking won't. It fucking
won't. It fucking won't. It fucking won't. It fucking
won't. It fucking won't. It fucking won't. It fucking
won't. It fucking won't. It fucking won't. It fucking
won't. It fucking won't. It fucking won't. It fucking
won't. It fucking won't. It fucking won't. It fucking
won't. It fucking won't. It fucking won't. It fucking
won't. It fucking won't. It fucking won't. It fucking
won't. It fucking won't. It fucking won't. It fucking
won't. It fucking won't. It fucking won't. It fucking
won't. It fucking won't. It fucking won't. It fucking
won't. It fucking won't. It fucking won't. It fucking
won't. It fucking won't. It fucking won't. It fucking
won't. It fucking won't. It fucking won't. It fucking
won't. It fucking won't. It fucking won't. It fucking
won't. It fucking won't. It fucking won't. It fucking
won't. It fucking won't. It fucking won't. It fucking

won't. It fucking won't. It fucking won't. It fucking
won't. It fucking won't. It fucking won't. It fucking
won't. It fucking won't. It fucking won't. It fucking
won't. It fucking won't. It fucking won't. It fucking
won't. It fucking won't. It fucking won't. It fucking
won't. It fucking won't. It fucking won't. It fucking
won't. It fucking won't. It fucking won't. It fucking
won't. It fucking won't. It fucking won't. It fucking
won't. It fucking won't. It fucking won't. It fucking
won't. It fucking won't. It fucking won't. It fucking
won't. It fucking won't. It fucking won't. It fucking
won't. It fucking won't. It fucking won't. It fucking
won't. It fucking won't. It fucking won't. It fucking
won't. It fucking won't. It fucking won't. It fucking
won't. It fucking won't. It fucking won't. It fucking
won't. It fucking won't. It fucking won't. It fucking
won't. It fucking won't. It fucking won't. It fucking
won't. It fucking won't. It fucking won't. It fucking
won't. It fucking won't. It fucking won't. It fucking
won't. It fucking won't. It fucking won't. It fucking
won't. It fucking won't. It fucking won't. It fucking
won't. It fucking won't. It fucking won't. It fucking
won't. It fucking won't. It fucking won't. It fucking
won't. It fucking won't. It fucking won't. It fucking
won't. It fucking won't. It fucking won't. It fucking
won't. It fucking won't. It fucking won't. It fucking
won't. It fucking won't. It fucking won't. It fucking
won't. It fucking won't. It fucking won't. It fucking
won't. It fucking won't. It fucking won't. It fucking
won't. It fucking won't. It fucking won't. It fucking
won't. It fucking won't. It fucking won't. It fucking

won't. It fucking won't. It fucking won't. It fucking
won't. It fucking won't. It fucking won't. It fucking
won't. It fucking won't. It fucking won't. It fucking
won't. It fucking won't. It fucking won't. It fucking
won't. It fucking won't. It fucking won't. It fucking
won't. It fucking won't. It fucking won't. It fucking
won't. It fucking won't. It fucking won't. It fucking
won't. It fucking won't. It fucking won't. It fucking
won't. It fucking won't. It fucking won't. It fucking
won't. It fucking won't. It fucking won't. It fucking
won't. It fucking won't. It fucking won't. It fucking
won't. It fucking won't. It fucking won't. It fucking
won't. It fucking won't. It fucking won't. It fucking
won't. It fucking won't. It fucking won't. It fucking
won't. It fucking won't. It fucking won't. It fucking
won't. It fucking won't. It fucking won't. It fucking
won't. It fucking won't. It fucking won't. It fucking
won't. It fucking won't. It fucking won't. It fucking
won't. It fucking won't. It fucking won't. It fucking
won't. It fucking won't. It fucking won't. It fucking
won't. It fucking won't. It fucking won't. It fucking
won't. It fucking won't. It fucking won't. It fucking
won't. It fucking won't. It fucking won't. It fucking
won't. It fucking won't. It fucking won't. It fucking
won't. It fucking won't. It fucking won't. It fucking
won't. It fucking won't. It fucking won't. It fucking
won't. It fucking won't. It fucking won't. It fucking
won't. It fucking won't. It fucking won't. It fucking
won't. It fucking won't. It fucking won't. It fucking
won't. It fucking won't. It fucking won't. It fucking

won't. It fucking won't. It fucking won't. It fucking
won't. It fucking won't. It fucking won't. It fucking
won't. It fucking won't. It fucking won't. It fucking
won't. It fucking won't. It fucking won't. It fucking
won't. It fucking won't. It fucking won't. It fucking
won't. It fucking won't. It fucking won't. It fucking
won't. It fucking won't. It fucking won't. It fucking
won't. It fucking won't. It fucking won't. It fucking
won't. It fucking won't. It fucking won't. It fucking
won't. It fucking won't. It fucking won't. It fucking
won't. It fucking won't. It fucking won't. It fucking
won't. It fucking won't. It fucking won't. It fucking
won't. It fucking won't. It fucking won't. It fucking
won't. It fucking won't. It fucking won't. It fucking
won't. It fucking won't. It fucking won't. It fucking
won't. It fucking won't. It fucking won't. It fucking
won't. It fucking won't. It fucking won't. It fucking
won't. It fucking won't. It fucking won't. It fucking
won't. It fucking won't. It fucking won't. It fucking
won't. It fucking won't. It fucking won't. It fucking
won't. It fucking won't. It fucking won't. It fucking
won't. It fucking won't. It fucking won't. It fucking
won't. It fucking won't. It fucking won't. It fucking
won't. It fucking won't. It fucking won't. It fucking
won't. It fucking won't. It fucking won't. It fucking
won't. It fucking won't. It fucking won't. It fucking
won't. It fucking won't. It fucking won't. It fucking
won't. It fucking won't. It fucking won't. It fucking
won't. It fucking won't. It fucking won't. It fucking
won't. It fucking won't. It fucking won't. It fucking

won't. It fucking won't. It fucking won't. It fucking
won't. It fucking won't. It fucking won't. It fucking
won't. It fucking won't. It fucking won't. It fucking
won't. It fucking won't. It fucking won't. It fucking
won't. It fucking won't. It fucking won't. It fucking
won't. It fucking won't. It fucking won't. It fucking
won't. It fucking won't. It fucking won't. It fucking
won't. It fucking won't. It fucking won't. It fucking
won't. It fucking won't. It fucking won't. It fucking
won't. It fucking won't. It fucking won't. It fucking
won't. It fucking won't. It fucking won't. It fucking
won't. It fucking won't. It fucking won't. It fucking
won't. It fucking won't. It fucking won't. It fucking
won't. It fucking won't. It fucking won't. It fucking
won't. It fucking won't. It fucking won't. It fucking
won't. It fucking won't. It fucking won't. It fucking
won't. It fucking won't. It fucking won't. It fucking
won't. It fucking won't. It fucking won't. It fucking
won't. It fucking won't. It fucking won't. It fucking
won't. It fucking won't. It fucking won't. It fucking
won't. It fucking won't. It fucking won't. It fucking
won't. It fucking won't. It fucking won't. It fucking
won't. It fucking won't. It fucking won't. It fucking
won't. It fucking won't. It fucking won't. It fucking
won't. It fucking won't. It fucking won't. It fucking
won't. It fucking won't. It fucking won't. It fucking
won't. It fucking won't. It fucking won't. It fucking
won't. It fucking won't. It fucking won't. It fucking
won't. It fucking won't. It fucking won't. It fucking
won't. It fucking won't. It fucking won't. It fucking

won't. It fucking won't. It fucking won't. It fucking
won't. It fucking won't. It fucking won't. It fucking
won't. It fucking won't. It fucking won't. It fucking
won't. It fucking won't. It fucking won't. It fucking
won't. It fucking won't. It fucking won't. It fucking
won't. It fucking won't. It fucking won't. It fucking
won't. It fucking won't. It fucking won't. It fucking
won't. It fucking won't. It fucking won't. It fucking
won't. It fucking won't. It fucking won't. It fucking
won't. It fucking won't. It fucking won't. It fucking
won't. It fucking won't. It fucking won't. It fucking
won't. It fucking won't. It fucking won't. It fucking
won't. It fucking won't. It fucking won't. It fucking
won't. It fucking won't. It fucking won't. It fucking
won't. It fucking won't. It fucking won't. It fucking
won't. It fucking won't. It fucking won't. It fucking
won't. It fucking won't. It fucking won't. It fucking
won't. It fucking won't. It fucking won't. It fucking
won't. It fucking won't. It fucking won't. It fucking
won't. It fucking won't. It fucking won't. It fucking
won't. It fucking won't. It fucking won't. It fucking
won't. It fucking won't. It fucking won't. It fucking
won't. It fucking won't. It fucking won't. It fucking
won't. It fucking won't. It fucking won't. It fucking
won't. It fucking won't. It fucking won't. It fucking
won't. It fucking won't. It fucking won't. It fucking
won't. It fucking won't. It fucking won't. It fucking
won't. It fucking won't. It fucking won't. It fucking
won't. It fucking won't. It fucking won't. It fucking
won't. It fucking won't. It fucking won't. It fucking
won't. It fucking won't. It fucking won't. It fucking
won't. It fucking won't. It fucking won't. It fucking

won't. It fucking won't. It fucking won't. It fucking
won't. It fucking won't. It fucking won't. It fucking
won't. It fucking won't. It fucking won't. It fucking
won't. It fucking won't. It fucking won't. It fucking
won't. It fucking won't. It fucking won't. It fucking
won't. It fucking won't. It fucking won't. It fucking
won't. It fucking won't. It fucking won't. It fucking
won't. It fucking won't. It fucking won't. It fucking
won't. It fucking won't. It fucking won't. It fucking
won't. It fucking won't. It fucking won't. It fucking
won't. It fucking won't. It fucking won't. It fucking
won't. It fucking won't. It fucking won't. It fucking
won't. It fucking won't. It fucking won't. It fucking
won't. It fucking won't. It fucking won't. It fucking
won't. It fucking won't. It fucking won't. It fucking
won't. It fucking won't. It fucking won't. It fucking
won't. It fucking won't. It fucking won't. It fucking
won't. It fucking won't. It fucking won't. It fucking
won't. It fucking won't. It fucking won't. It fucking
won't. It fucking won't. It fucking won't. It fucking
won't. It fucking won't. It fucking won't. It fucking
won't. It fucking won't. It fucking won't. It fucking
won't. It fucking won't. It fucking won't. It fucking
won't. It fucking won't. It fucking won't. It fucking
won't. It fucking won't. It fucking won't. It fucking
won't. It fucking won't. It fucking won't. It fucking
won't. It fucking won't. It fucking won't. It fucking
won't. It fucking won't. It fucking won't. It fucking
won't. It fucking won't. It fucking won't. It fucking
won't. It fucking won't. It fucking won't. It fucking

won't. It fucking won't. It fucking won't. It fucking
won't. It fucking won't. It fucking won't. It fucking
won't. It fucking won't. It fucking won't. It fucking
won't. It fucking won't. It fucking won't. It fucking
won't. It fucking won't. It fucking won't. It fucking
won't. It fucking won't. It fucking won't. It fucking
won't. It fucking won't. It fucking won't. It fucking
won't. It fucking won't. It fucking won't. It fucking
won't. It fucking won't. It fucking won't. It fucking
won't. It fucking won't. It fucking won't. It fucking
won't. It fucking won't. It fucking won't. It fucking
won't. It fucking won't. It fucking won't. It fucking
won't. It fucking won't. It fucking won't. It fucking
won't. It fucking won't. It fucking won't. It fucking
won't. It fucking won't. It fucking won't. It fucking
won't. It fucking won't. It fucking won't. It fucking
won't. It fucking won't. It fucking won't. It fucking
won't. It fucking won't. It fucking won't. It fucking
won't. It fucking won't. It fucking won't. It fucking
won't. It fucking won't. It fucking won't. It fucking
won't. It fucking won't. It fucking won't. It fucking
won't. It fucking won't. It fucking won't. It fucking
won't. It fucking won't. It fucking won't. It fucking
won't. It fucking won't. It fucking won't. It fucking
won't. It fucking won't. It fucking won't. It fucking
won't. It fucking won't. It fucking won't. It fucking
won't. It fucking won't. It fucking won't.

It fucking won't. It fucking won't. It fucking won't. It
fucking won't. It fucking won't. It fucking won't. It
fucking won't. It fucking won't. It fucking won't. It

fucking won't. It fucking won't. It fucking won't. It
fucking won't. It fucking won't. It fucking won't. It
fucking won't. It fucking won't. It fucking won't. It
fucking won't. It fucking won't. It fucking won't. It
fucking won't. It fucking won't. It fucking won't. It
fucking won't. It fucking won't. It fucking won't. It
fucking won't. It fucking won't. It fucking won't. It
fucking won't. It fucking won't. It fucking won't. It
fucking won't. It fucking won't. It fucking won't. It
fucking won't. It fucking won't. It fucking won't. It
fucking won't. It fucking won't. It fucking won't. It
fucking won't. It fucking won't. It fucking won't. It
fucking won't. It fucking won't. It fucking won't. It
fucking won't. It fucking won't. It fucking won't. It
fucking won't. It fucking won't. It fucking won't. It
fucking won't. It fucking won't. It fucking won't. It
fucking won't. It fucking won't. It fucking won't. It
fucking won't. It fucking won't. It fucking won't. It
fucking won't. It fucking won't. It fucking won't. It
fucking won't. It fucking won't. It fucking won't. It
fucking won't. It fucking won't. It fucking won't. It
fucking won't. It fucking won't. It fucking won't. It
fucking won't. It fucking won't. It fucking won't. It
fucking won't. It fucking won't. It fucking won't. It
fucking won't. It fucking won't. It fucking won't. It
fucking won't. It fucking won't. It fucking won't. It
fucking won't. It fucking won't. It fucking won't. It
fucking won't. It fucking won't. It fucking won't. It
fucking won't. It fucking won't. It fucking won't. It
fucking won't. It fucking won't. It fucking won't. It

fucking won't. It fucking won't. It fucking won't. It
fucking won't. It fucking won't. It fucking won't. It
fucking won't. It fucking won't. It fucking won't. It
fucking won't. It fucking won't. It fucking won't. It
fucking won't. It fucking won't. It fucking won't. It
fucking won't. It fucking won't. It fucking won't. It
fucking won't. It fucking won't. It fucking won't. It
fucking won't. It fucking won't. It fucking won't. It
fucking won't. It fucking won't. It fucking won't. It
fucking won't. It fucking won't. It fucking won't. It
fucking won't. It fucking won't. It fucking won't. It
fucking won't. It fucking won't. It fucking won't. It
fucking won't. It fucking won't. It fucking won't. It
fucking won't. It fucking won't. It fucking won't. It
fucking won't. It fucking won't. It fucking won't. It
fucking won't. It fucking won't. It fucking won't. It
fucking won't. It fucking won't. It fucking won't. It
fucking won't. It fucking won't. It fucking won't. It
fucking won't. It fucking won't. It fucking won't. It
fucking won't. It fucking won't. It fucking won't. It
fucking won't. It fucking won't. It fucking won't. It
fucking won't. It fucking won't. It fucking won't. It
fucking won't. It fucking won't. It fucking won't. It
fucking won't. It fucking won't. It fucking won't. It
fucking won't. It fucking won't. It fucking won't. It
fucking won't. It fucking won't. It fucking won't. It
fucking won't. It fucking won't. It fucking won't. It
fucking won't. It fucking won't. It fucking won't. It
fucking won't. It fucking won't. It fucking won't. It
fucking won't. It fucking won't. It fucking won't. It
fucking won't. It fucking won't. It fucking won't. It
fucking won't. It fucking won't. It fucking won't. It

fucking won't. It fucking won't. It fucking won't. It
fucking won't. It fucking won't. It fucking won't. It
fucking won't. It fucking won't. It fucking won't. It
fucking won't. It fucking won't. It fucking won't. It
fucking won't. It fucking won't. It fucking won't. It
fucking won't. It fucking won't. It fucking won't. It
fucking won't. It fucking won't. It fucking won't. It
fucking won't. It fucking won't. It fucking won't. It
fucking won't. It fucking won't. It fucking won't. It
fucking won't. It fucking won't. It fucking won't. It
fucking won't. It fucking won't. It fucking won't. It
fucking won't. It fucking won't. It fucking won't. It
fucking won't. It fucking won't. It fucking won't. It
fucking won't. It fucking won't. It fucking won't. It
fucking won't. It fucking won't. It fucking won't. It
fucking won't. It fucking won't. It fucking won't. It
fucking won't. It fucking won't. It fucking won't. It
fucking won't. It fucking won't. It fucking won't. It
fucking won't. It fucking won't. It fucking won't. It
fucking won't. It fucking won't. It fucking won't. It
fucking won't. It fucking won't. It fucking won't. It
fucking won't. It fucking won't. It fucking won't. It
fucking won't. It fucking won't. It fucking won't. It
fucking won't. It fucking won't. It fucking won't. It
fucking won't. It fucking won't. It fucking won't. It
fucking won't. It fucking won't. It fucking won't. It
fucking won't. It fucking won't. It fucking won't. It
fucking won't. It fucking won't. It fucking won't. It
fucking won't. It fucking won't. It fucking won't. It
fucking won't. It fucking won't. It fucking won't. It

fucking won't. It fucking won't. It fucking won't. It
fucking won't. It fucking won't. It fucking won't. It
fucking won't. It fucking won't. It fucking won't. It
fucking won't. It fucking won't. It fucking won't. It
fucking won't. It fucking won't. It fucking won't. It
fucking won't. It fucking won't. It fucking won't. It
fucking won't. It fucking won't. It fucking won't. It
fucking won't. It fucking won't. It fucking won't. It
fucking won't. It fucking won't. It fucking won't. It
fucking won't. It fucking won't. It fucking won't. It
fucking won't. It fucking won't. It fucking won't. It
fucking won't. It fucking won't. It fucking won't. It
fucking won't. It fucking won't. It fucking won't. It
fucking won't. It fucking won't. It fucking won't. It
fucking won't. It fucking won't. It fucking won't. It
fucking won't. It fucking won't. It fucking won't. It
fucking won't. It fucking won't. It fucking won't. It
fucking won't. It fucking won't. It fucking won't. It
fucking won't. It fucking won't. It fucking won't. It
fucking won't. It fucking won't. It fucking won't. It
fucking won't. It fucking won't. It fucking won't. It
fucking won't. It fucking won't. It fucking won't. It
fucking won't. It fucking won't. It fucking won't. It
fucking won't. It fucking won't. It fucking won't. It
fucking won't. It fucking won't. It fucking won't. It
fucking won't. It fucking won't. It fucking won't. It
fucking won't. It fucking won't. It fucking won't. It
fucking won't. It fucking won't. It fucking won't. It
fucking won't. It fucking won't. It fucking won't. It
fucking won't. It fucking won't. It fucking won't. It
fucking won't. It fucking won't. It fucking won't. It
fucking won't. It fucking won't. It fucking won't. It

fucking won't. It fucking won't. It fucking won't. It
fucking won't. It fucking won't. It fucking won't. It
fucking won't. It fucking won't. It fucking won't. It
fucking won't. It fucking won't. It fucking won't. It
fucking won't. It fucking won't. It fucking won't. It
fucking won't. It fucking won't. It fucking won't. It
fucking won't. It fucking won't. It fucking won't. It
fucking won't. It fucking won't. It fucking won't. It
fucking won't. It fucking won't. It fucking won't. It
fucking won't. It fucking won't. It fucking won't. It
fucking won't. It fucking won't. It fucking won't. It
fucking won't. It fucking won't. It fucking won't. It
fucking won't. It fucking won't. It fucking won't. It
fucking won't. It fucking won't. It fucking won't. It
fucking won't. It fucking won't. It fucking won't. It
fucking won't. It fucking won't. It fucking won't. It
fucking won't. It fucking won't. It fucking won't. It
fucking won't. It fucking won't. It fucking won't. It
fucking won't. It fucking won't. It fucking won't. It
fucking won't. It fucking won't. It fucking won't. It
fucking won't. It fucking won't. It fucking won't. It
fucking won't. It fucking won't. It fucking won't. It
fucking won't. It fucking won't. It fucking won't. It
fucking won't. It fucking won't. It fucking won't. It
fucking won't. It fucking won't. It fucking won't. It
fucking won't. It fucking won't. It fucking won't. It
fucking won't. It fucking won't. It fucking won't. It
fucking won't. It fucking won't. It fucking won't. It
fucking won't. It fucking won't. It fucking won't. It
fucking won't. It fucking won't. It fucking won't. It
fucking won't. It fucking won't. It fucking won't. It

fucking won't. It fucking won't. It fucking won't. It
fucking won't. It fucking won't. It fucking won't. It
fucking won't. It fucking won't. It fucking won't. It
fucking won't. It fucking won't. It fucking won't. It
fucking won't. It fucking won't. It fucking won't. It
fucking won't. It fucking won't. It fucking won't. It
fucking won't. It fucking won't. It fucking won't. It
fucking won't. It fucking won't. It fucking won't. It
fucking won't. It fucking won't. It fucking won't. It
fucking won't. It fucking won't. It fucking won't. It
fucking won't. It fucking won't. It fucking won't. It
fucking won't. It fucking won't. It fucking won't. It
fucking won't. It fucking won't. It fucking won't. It
fucking won't. It fucking won't. It fucking won't. It
fucking won't. It fucking won't. It fucking won't. It
fucking won't. It fucking won't. It fucking won't. It
fucking won't. It fucking won't. It fucking won't. It
fucking won't. It fucking won't. It fucking won't. It
fucking won't. It fucking won't. It fucking won't. It
fucking won't. It fucking won't. It fucking won't. It
fucking won't. It fucking won't. It fucking won't. It
fucking won't. It fucking won't. It fucking won't. It
fucking won't. It fucking won't. It fucking won't. It
fucking won't. It fucking won't. It fucking won't. It
fucking won't. It fucking won't. It fucking won't. It
fucking won't. It fucking won't. It fucking won't. It
fucking won't. It fucking won't. It fucking won't. It
fucking won't. It fucking won't. It fucking won't. It
fucking won't. It fucking won't. It fucking won't. It
fucking won't. It fucking won't. It fucking won't. It
fucking won't. It fucking won't. It fucking won't. It
fucking won't. It fucking won't. It fucking won't. It

fucking won't. It fucking won't. It fucking won't. It
fucking won't. It fucking won't. It fucking won't. It
fucking won't. It fucking won't. It fucking won't. It
fucking won't. It fucking won't. It fucking won't. It
fucking won't. It fucking won't. It fucking won't. It
fucking won't. It fucking won't. It fucking won't. It
fucking won't. It fucking won't. It fucking won't. It
fucking won't. It fucking won't. It fucking won't. It
fucking won't. It fucking won't. It fucking won't. It
fucking won't. It fucking won't. It fucking won't. It
fucking won't. It fucking won't. It fucking won't. It
fucking won't. It fucking won't. It fucking won't. It
fucking won't. It fucking won't. It fucking won't. It
fucking won't. It fucking won't. It fucking won't. It
fucking won't. It fucking won't. It fucking won't. It
fucking won't. It fucking won't. It fucking won't. It
fucking won't. It fucking won't. It fucking won't. It
fucking won't. It fucking won't. It fucking won't. It
fucking won't. It fucking won't. It fucking won't. It
fucking won't. It fucking won't. It fucking won't. It
fucking won't. It fucking won't. It fucking won't. It
fucking won't. It fucking won't. It fucking won't. It
fucking won't. It fucking won't. It fucking won't. It
fucking won't. It fucking won't. It fucking won't. It
fucking won't. It fucking won't. It fucking won't. It
fucking won't. It fucking won't. It fucking won't. It
fucking won't. It fucking won't. It fucking won't. It
fucking won't. It fucking won't. It fucking won't. It
fucking won't. It fucking won't. It fucking won't. It
fucking won't. It fucking won't. It fucking won't. It

fucking won't. It fucking won't. It fucking won't. It
fucking won't. It fucking won't. It fucking won't. It
fucking won't. It fucking won't. It fucking won't. It
fucking won't. It fucking won't. It fucking won't. It
fucking won't. It fucking won't. It fucking won't. It
fucking won't. It fucking won't. It fucking won't. It
fucking won't. It fucking won't. It fucking won't. It
fucking won't. It fucking won't. It fucking won't. It
fucking won't. It fucking won't. It fucking won't. It
fucking won't. It fucking won't. It fucking won't. It
fucking won't. It fucking won't. It fucking won't. It
fucking won't. It fucking won't. It fucking won't. It
fucking won't. It fucking won't. It fucking won't. It
fucking won't. It fucking won't. It fucking won't. It
fucking won't. It fucking won't. It fucking won't. It
fucking won't. It fucking won't. It fucking won't. It
fucking won't. It fucking won't. It fucking won't. It
fucking won't. It fucking won't. It fucking won't. It
fucking won't. It fucking won't. It fucking won't. It
fucking won't. It fucking won't. It fucking won't. It
fucking won't. It fucking won't. It fucking won't. It
fucking won't. It fucking won't. It fucking won't. It
fucking won't. It fucking won't. It fucking won't. It
fucking won't. It fucking won't. It fucking won't. It
fucking won't. It fucking won't. It fucking won't. It
fucking won't. It fucking won't. It fucking won't. It
fucking won't. It fucking won't. It fucking won't. It
fucking won't. It fucking won't. It fucking won't. It
fucking won't. It fucking won't. It fucking won't. It
fucking won't. It fucking won't. It fucking won't. It
fucking won't. It fucking won't. It fucking won't. It

fucking won't. It fucking won't. It fucking won't. It
fucking won't. It fucking won't. It fucking won't. It
fucking won't. It fucking won't. It fucking won't. It
fucking won't. It fucking won't. It fucking won't. It
fucking won't. It fucking won't. It fucking won't. It
fucking won't. It fucking won't. It fucking won't. It
fucking won't. It fucking won't. It fucking won't. It
fucking won't. It fucking won't. It fucking won't. It
fucking won't. It fucking won't. It fucking won't. It
fucking won't. It fucking won't. It fucking won't. It
fucking won't. It fucking won't. It fucking won't. It
fucking won't. It fucking won't. It fucking won't. It
fucking won't. It fucking won't. It fucking won't. It
fucking won't. It fucking won't. It fucking won't. It
fucking won't. It fucking won't. It fucking won't. It
fucking won't. It fucking won't. It fucking won't. It
fucking won't. It fucking won't. It fucking won't. It
fucking won't. It fucking won't. It fucking won't. It
fucking won't. It fucking won't. It fucking won't. It
fucking won't. It fucking won't. It fucking won't. It
fucking won't. It fucking won't. It fucking won't. It
fucking won't. It fucking won't. It fucking won't. It
fucking won't. It fucking won't. It fucking won't. It
fucking won't. It fucking won't. It fucking won't. It
fucking won't. It fucking won't. It fucking won't. It
fucking won't. It fucking won't. It fucking won't. It
fucking won't. It fucking won't. It fucking won't. It
fucking won't. It fucking won't. It fucking won't. It
fucking won't. It fucking won't. It fucking won't. It
fucking won't. It fucking won't. It fucking won't. It
fucking won't. It fucking won't. It fucking won't. It

fucking won't. It fucking won't. It fucking won't. It
fucking won't. It fucking won't. It fucking won't. It
fucking won't. It fucking won't. It fucking won't. It
fucking won't. It fucking won't. It fucking won't. It
fucking won't. It fucking won't. It fucking won't. It
fucking won't. It fucking won't. It fucking won't. It
fucking won't. It fucking won't. It fucking won't. It
fucking won't. It fucking won't. It fucking won't. It
fucking won't. It fucking won't. It fucking won't. It
fucking won't. It fucking won't. It fucking won't. It
fucking won't. It fucking won't. It fucking won't. It
fucking won't. It fucking won't. It fucking won't. It
fucking won't. It fucking won't. It fucking won't. It
fucking won't. It fucking won't. It fucking won't. It
fucking won't. It fucking won't. It fucking won't. It
fucking won't. It fucking won't. It fucking won't. It
fucking won't. It fucking won't. It fucking won't. It
fucking won't. It fucking won't. It fucking won't. It
fucking won't. It fucking won't. It fucking won't. It
fucking won't. It fucking won't. It fucking won't. It
fucking won't. It fucking won't. It fucking won't. It
fucking won't. It fucking won't. It fucking won't. It
fucking won't. It fucking won't. It fucking won't. It
fucking won't. It fucking won't. It fucking won't. It
fucking won't. It fucking won't. It fucking won't. It
fucking won't. It fucking won't. It fucking won't. It
fucking won't. It fucking won't. It fucking won't. It
fucking won't. It fucking won't. It fucking won't. It
fucking won't. It fucking won't. It fucking won't. It
fucking won't. It fucking won't. It fucking won't. It
fucking won't. It fucking won't. It fucking won't. It

fucking won't. It fucking won't. It fucking won't. It
fucking won't. It fucking won't. It fucking won't. It
fucking won't. It fucking won't. It fucking won't. It
fucking won't. It fucking won't. It fucking won't. It
fucking won't. It fucking won't. It fucking won't. It
fucking won't. It fucking won't. It fucking won't. It
fucking won't. It fucking won't. It fucking won't. It
fucking won't. It fucking won't. It fucking won't. It
fucking won't. It fucking won't. It fucking won't. It
fucking won't. It fucking won't. It fucking won't. It
fucking won't. It fucking won't. It fucking won't. It
fucking won't. It fucking won't. It fucking won't. It
fucking won't. It fucking won't. It fucking won't. It
fucking won't. It fucking won't. It fucking won't. It
fucking won't. It fucking won't. It fucking won't. It
fucking won't. It fucking won't. It fucking won't. It
fucking won't. It fucking won't. It fucking won't. It
fucking won't. It fucking won't. It fucking won't. It
fucking won't. It fucking won't. It fucking won't. It
fucking won't. It fucking won't. It fucking won't. It
fucking won't. It fucking won't. It fucking won't. It
fucking won't. It fucking won't. It fucking won't. It
fucking won't. It fucking won't. It fucking won't. It
fucking won't. It fucking won't. It fucking won't. It
fucking won't. It fucking won't. It fucking won't. It
fucking won't. It fucking won't. It fucking won't. It
fucking won't. It fucking won't. It fucking won't. It
fucking won't. It fucking won't. It fucking won't. It
fucking won't. It fucking won't. It fucking won't. It
fucking won't. It fucking won't. It fucking won't. It
fucking won't. It fucking won't. It fucking won't.

It fucking won't. It

fucking won't. It fucking won't. It fucking won't. It
fucking won't. It fucking won't. It fucking won't. It
fucking won't. It fucking won't. It fucking won't. It
fucking won't. It fucking won't. It fucking won't. It
fucking won't. It fucking won't. It fucking won't. It
fucking won't. It fucking won't. It fucking won't. It
fucking won't. It fucking won't. It fucking won't. It
fucking won't. It fucking won't. It fucking won't. It
fucking won't. It fucking won't. It fucking won't. It
fucking won't. It fucking won't. It fucking won't. It
fucking won't. It fucking won't. It fucking won't. It
fucking won't. It fucking won't. It fucking won't. It
fucking won't. It fucking won't. It fucking won't. It
fucking won't. It fucking won't. It fucking won't. It
fucking won't. It fucking won't. It fucking won't. It
fucking won't. It fucking won't. It fucking won't. It
fucking won't. It fucking won't. It fucking won't. It
fucking won't. It fucking won't. It fucking won't. It
fucking won't. It fucking won't. It fucking won't. It
fucking won't. It fucking won't. It fucking won't. It
fucking won't. It fucking won't. It fucking won't. It
fucking won't. It fucking won't. It fucking won't. It
fucking won't. It fucking won't. It fucking won't. It
fucking won't. It fucking won't. It fucking won't. It
fucking won't. It fucking won't. It fucking won't. It
fucking won't. It fucking won't. It fucking won't. It
fucking won't. It fucking won't. It fucking won't. It
fucking won't. It fucking won't. It fucking won't. It
fucking won't. It fucking won't. It fucking won't. It
fucking won't. It fucking won't. It fucking won't. It

fucking won't. It fucking won't. It fucking won't. It
fucking won't. It fucking won't. It fucking won't. It
fucking won't. It fucking won't. It fucking won't. It
fucking won't. It fucking won't. It fucking won't. It
fucking won't. It fucking won't. It fucking won't. It
fucking won't. It fucking won't. It fucking won't. It
fucking won't. It fucking won't. It fucking won't. It
fucking won't. It fucking won't. It fucking won't. It
fucking won't. It fucking won't. It fucking won't. It
fucking won't. It fucking won't. It fucking won't. It
fucking won't. It fucking won't. It fucking won't. It
fucking won't. It fucking won't. It fucking won't. It
fucking won't. It fucking won't. It fucking won't. It
fucking won't. It fucking won't. It fucking won't. It
fucking won't. It fucking won't. It fucking won't. It
fucking won't. It fucking won't. It fucking won't. It
fucking won't. It fucking won't. It fucking won't. It
fucking won't. It fucking won't. It fucking won't. It
fucking won't. It fucking won't. It fucking won't. It
fucking won't. It fucking won't. It fucking won't. It
fucking won't. It fucking won't. It fucking won't. It
fucking won't. It fucking won't. It fucking won't. It
fucking won't. It fucking won't. It fucking won't. It
fucking won't. It fucking won't. It fucking won't. It
fucking won't. It fucking won't. It fucking won't. It
fucking won't. It fucking won't. It fucking won't. It
fucking won't. It fucking won't. It fucking won't. It
fucking won't. It fucking won't. It fucking won't. It
fucking won't. It fucking won't. It fucking won't. It
fucking won't. It fucking won't. It fucking won't. It

fucking won't. It fucking won't. It fucking won't. It
fucking won't. It fucking won't. It fucking won't. It
fucking won't. It fucking won't. It fucking won't. It
fucking won't. It fucking won't. It fucking won't. It
fucking won't. It fucking won't. It fucking won't. It
fucking won't. It fucking won't. It fucking won't. It
fucking won't. It fucking won't. It fucking won't. It
fucking won't. It fucking won't. It fucking won't. It
fucking won't. It fucking won't. It fucking won't. It
fucking won't. It fucking won't. It fucking won't. It
fucking won't. It fucking won't. It fucking won't. It
fucking won't. It fucking won't. It fucking won't. It
fucking won't. It fucking won't. It fucking won't. It
fucking won't. It fucking won't. It fucking won't. It
fucking won't. It fucking won't. It fucking won't. It
fucking won't. It fucking won't. It fucking won't. It
fucking won't. It fucking won't. It fucking won't. It
fucking won't. It fucking won't. It fucking won't. It
fucking won't. It fucking won't. It fucking won't. It
fucking won't. It fucking won't. It fucking won't. It
fucking won't. It fucking won't. It fucking won't. It
fucking won't. It fucking won't. It fucking won't. It
fucking won't. It fucking won't. It fucking won't. It
fucking won't. It fucking won't. It fucking won't. It
fucking won't. It fucking won't. It fucking won't. It
fucking won't. It fucking won't. It fucking won't. It
fucking won't. It fucking won't. It fucking won't. It
fucking won't. It fucking won't. It fucking won't. It
fucking won't. It fucking won't. It fucking won't. It
fucking won't. It fucking won't. It fucking won't. It
fucking won't. It fucking won't. It fucking won't. It

fucking won't. It fucking won't. It fucking won't. It
fucking won't. It fucking won't. It fucking won't. It
fucking won't. It fucking won't. It fucking won't. It
fucking won't. It fucking won't. It fucking won't. It
fucking won't. It fucking won't. It fucking won't. It
fucking won't. It fucking won't. It fucking won't. It
fucking won't. It fucking won't. It fucking won't. It
fucking won't. It fucking won't. It fucking won't. It
fucking won't. It fucking won't. It fucking won't. It
fucking won't. It fucking won't. It fucking won't. It
fucking won't. It fucking won't. It fucking won't. It
fucking won't. It fucking won't. It fucking won't. It
fucking won't. It fucking won't. It fucking won't. It
fucking won't. It fucking won't. It fucking won't. It
fucking won't. It fucking won't. It fucking won't. It
fucking won't. It fucking won't. It fucking won't. It
fucking won't. It fucking won't. It fucking won't. It
fucking won't. It fucking won't. It fucking won't. It
fucking won't. It fucking won't. It fucking won't. It
fucking won't. It fucking won't. It fucking won't. It
fucking won't. It fucking won't. It fucking won't. It
fucking won't. It fucking won't. It fucking won't. It
fucking won't. It fucking won't. It fucking won't. It
fucking won't. It fucking won't. It fucking won't. It
fucking won't. It fucking won't. It fucking won't. It
fucking won't. It fucking won't. It fucking won't. It
fucking won't. It fucking won't. It fucking won't. It
fucking won't. It fucking won't. It fucking won't. It
fucking won't. It fucking won't. It fucking won't. It
fucking won't. It fucking won't. It fucking won't. It
fucking won't. It fucking won't. It fucking won't. It

fucking won't. It fucking won't. It fucking won't. It
fucking won't. It fucking won't. It fucking won't. It
fucking won't. It fucking won't. It fucking won't. It
fucking won't. It fucking won't. It fucking won't. It
fucking won't. It fucking won't. It fucking won't. It
fucking won't. It fucking won't. It fucking won't. It
fucking won't. It fucking won't. It fucking won't. It
fucking won't. It fucking won't. It fucking won't. It
fucking won't. It fucking won't. It fucking won't. It
fucking won't. It fucking won't. It fucking won't. It
fucking won't. It fucking won't. It fucking won't. It
fucking won't. It fucking won't. It fucking won't. It
fucking won't. It fucking won't. It fucking won't. It
fucking won't. It fucking won't. It fucking won't. It
fucking won't. It fucking won't. It fucking won't. It
fucking won't. It fucking won't. It fucking won't. It
fucking won't. It fucking won't. It fucking won't. It
fucking won't. It fucking won't. It fucking won't. It
fucking won't. It fucking won't. It fucking won't. It
fucking won't. It fucking won't. It fucking won't. It
fucking won't. It fucking won't. It fucking won't. It
fucking won't. It fucking won't. It fucking won't. It
fucking won't. It fucking won't. It fucking won't. It
fucking won't. It fucking won't. It fucking won't. It
fucking won't. It fucking won't. It fucking won't. It
fucking won't. It fucking won't. It fucking won't. It
fucking won't. It fucking won't. It fucking won't. It
fucking won't. It fucking won't. It fucking won't. It
fucking won't. It fucking won't. It fucking won't. It
fucking won't. It fucking won't. It fucking won't. It

fucking won't. It fucking won't. It fucking won't. It
fucking won't. It fucking won't. It fucking won't. It
fucking won't. It fucking won't. It fucking won't. It
fucking won't. It fucking won't. It fucking won't. It
fucking won't. It fucking won't. It fucking won't. It
fucking won't. It fucking won't. It fucking won't. It
fucking won't. It fucking won't. It fucking won't. It
fucking won't. It fucking won't. It fucking won't. It
fucking won't. It fucking won't. It fucking won't. It
fucking won't. It fucking won't. It fucking won't. It
fucking won't. It fucking won't. It fucking won't. It
fucking won't. It fucking won't. It fucking won't. It
fucking won't. It fucking won't. It fucking won't. It
fucking won't. It fucking won't. It fucking won't. It
fucking won't. It fucking won't. It fucking won't. It
fucking won't. It fucking won't. It fucking won't. It
fucking won't. It fucking won't. It fucking won't. It
fucking won't. It fucking won't. It fucking won't. It
fucking won't. It fucking won't. It fucking won't. It
fucking won't. It fucking won't. It fucking won't. It
fucking won't. It fucking won't. It fucking won't. It
fucking won't. It fucking won't. It fucking won't. It
fucking won't. It fucking won't. It fucking won't. It
fucking won't. It fucking won't. It fucking won't. It
fucking won't. It fucking won't. It fucking won't. It
fucking won't. It fucking won't. It fucking won't. It
fucking won't. It fucking won't. It fucking won't. It
fucking won't. It fucking won't. It fucking won't. It
fucking won't. It fucking won't. It fucking won't. It
fucking won't. It fucking won't. It fucking won't. It
fucking won't. It fucking won't. It fucking won't. It

fucking won't. It fucking won't. It fucking won't. It
fucking won't. It fucking won't. It fucking won't. It
fucking won't. It fucking won't. It fucking won't. It
fucking won't. It fucking won't. It fucking won't. It
fucking won't. It fucking won't. It fucking won't. It
fucking won't. It fucking won't. It fucking won't. It
fucking won't. It fucking won't. It fucking won't. It
fucking won't. It fucking won't. It fucking won't. It
fucking won't. It fucking won't. It fucking won't. It
fucking won't. It fucking won't. It fucking won't. It
fucking won't. It fucking won't. It fucking won't. It
fucking won't. It fucking won't. It fucking won't. It
fucking won't. It fucking won't. It fucking won't. It
fucking won't. It fucking won't. It fucking won't. It
fucking won't. It fucking won't. It fucking won't. It
fucking won't. It fucking won't. It fucking won't. It
fucking won't. It fucking won't. It fucking won't. It
fucking won't. It fucking won't. It fucking won't. It
fucking won't. It fucking won't. It fucking won't. It
fucking won't. It fucking won't. It fucking won't. It
fucking won't. It fucking won't. It fucking won't. It
fucking won't. It fucking won't. It fucking won't. It
fucking won't. It fucking won't. It fucking won't. It
fucking won't. It fucking won't. It fucking won't. It
fucking won't. It fucking won't. It fucking won't. It
fucking won't. It fucking won't. It fucking won't. It
fucking won't. It fucking won't. It fucking won't. It
fucking won't. It fucking won't. It fucking won't. It
fucking won't. It fucking won't. It fucking won't. It
fucking won't. It fucking won't. It fucking won't. It

fucking won't. It fucking won't. It fucking won't. It
fucking won't. It fucking won't. It fucking won't. It
fucking won't. It fucking won't. It fucking won't. It
fucking won't. It fucking won't. It fucking won't. It
fucking won't. It fucking won't. It fucking won't. It
fucking won't. It fucking won't. It fucking won't. It
fucking won't. It fucking won't. It fucking won't. It
fucking won't. It fucking won't. It fucking won't. It
fucking won't. It fucking won't. It fucking won't. It
fucking won't. It fucking won't. It fucking won't. It
fucking won't. It fucking won't. It fucking won't. It
fucking won't. It fucking won't. It fucking won't. It
fucking won't. It fucking won't. It fucking won't. It
fucking won't. It fucking won't. It fucking won't. It
fucking won't. It fucking won't. It fucking won't. It
fucking won't. It fucking won't. It fucking won't. It
fucking won't. It fucking won't. It fucking won't. It
fucking won't. It fucking won't. It fucking won't. It
fucking won't. It fucking won't. It fucking won't. It
fucking won't. It fucking won't. It fucking won't. It
fucking won't. It fucking won't. It fucking won't. It
fucking won't. It fucking won't. It fucking won't. It
fucking won't. It fucking won't. It fucking won't. It
fucking won't. It fucking won't. It fucking won't. It
fucking won't. It fucking won't. It fucking won't. It
fucking won't. It fucking won't. It fucking won't. It
fucking won't. It fucking won't. It fucking won't. It
fucking won't. It fucking won't. It fucking won't. It
fucking won't. It fucking won't. It fucking won't. It
fucking won't. It fucking won't. It fucking won't. It

fucking won't. It fucking won't. It fucking won't. It
fucking won't. It fucking won't. It fucking won't. It
fucking won't. It fucking won't. It fucking won't. It
fucking won't. It fucking won't. It fucking won't. It
fucking won't. It fucking won't. It fucking won't. It
fucking won't. It fucking won't. It fucking won't. It
fucking won't. It fucking won't. It fucking won't. It
fucking won't. It fucking won't. It fucking won't. It
fucking won't. It fucking won't. It fucking won't. It
fucking won't. It fucking won't. It fucking won't. It
fucking won't. It fucking won't. It fucking won't. It
fucking won't. It fucking won't. It fucking won't. It
fucking won't. It fucking won't. It fucking won't. It
fucking won't. It fucking won't. It fucking won't. It
fucking won't. It fucking won't. It fucking won't. It
fucking won't. It fucking won't. It fucking won't. It
fucking won't. It fucking won't. It fucking won't. It
fucking won't. It fucking won't. It fucking won't. It
fucking won't. It fucking won't. It fucking won't. It
fucking won't. It fucking won't. It fucking won't. It
fucking won't. It fucking won't. It fucking won't. It
fucking won't. It fucking won't. It fucking won't. It
fucking won't. It fucking won't. It fucking won't. It
fucking won't. It fucking won't. It fucking won't. It
fucking won't. It fucking won't. It fucking won't. It
fucking won't. It fucking won't. It fucking won't. It
fucking won't. It fucking won't. It fucking won't. It
fucking won't. It fucking won't. It fucking won't. It
fucking won't. It fucking won't. It fucking won't. It
fucking won't. It fucking won't. It fucking won't. It

fucking won't. It fucking won't. It fucking won't. It
fucking won't. It fucking won't. It fucking won't. It
fucking won't. It fucking won't. It fucking won't. It
fucking won't. It fucking won't. It fucking won't. It
fucking won't. It fucking won't. It fucking won't. It
fucking won't. It fucking won't. It fucking won't. It
fucking won't. It fucking won't. It fucking won't. It
fucking won't. It fucking won't. It fucking won't. It
fucking won't. It fucking won't. It fucking won't. It
fucking won't. It fucking won't. It fucking won't. It
fucking won't. It fucking won't. It fucking won't. It
fucking won't. It fucking won't. It fucking won't. It
fucking won't. It fucking won't. It fucking won't. It
fucking won't. It fucking won't. It fucking won't. It
fucking won't. It fucking won't. It fucking won't. It
fucking won't. It fucking won't. It fucking won't. It
fucking won't. It fucking won't. It fucking won't. It
fucking won't. It fucking won't. It fucking won't. It
fucking won't. It fucking won't. It fucking won't. It
fucking won't. It fucking won't. It fucking won't. It
fucking won't. It fucking won't. It fucking won't. It
fucking won't. It fucking won't. It fucking won't. It
fucking won't. It fucking won't. It fucking won't. It
fucking won't. It fucking won't. It fucking won't. It
fucking won't. It fucking won't. It fucking won't. It
fucking won't. It fucking won't. It fucking won't. It
fucking won't. It fucking won't. It fucking won't. It
fucking won't. It fucking won't. It fucking won't. It
fucking won't. It fucking won't. It fucking won't. It
fucking won't. It fucking won't. It fucking won't. It

fucking won't. It fucking won't. It fucking won't. It fucking won't. It fucking won't. It fucking won't. It fucking won't. It fucking won't. It fucking won't.

It fucking won't. It

fucking won't. It fucking won't. It fucking won't. It
fucking won't. It fucking won't. It fucking won't. It
fucking won't. It fucking won't. It fucking won't. It
fucking won't. It fucking won't. It fucking won't. It
fucking won't. It fucking won't. It fucking won't. It
fucking won't. It fucking won't. It fucking won't. It
fucking won't. It fucking won't. It fucking won't. It
fucking won't. It fucking won't. It fucking won't. It
fucking won't. It fucking won't. It fucking won't. It
fucking won't. It fucking won't. It fucking won't. It
fucking won't. It fucking won't. It fucking won't. It
fucking won't. It fucking won't. It fucking won't. It
fucking won't. It fucking won't. It fucking won't. It
fucking won't. It fucking won't. It fucking won't. It
fucking won't. It fucking won't. It fucking won't. It
fucking won't. It fucking won't. It fucking won't. It
fucking won't. It fucking won't. It fucking won't. It
fucking won't. It fucking won't. It fucking won't. It
fucking won't. It fucking won't. It fucking won't. It
fucking won't. It fucking won't. It fucking won't. It
fucking won't. It fucking won't. It fucking won't. It
fucking won't. It fucking won't. It fucking won't. It
fucking won't. It fucking won't. It fucking won't. It
fucking won't. It fucking won't. It fucking won't. It
fucking won't. It fucking won't. It fucking won't. It
fucking won't. It fucking won't. It fucking won't. It
fucking won't. It fucking won't. It fucking won't. It
fucking won't. It fucking won't. It fucking won't. It
fucking won't. It fucking won't. It fucking won't. It
fucking won't. It fucking won't. It fucking won't. It

fucking won't. It fucking won't. It fucking won't. It
fucking won't. It fucking won't. It fucking won't. It
fucking won't. It fucking won't. It fucking won't. It
fucking won't. It fucking won't. It fucking won't. It
fucking won't. It fucking won't. It fucking won't. It
fucking won't. It fucking won't. It fucking won't. It
fucking won't. It fucking won't. It fucking won't. It
fucking won't. It fucking won't. It fucking won't. It
fucking won't. It fucking won't. It fucking won't. It
fucking won't. It fucking won't. It fucking won't. It
fucking won't. It fucking won't. It fucking won't. It
fucking won't. It fucking won't. It fucking won't. It
fucking won't. It fucking won't. It fucking won't. It
fucking won't. It fucking won't. It fucking won't. It
fucking won't. It fucking won't. It fucking won't. It
fucking won't. It fucking won't. It fucking won't. It
fucking won't. It fucking won't. It fucking won't. It
fucking won't. It fucking won't. It fucking won't. It
fucking won't. It fucking won't. It fucking won't. It
fucking won't. It fucking won't. It fucking won't. It
fucking won't. It fucking won't. It fucking won't. It
fucking won't. It fucking won't. It fucking won't. It
fucking won't. It fucking won't. It fucking won't. It
fucking won't. It fucking won't. It fucking won't. It
fucking won't. It fucking won't. It fucking won't. It
fucking won't. It fucking won't. It fucking won't. It
fucking won't. It fucking won't. It fucking won't. It
fucking won't. It fucking won't. It fucking won't. It
fucking won't. It fucking won't. It fucking won't. It
fucking won't. It fucking won't. It fucking won't. It

fucking won't. It fucking won't. It fucking won't. It
fucking won't. It fucking won't. It fucking won't. It
fucking won't. It fucking won't. It fucking won't. It
fucking won't. It fucking won't. It fucking won't. It
fucking won't. It fucking won't. It fucking won't. It
fucking won't. It fucking won't. It fucking won't. It
fucking won't. It fucking won't. It fucking won't. It
fucking won't. It fucking won't. It fucking won't. It
fucking won't. It fucking won't. It fucking won't. It
fucking won't. It fucking won't. It fucking won't. It
fucking won't. It fucking won't. It fucking won't. It
fucking won't. It fucking won't. It fucking won't. It
fucking won't. It fucking won't. It fucking won't. It
fucking won't. It fucking won't. It fucking won't. It
fucking won't. It fucking won't. It fucking won't. It
fucking won't. It fucking won't. It fucking won't. It
fucking won't. It fucking won't. It fucking won't. It
fucking won't. It fucking won't. It fucking won't. It
fucking won't. It fucking won't. It fucking won't. It
fucking won't. It fucking won't. It fucking won't. It
fucking won't. It fucking won't. It fucking won't. It
fucking won't. It fucking won't. It fucking won't. It
fucking won't. It fucking won't. It fucking won't. It
fucking won't. It fucking won't. It fucking won't. It
fucking won't. It fucking won't. It fucking won't. It
fucking won't. It fucking won't. It fucking won't. It
fucking won't. It fucking won't. It fucking won't. It
fucking won't. It fucking won't. It fucking won't. It
fucking won't. It fucking won't. It fucking won't. It
fucking won't. It fucking won't. It fucking won't. It
fucking won't. It fucking won't. It fucking won't. It

fucking won't. It fucking won't. It fucking won't. It
fucking won't. It fucking won't. It fucking won't. It
fucking won't. It fucking won't. It fucking won't. It
fucking won't. It fucking won't. It fucking won't. It
fucking won't. It fucking won't. It fucking won't. It
fucking won't. It fucking won't. It fucking won't. It
fucking won't. It fucking won't. It fucking won't. It
fucking won't. It fucking won't. It fucking won't. It
fucking won't. It fucking won't. It fucking won't. It
fucking won't. It fucking won't. It fucking won't. It
fucking won't. It fucking won't. It fucking won't. It
fucking won't. It fucking won't. It fucking won't. It
fucking won't. It fucking won't. It fucking won't. It
fucking won't. It fucking won't. It fucking won't. It
fucking won't. It fucking won't. It fucking won't. It
fucking won't. It fucking won't. It fucking won't. It
fucking won't. It fucking won't. It fucking won't. It
fucking won't. It fucking won't. It fucking won't. It
fucking won't. It fucking won't. It fucking won't. It
fucking won't. It fucking won't. It fucking won't. It
fucking won't. It fucking won't. It fucking won't. It
fucking won't. It fucking won't. It fucking won't. It
fucking won't. It fucking won't. It fucking won't. It
fucking won't. It fucking won't. It fucking won't. It
fucking won't. It fucking won't. It fucking won't. It
fucking won't. It fucking won't. It fucking won't. It
fucking won't. It fucking won't. It fucking won't. It
fucking won't. It fucking won't. It fucking won't. It
fucking won't. It fucking won't. It fucking won't. It
fucking won't. It fucking won't. It fucking won't. It

fucking won't. It fucking won't. It fucking won't. It
fucking won't. It fucking won't. It fucking won't. It
fucking won't. It fucking won't. It fucking won't. It
fucking won't. It fucking won't. It fucking won't. It
fucking won't. It fucking won't. It fucking won't. It
fucking won't. It fucking won't. It fucking won't. It
fucking won't. It fucking won't. It fucking won't. It
fucking won't. It fucking won't. It fucking won't. It
fucking won't. It fucking won't. It fucking won't. It
fucking won't. It fucking won't. It fucking won't. It
fucking won't. It fucking won't. It fucking won't. It
fucking won't. It fucking won't. It fucking won't. It
fucking won't. It fucking won't. It fucking won't. It
fucking won't. It fucking won't. It fucking won't. It
fucking won't. It fucking won't. It fucking won't. It
fucking won't. It fucking won't. It fucking won't. It
fucking won't. It fucking won't. It fucking won't. It
fucking won't. It fucking won't. It fucking won't. It
fucking won't. It fucking won't. It fucking won't. It
fucking won't. It fucking won't. It fucking won't. It
fucking won't. It fucking won't. It fucking won't. It
fucking won't. It fucking won't. It fucking won't. It
fucking won't. It fucking won't. It fucking won't. It
fucking won't. It fucking won't. It fucking won't. It
fucking won't. It fucking won't. It fucking won't. It
fucking won't. It fucking won't. It fucking won't. It
fucking won't. It fucking won't. It fucking won't. It
fucking won't. It fucking won't. It fucking won't. It
fucking won't. It fucking won't. It fucking won't. It
fucking won't. It fucking won't. It fucking won't. It

fucking won't. It fucking won't. It fucking won't. It
fucking won't. It fucking won't. It fucking won't. It
fucking won't. It fucking won't. It fucking won't. It
fucking won't. It fucking won't. It fucking won't. It
fucking won't. It fucking won't. It fucking won't. It
fucking won't. It fucking won't. It fucking won't. It
fucking won't. It fucking won't. It fucking won't. It
fucking won't. It fucking won't. It fucking won't. It
fucking won't. It fucking won't. It fucking won't. It
fucking won't. It fucking won't. It fucking won't. It
fucking won't. It fucking won't. It fucking won't. It
fucking won't. It fucking won't. It fucking won't. It
fucking won't. It fucking won't. It fucking won't. It
fucking won't. It fucking won't. It fucking won't. It
fucking won't. It fucking won't. It fucking won't. It
fucking won't. It fucking won't. It fucking won't. It
fucking won't. It fucking won't. It fucking won't. It
fucking won't. It fucking won't. It fucking won't. It
fucking won't. It fucking won't. It fucking won't. It
fucking won't. It fucking won't. It fucking won't. It
fucking won't. It fucking won't. It fucking won't. It
fucking won't. It fucking won't. It fucking won't. It
fucking won't. It fucking won't. It fucking won't. It
fucking won't. It fucking won't. It fucking won't. It
fucking won't. It fucking won't. It fucking won't. It
fucking won't. It fucking won't. It fucking won't. It
fucking won't. It fucking won't. It fucking won't. It
fucking won't. It fucking won't. It fucking won't. It
fucking won't. It fucking won't. It fucking won't. It
fucking won't. It fucking won't. It fucking won't. It
fucking won't. It fucking won't. It fucking won't. It

fucking won't. It fucking won't. It fucking won't. It
fucking won't. It fucking won't. It fucking won't. It
fucking won't. It fucking won't. It fucking won't. It
fucking won't. It fucking won't. It fucking won't. It
fucking won't. It fucking won't. It fucking won't. It
fucking won't. It fucking won't. It fucking won't. It
fucking won't. It fucking won't. It fucking won't. It
fucking won't. It fucking won't. It fucking won't. It
fucking won't. It fucking won't. It fucking won't. It
fucking won't. It fucking won't. It fucking won't. It
fucking won't. It fucking won't. It fucking won't. It
fucking won't. It fucking won't. It fucking won't. It
fucking won't. It fucking won't. It fucking won't. It
fucking won't. It fucking won't. It fucking won't. It
fucking won't. It fucking won't. It fucking won't. It
fucking won't. It fucking won't. It fucking won't. It
fucking won't. It fucking won't. It fucking won't. It
fucking won't. It fucking won't. It fucking won't. It
fucking won't. It fucking won't. It fucking won't. It
fucking won't. It fucking won't. It fucking won't. It
fucking won't. It fucking won't. It fucking won't. It
fucking won't. It fucking won't. It fucking won't. It
fucking won't. It fucking won't. It fucking won't. It
fucking won't. It fucking won't. It fucking won't. It
fucking won't. It fucking won't. It fucking won't. It
fucking won't. It fucking won't. It fucking won't. It
fucking won't. It fucking won't. It fucking won't. It
fucking won't. It fucking won't. It fucking won't. It
fucking won't. It fucking won't. It fucking won't. It
fucking won't. It fucking won't. It fucking won't. It
fucking won't. It fucking won't. It fucking won't. It

fucking won't. It fucking won't. It fucking won't. It
fucking won't. It fucking won't. It fucking won't. It
fucking won't. It fucking won't. It fucking won't. It
fucking won't. It fucking won't. It fucking won't. It
fucking won't. It fucking won't. It fucking won't. It
fucking won't. It fucking won't. It fucking won't. It
fucking won't. It fucking won't. It fucking won't. It
fucking won't. It fucking won't. It fucking won't. It
fucking won't. It fucking won't. It fucking won't. It
fucking won't. It fucking won't. It fucking won't. It
fucking won't. It fucking won't. It fucking won't. It
fucking won't. It fucking won't. It fucking won't. It
fucking won't. It fucking won't. It fucking won't. It
fucking won't. It fucking won't. It fucking won't. It
fucking won't. It fucking won't. It fucking won't. It
fucking won't. It fucking won't. It fucking won't. It
fucking won't. It fucking won't. It fucking won't. It
fucking won't. It fucking won't. It fucking won't. It
fucking won't. It fucking won't. It fucking won't. It
fucking won't. It fucking won't. It fucking won't. It
fucking won't. It fucking won't. It fucking won't. It
fucking won't. It fucking won't. It fucking won't. It
fucking won't. It fucking won't. It fucking won't. It
fucking won't. It fucking won't. It fucking won't. It
fucking won't. It fucking won't. It fucking won't. It
fucking won't. It fucking won't. It fucking won't. It
fucking won't. It fucking won't. It fucking won't. It
fucking won't. It fucking won't. It fucking won't. It
fucking won't. It fucking won't. It fucking won't. It
fucking won't. It fucking won't. It fucking won't. It

fucking won't. It fucking won't. It fucking won't. It
fucking won't. It fucking won't. It fucking won't. It
fucking won't. It fucking won't. It fucking won't. It
fucking won't. It fucking won't. It fucking won't. It
fucking won't. It fucking won't. It fucking won't. It
fucking won't. It fucking won't. It fucking won't. It
fucking won't. It fucking won't. It fucking won't. It
fucking won't. It fucking won't. It fucking won't. It
fucking won't. It fucking won't. It fucking won't. It
fucking won't. It fucking won't. It fucking won't. It
fucking won't. It fucking won't. It fucking won't. It
fucking won't. It fucking won't. It fucking won't. It
fucking won't. It fucking won't. It fucking won't. It
fucking won't. It fucking won't. It fucking won't. It
fucking won't. It fucking won't. It fucking won't. It
fucking won't. It fucking won't. It fucking won't. It
fucking won't. It fucking won't. It fucking won't. It
fucking won't. It fucking won't. It fucking won't. It
fucking won't. It fucking won't. It fucking won't. It
fucking won't. It fucking won't. It fucking won't. It
fucking won't. It fucking won't. It fucking won't. It
fucking won't. It fucking won't. It fucking won't. It
fucking won't. It fucking won't. It fucking won't. It
fucking won't. It fucking won't. It fucking won't. It
fucking won't. It fucking won't. It fucking won't. It
fucking won't. It fucking won't. It fucking won't. It
fucking won't. It fucking won't. It fucking won't. It
fucking won't. It fucking won't. It fucking won't. It
fucking won't. It fucking won't. It fucking won't. It

fucking won't. It fucking won't. It fucking won't. It
fucking won't. It fucking won't. It fucking won't. It
fucking won't. It fucking won't. It fucking won't. It
fucking won't. It fucking won't. It fucking won't. It
fucking won't. It fucking won't. It fucking won't. It
fucking won't. It fucking won't. It fucking won't. It
fucking won't. It fucking won't. It fucking won't. It
fucking won't. It fucking won't. It fucking won't. It
fucking won't. It fucking won't. It fucking won't. It
fucking won't. It fucking won't. It fucking won't. It
fucking won't. It fucking won't. It fucking won't. It
fucking won't. It fucking won't. It fucking won't. It
fucking won't. It fucking won't. It fucking won't. It
fucking won't. It fucking won't. It fucking won't. It
fucking won't. It fucking won't. It fucking won't. It
fucking won't. It fucking won't. It fucking won't. It
fucking won't. It fucking won't. It fucking won't. It
fucking won't. It fucking won't. It fucking won't. It
fucking won't. It fucking won't. It fucking won't. It
fucking won't. It fucking won't. It fucking won't. It
fucking won't. It fucking won't. It fucking won't. It
fucking won't. It fucking won't. It fucking won't. It
fucking won't. It fucking won't. It fucking won't. It
fucking won't. It fucking won't. It fucking won't. It
fucking won't. It fucking won't. It fucking won't. It
fucking won't. It fucking won't. It fucking won't. It
fucking won't. It fucking won't. It fucking won't. It
fucking won't. It fucking won't. It fucking won't. It
fucking won't. It fucking won't. It fucking won't. It
fucking won't. It fucking won't. It fucking won't. It

fucking won't. It fucking won't.

It fucking won't. It

fucking won't. It fucking won't. It fucking won't. It
fucking won't. It fucking won't. It fucking won't. It
fucking won't. It fucking won't. It fucking won't. It
fucking won't. It fucking won't. It fucking won't. It
fucking won't. It fucking won't. It fucking won't. It
fucking won't. It fucking won't. It fucking won't. It
fucking won't. It fucking won't. It fucking won't. It
fucking won't. It fucking won't. It fucking won't. It
fucking won't. It fucking won't. It fucking won't. It
fucking won't. It fucking won't. It fucking won't. It
fucking won't. It fucking won't. It fucking won't. It
fucking won't. It fucking won't. It fucking won't. It
fucking won't. It fucking won't. It fucking won't. It
fucking won't. It fucking won't. It fucking won't. It
fucking won't. It fucking won't. It fucking won't. It
fucking won't. It fucking won't. It fucking won't. It
fucking won't. It fucking won't. It fucking won't. It
fucking won't. It fucking won't. It fucking won't. It
fucking won't. It fucking won't. It fucking won't. It
fucking won't. It fucking won't. It fucking won't. It
fucking won't. It fucking won't. It fucking won't. It
fucking won't. It fucking won't. It fucking won't. It
fucking won't. It fucking won't. It fucking won't. It
fucking won't. It fucking won't. It fucking won't. It
fucking won't. It fucking won't. It fucking won't. It
fucking won't. It fucking won't. It fucking won't. It
fucking won't. It fucking won't. It fucking won't. It
fucking won't. It fucking won't. It fucking won't. It
fucking won't. It fucking won't. It fucking won't. It
fucking won't. It fucking won't. It fucking won't. It

fucking won't. It fucking won't. It fucking won't. It
fucking won't. It fucking won't. It fucking won't. It
fucking won't. It fucking won't. It fucking won't. It
fucking won't. It fucking won't. It fucking won't. It
fucking won't. It fucking won't. It fucking won't. It
fucking won't. It fucking won't. It fucking won't. It
fucking won't. It fucking won't. It fucking won't. It
fucking won't. It fucking won't. It fucking won't. It
fucking won't. It fucking won't. It fucking won't. It
fucking won't. It fucking won't. It fucking won't. It
fucking won't. It fucking won't. It fucking won't. It
fucking won't. It fucking won't. It fucking won't. It
fucking won't. It fucking won't. It fucking won't. It
fucking won't. It fucking won't. It fucking won't. It
fucking won't. It fucking won't. It fucking won't. It
fucking won't. It fucking won't. It fucking won't. It
fucking won't. It fucking won't. It fucking won't. It
fucking won't. It fucking won't. It fucking won't. It
fucking won't. It fucking won't. It fucking won't. It
fucking won't. It fucking won't. It fucking won't. It
fucking won't. It fucking won't. It fucking won't. It
fucking won't. It fucking won't. It fucking won't. It
fucking won't. It fucking won't. It fucking won't. It
fucking won't. It fucking won't. It fucking won't. It
fucking won't. It fucking won't. It fucking won't. It
fucking won't. It fucking won't. It fucking won't. It
fucking won't. It fucking won't. It fucking won't. It
fucking won't. It fucking won't. It fucking won't. It
fucking won't. It fucking won't. It fucking won't. It
fucking won't. It fucking won't. It fucking won't. It

fucking won't. It fucking won't. It fucking won't. It
fucking won't. It fucking won't. It fucking won't. It
fucking won't. It fucking won't. It fucking won't. It
fucking won't. It fucking won't. It fucking won't. It
fucking won't. It fucking won't. It fucking won't. It
fucking won't. It fucking won't. It fucking won't. It
fucking won't. It fucking won't. It fucking won't. It
fucking won't. It fucking won't. It fucking won't. It
fucking won't. It fucking won't. It fucking won't. It
fucking won't. It fucking won't. It fucking won't. It
fucking won't. It fucking won't. It fucking won't. It
fucking won't. It fucking won't. It fucking won't. It
fucking won't. It fucking won't. It fucking won't. It
fucking won't. It fucking won't. It fucking won't. It
fucking won't. It fucking won't. It fucking won't. It
fucking won't. It fucking won't. It fucking won't. It
fucking won't. It fucking won't. It fucking won't. It
fucking won't. It fucking won't. It fucking won't. It
fucking won't. It fucking won't. It fucking won't. It
fucking won't. It fucking won't. It fucking won't. It
fucking won't. It fucking won't. It fucking won't. It
fucking won't. It fucking won't. It fucking won't. It
fucking won't. It fucking won't. It fucking won't. It
fucking won't. It fucking won't. It fucking won't. It
fucking won't. It fucking won't. It fucking won't. It
fucking won't. It fucking won't. It fucking won't. It
fucking won't. It fucking won't. It fucking won't. It
fucking won't. It fucking won't. It fucking won't. It
fucking won't. It fucking won't. It fucking won't. It
fucking won't. It fucking won't. It fucking won't. It

fucking won't. It fucking won't. It fucking won't. It
fucking won't. It fucking won't. It fucking won't. It
fucking won't. It fucking won't. It fucking won't. It
fucking won't. It fucking won't. It fucking won't. It
fucking won't. It fucking won't. It fucking won't. It
fucking won't. It fucking won't. It fucking won't. It
fucking won't. It fucking won't. It fucking won't. It
fucking won't. It fucking won't. It fucking won't. It
fucking won't. It fucking won't. It fucking won't. It
fucking won't. It fucking won't. It fucking won't. It
fucking won't. It fucking won't. It fucking won't. It
fucking won't. It fucking won't. It fucking won't. It
fucking won't. It fucking won't. It fucking won't. It
fucking won't. It fucking won't. It fucking won't. It
fucking won't. It fucking won't. It fucking won't. It
fucking won't. It fucking won't. It fucking won't. It
fucking won't. It fucking won't. It fucking won't. It
fucking won't. It fucking won't. It fucking won't. It
fucking won't. It fucking won't. It fucking won't. It
fucking won't. It fucking won't. It fucking won't. It
fucking won't. It fucking won't. It fucking won't. It
fucking won't. It fucking won't. It fucking won't. It
fucking won't. It fucking won't. It fucking won't. It
fucking won't. It fucking won't. It fucking won't. It
fucking won't. It fucking won't. It fucking won't. It
fucking won't. It fucking won't. It fucking won't. It
fucking won't. It fucking won't. It fucking won't. It
fucking won't. It fucking won't. It fucking won't. It
fucking won't. It fucking won't. It fucking won't. It
fucking won't. It fucking won't. It fucking won't. It

fucking won't. It fucking won't. It fucking won't. It
fucking won't. It fucking won't. It fucking won't. It
fucking won't. It fucking won't. It fucking won't. It
fucking won't. It fucking won't. It fucking won't. It
fucking won't. It fucking won't. It fucking won't. It
fucking won't. It fucking won't. It fucking won't. It
fucking won't. It fucking won't. It fucking won't. It
fucking won't. It fucking won't. It fucking won't. It
fucking won't. It fucking won't. It fucking won't. It
fucking won't. It fucking won't. It fucking won't. It
fucking won't. It fucking won't. It fucking won't. It
fucking won't. It fucking won't. It fucking won't. It
fucking won't. It fucking won't. It fucking won't. It
fucking won't. It fucking won't. It fucking won't. It
fucking won't. It fucking won't. It fucking won't. It
fucking won't. It fucking won't. It fucking won't. It
fucking won't. It fucking won't. It fucking won't. It
fucking won't. It fucking won't. It fucking won't. It
fucking won't. It fucking won't. It fucking won't. It
fucking won't. It fucking won't. It fucking won't. It
fucking won't. It fucking won't. It fucking won't. It
fucking won't. It fucking won't. It fucking won't. It
fucking won't. It fucking won't. It fucking won't. It
fucking won't. It fucking won't. It fucking won't. It
fucking won't. It fucking won't. It fucking won't. It
fucking won't. It fucking won't. It fucking won't. It
fucking won't. It fucking won't. It fucking won't. It
fucking won't. It fucking won't. It fucking won't. It
fucking won't. It fucking won't. It fucking won't. It
fucking won't. It fucking won't. It fucking won't. It

fucking won't. It fucking won't. It fucking won't. It
fucking won't. It fucking won't. It fucking won't. It
fucking won't. It fucking won't. It fucking won't. It
fucking won't. It fucking won't. It fucking won't. It
fucking won't. It fucking won't. It fucking won't. It
fucking won't. It fucking won't. It fucking won't. It
fucking won't. It fucking won't. It fucking won't. It
fucking won't. It fucking won't. It fucking won't. It
fucking won't. It fucking won't. It fucking won't. It
fucking won't. It fucking won't. It fucking won't. It
fucking won't. It fucking won't. It fucking won't. It
fucking won't. It fucking won't. It fucking won't. It
fucking won't. It fucking won't. It fucking won't. It
fucking won't. It fucking won't. It fucking won't. It
fucking won't. It fucking won't. It fucking won't. It
fucking won't. It fucking won't. It fucking won't. It
fucking won't. It fucking won't. It fucking won't. It
fucking won't. It fucking won't. It fucking won't. It
fucking won't. It fucking won't. It fucking won't. It
fucking won't. It fucking won't. It fucking won't. It
fucking won't. It fucking won't. It fucking won't. It
fucking won't. It fucking won't. It fucking won't. It
fucking won't. It fucking won't. It fucking won't. It
fucking won't. It fucking won't. It fucking won't. It
fucking won't. It fucking won't. It fucking won't. It
fucking won't. It fucking won't. It fucking won't. It
fucking won't. It fucking won't. It fucking won't. It
fucking won't. It fucking won't. It fucking won't. It
fucking won't. It fucking won't. It fucking won't. It
fucking won't. It fucking won't. It fucking won't. It

fucking won't. It fucking won't. It fucking won't. It
fucking won't. It fucking won't. It fucking won't. It
fucking won't. It fucking won't. It fucking won't. It
fucking won't. It fucking won't. It fucking won't. It
fucking won't. It fucking won't. It fucking won't. It
fucking won't. It fucking won't. It fucking won't. It
fucking won't. It fucking won't. It fucking won't. It
fucking won't. It fucking won't. It fucking won't. It
fucking won't. It fucking won't. It fucking won't. It
fucking won't. It fucking won't. It fucking won't. It
fucking won't. It fucking won't. It fucking won't. It
fucking won't. It fucking won't. It fucking won't. It
fucking won't. It fucking won't. It fucking won't. It
fucking won't. It fucking won't. It fucking won't. It
fucking won't. It fucking won't. It fucking won't. It
fucking won't. It fucking won't. It fucking won't. It
fucking won't. It fucking won't. It fucking won't. It
fucking won't. It fucking won't. It fucking won't. It
fucking won't. It fucking won't. It fucking won't. It
fucking won't. It fucking won't. It fucking won't. It
fucking won't. It fucking won't. It fucking won't. It
fucking won't. It fucking won't. It fucking won't. It
fucking won't. It fucking won't. It fucking won't. It
fucking won't. It fucking won't. It fucking won't. It
fucking won't. It fucking won't. It fucking won't. It
fucking won't. It fucking won't. It fucking won't. It
fucking won't. It fucking won't. It fucking won't. It
fucking won't. It fucking won't. It fucking won't. It
fucking won't. It fucking won't. It fucking won't. It
fucking won't. It fucking won't. It fucking won't. It
fucking won't. It fucking won't. It fucking won't. It

fucking won't. It fucking won't. It fucking won't. It
fucking won't. It fucking won't. It fucking won't. It
fucking won't. It fucking won't. It fucking won't. It
fucking won't. It fucking won't. It fucking won't. It
fucking won't. It fucking won't. It fucking won't. It
fucking won't. It fucking won't. It fucking won't. It
fucking won't. It fucking won't. It fucking won't. It
fucking won't. It fucking won't. It fucking won't. It
fucking won't. It fucking won't. It fucking won't. It
fucking won't. It fucking won't. It fucking won't. It
fucking won't. It fucking won't. It fucking won't. It
fucking won't. It fucking won't. It fucking won't. It
fucking won't. It fucking won't. It fucking won't. It
fucking won't. It fucking won't. It fucking won't. It
fucking won't. It fucking won't. It fucking won't. It
fucking won't. It fucking won't. It fucking won't. It
fucking won't. It fucking won't. It fucking won't. It
fucking won't. It fucking won't. It fucking won't. It
fucking won't. It fucking won't. It fucking won't. It
fucking won't. It fucking won't. It fucking won't. It
fucking won't. It fucking won't. It fucking won't. It
fucking won't. It fucking won't. It fucking won't. It
fucking won't. It fucking won't. It fucking won't. It
fucking won't. It fucking won't. It fucking won't. It
fucking won't. It fucking won't. It fucking won't. It
fucking won't. It fucking won't. It fucking won't. It
fucking won't. It fucking won't. It fucking won't. It
fucking won't. It fucking won't. It fucking won't. It
fucking won't. It fucking won't. It fucking won't. It
fucking won't. It fucking won't. It fucking won't. It

fucking won't. It fucking won't. It fucking won't. It
fucking won't. It fucking won't. It fucking won't. It
fucking won't. It fucking won't. It fucking won't. It
fucking won't. It fucking won't. It fucking won't. It
fucking won't. It fucking won't. It fucking won't. It
fucking won't. It fucking won't. It fucking won't. It
fucking won't. It fucking won't. It fucking won't. It
fucking won't. It fucking won't. It fucking won't. It
fucking won't. It fucking won't. It fucking won't. It
fucking won't. It fucking won't. It fucking won't. It
fucking won't. It fucking won't. It fucking won't. It
fucking won't. It fucking won't. It fucking won't. It
fucking won't. It fucking won't. It fucking won't. It
fucking won't. It fucking won't. It fucking won't. It
fucking won't. It fucking won't. It fucking won't. It
fucking won't. It fucking won't. It fucking won't. It
fucking won't. It fucking won't. It fucking won't. It
fucking won't. It fucking won't. It fucking won't. It
fucking won't. It fucking won't. It fucking won't. It
fucking won't. It fucking won't. It fucking won't. It
fucking won't. It fucking won't. It fucking won't. It
fucking won't. It fucking won't. It fucking won't. It
fucking won't. It fucking won't. It fucking won't. It
fucking won't. It fucking won't. It fucking won't. It
fucking won't. It fucking won't. It fucking won't. It
fucking won't. It fucking won't. It fucking won't. It
fucking won't. It fucking won't. It fucking won't. It
fucking won't. It fucking won't. It fucking won't. It
fucking won't. It fucking won't. It fucking won't. It
fucking won't. It fucking won't. It fucking won't. It

fucking won't. It fucking won't. It fucking won't. It
fucking won't. It fucking won't. It fucking won't. It
fucking won't. It fucking won't. It fucking won't. It
fucking won't. It fucking won't. It fucking won't. It
fucking won't. It fucking won't. It fucking won't. It
fucking won't. It fucking won't. It fucking won't. It
fucking won't. It fucking won't. It fucking won't. It
fucking won't. It fucking won't. It fucking won't. It
fucking won't. It fucking won't. It fucking won't. It
fucking won't. It fucking won't. It fucking won't. It
fucking won't. It fucking won't. It fucking won't. It
fucking won't. It fucking won't. It fucking won't. It
fucking won't. It fucking won't. It fucking won't. It
fucking won't. It fucking won't. It fucking won't. It
fucking won't. It fucking won't. It fucking won't. It
fucking won't. It fucking won't. It fucking won't. It
fucking won't. It fucking won't. It fucking won't. It
fucking won't. It fucking won't. It fucking won't. It
fucking won't. It fucking won't. It fucking won't. It
fucking won't. It fucking won't. It fucking won't. It
fucking won't. It fucking won't. It fucking won't. It
fucking won't. It fucking won't. It fucking won't. It
fucking won't. It fucking won't. It fucking won't. It
fucking won't. It fucking won't. It fucking won't. It
fucking won't. It fucking won't. It fucking won't. It
fucking won't. It fucking won't. It fucking won't. It
fucking won't. It fucking won't. It fucking won't. It
fucking won't. It fucking won't. It fucking won't. It
fucking won't. It fucking won't. It fucking won't. It
fucking won't. It fucking won't. It fucking won't. It

fucking won't. It fucking won't. It fucking won't. It
fucking won't. It fucking won't. It fucking won't. It
fucking won't. It fucking won't. It fucking won't. It
fucking won't. It fucking won't. It fucking won't. It
fucking won't. It fucking won't. It fucking won't. It
fucking won't. It fucking won't. It fucking won't. It
fucking won't. It fucking won't. It fucking won't. It
fucking won't. It fucking won't. It fucking won't. It
fucking won't. It fucking won't. It fucking won't. It
fucking won't. It fucking won't. It fucking won't. It
fucking won't. It fucking won't. It fucking won't.

It fucking won't. It fucking won't. It fucking won't. It
fucking won't. It fucking won't. It fucking won't. It
fucking won't. It fucking won't. It fucking won't. It
fucking won't. It fucking won't. It fucking won't. It
fucking won't. It fucking won't. It fucking won't. It
fucking won't. It fucking won't. It fucking won't. It
fucking won't. It fucking won't. It fucking won't. It
fucking won't. It fucking won't. It fucking won't. It
fucking won't. It fucking won't. It fucking won't. It
fucking won't. It fucking won't. It fucking won't. It
fucking won't. It fucking won't. It fucking won't. It
fucking won't. It fucking won't. It fucking won't. It
fucking won't. It fucking won't. It fucking won't. It
fucking won't. It fucking won't. It fucking won't. It
fucking won't. It fucking won't. It fucking won't. It
fucking won't. It fucking won't. It fucking won't. It
fucking won't. It fucking won't. It fucking won't. It
fucking won't. It fucking won't. It fucking won't. It
fucking won't. It fucking won't. It fucking won't. It

fucking won't. It fucking won't. It fucking won't. It
fucking won't. It fucking won't. It fucking won't. It
fucking won't. It fucking won't. It fucking won't. It
fucking won't. It fucking won't. It fucking won't. It
fucking won't. It fucking won't. It fucking won't. It
fucking won't. It fucking won't. It fucking won't. It
fucking won't. It fucking won't. It fucking won't. It
fucking won't. It fucking won't. It fucking won't. It
fucking won't. It fucking won't. It fucking won't. It
fucking won't. It fucking won't. It fucking won't. It
fucking won't. It fucking won't. It fucking won't. It
fucking won't. It fucking won't. It fucking won't. It
fucking won't. It fucking won't. It fucking won't. It
fucking won't. It fucking won't. It fucking won't. It
fucking won't. It fucking won't. It fucking won't. It
fucking won't. It fucking won't. It fucking won't. It
fucking won't. It fucking won't. It fucking won't. It
fucking won't. It fucking won't. It fucking won't. It
fucking won't. It fucking won't. It fucking won't. It
fucking won't. It fucking won't. It fucking won't. It
fucking won't. It fucking won't. It fucking won't. It
fucking won't. It fucking won't. It fucking won't. It
fucking won't. It fucking won't. It fucking won't. It
fucking won't. It fucking won't. It fucking won't. It
fucking won't. It fucking won't. It fucking won't. It
fucking won't. It fucking won't. It fucking won't. It
fucking won't. It fucking won't. It fucking won't. It
fucking won't. It fucking won't. It fucking won't. It
fucking won't. It fucking won't. It fucking won't. It
fucking won't. It fucking won't. It fucking won't. It

fucking won't. It fucking won't. It fucking won't. It
fucking won't. It fucking won't. It fucking won't. It
fucking won't. It fucking won't. It fucking won't. It
fucking won't. It fucking won't. It fucking won't. It
fucking won't. It fucking won't. It fucking won't. It
fucking won't. It fucking won't. It fucking won't. It
fucking won't. It fucking won't. It fucking won't. It
fucking won't. It fucking won't. It fucking won't. It
fucking won't. It fucking won't. It fucking won't. It
fucking won't. It fucking won't. It fucking won't. It
fucking won't. It fucking won't. It fucking won't. It
fucking won't. It fucking won't. It fucking won't. It
fucking won't. It fucking won't. It fucking won't. It
fucking won't. It fucking won't. It fucking won't. It
fucking won't. It fucking won't. It fucking won't. It
fucking won't. It fucking won't. It fucking won't. It
fucking won't. It fucking won't. It fucking won't. It
fucking won't. It fucking won't. It fucking won't. It
fucking won't. It fucking won't. It fucking won't. It
fucking won't. It fucking won't. It fucking won't. It
fucking won't. It fucking won't. It fucking won't. It
fucking won't. It fucking won't. It fucking won't. It
fucking won't. It fucking won't. It fucking won't. It
fucking won't. It fucking won't. It fucking won't. It
fucking won't. It fucking won't. It fucking won't. It
fucking won't. It fucking won't. It fucking won't. It
fucking won't. It fucking won't. It fucking won't. It
fucking won't. It fucking won't. It fucking won't. It
fucking won't. It fucking won't. It fucking won't. It
fucking won't. It fucking won't. It fucking won't. It

fucking won't. It fucking won't. It fucking won't. It
fucking won't. It fucking won't. It fucking won't. It
fucking won't. It fucking won't. It fucking won't. It
fucking won't. It fucking won't. It fucking won't. It
fucking won't. It fucking won't. It fucking won't. It
fucking won't. It fucking won't. It fucking won't. It
fucking won't. It fucking won't. It fucking won't. It
fucking won't. It fucking won't. It fucking won't. It
fucking won't. It fucking won't. It fucking won't. It
fucking won't. It fucking won't. It fucking won't. It
fucking won't. It fucking won't. It fucking won't. It
fucking won't. It fucking won't. It fucking won't. It
fucking won't. It fucking won't. It fucking won't. It
fucking won't. It fucking won't. It fucking won't. It
fucking won't. It fucking won't. It fucking won't. It
fucking won't. It fucking won't. It fucking won't. It
fucking won't. It fucking won't. It fucking won't. It
fucking won't. It fucking won't. It fucking won't. It
fucking won't. It fucking won't. It fucking won't. It
fucking won't. It fucking won't. It fucking won't. It
fucking won't. It fucking won't. It fucking won't. It
fucking won't. It fucking won't. It fucking won't. It
fucking won't. It fucking won't. It fucking won't. It
fucking won't. It fucking won't. It fucking won't. It
fucking won't. It fucking won't. It fucking won't. It
fucking won't. It fucking won't. It fucking won't. It
fucking won't. It fucking won't. It fucking won't. It
fucking won't. It fucking won't. It fucking won't. It
fucking won't. It fucking won't. It fucking won't. It
fucking won't. It fucking won't. It fucking won't. It
fucking won't. It fucking won't. It fucking won't. It
fucking won't. It fucking won't. It fucking won't. It

fucking won't. It fucking won't. It fucking won't. It
fucking won't. It fucking won't. It fucking won't. It
fucking won't. It fucking won't. It fucking won't. It
fucking won't. It fucking won't. It fucking won't. It
fucking won't. It fucking won't. It fucking won't. It
fucking won't. It fucking won't. It fucking won't. It
fucking won't. It fucking won't. It fucking won't. It
fucking won't. It fucking won't. It fucking won't. It
fucking won't. It fucking won't. It fucking won't. It
fucking won't. It fucking won't. It fucking won't. It
fucking won't. It fucking won't. It fucking won't. It
fucking won't. It fucking won't. It fucking won't. It
fucking won't. It fucking won't. It fucking won't. It
fucking won't. It fucking won't. It fucking won't. It
fucking won't. It fucking won't. It fucking won't. It
fucking won't. It fucking won't. It fucking won't. It
fucking won't. It fucking won't. It fucking won't. It
fucking won't. It fucking won't. It fucking won't. It
fucking won't. It fucking won't. It fucking won't. It
fucking won't. It fucking won't. It fucking won't. It
fucking won't. It fucking won't. It fucking won't. It
fucking won't. It fucking won't. It fucking won't. It
fucking won't. It fucking won't. It fucking won't. It
fucking won't. It fucking won't. It fucking won't. It
fucking won't. It fucking won't. It fucking won't. It
fucking won't. It fucking won't. It fucking won't. It
fucking won't. It fucking won't. It fucking won't. It
fucking won't. It fucking won't. It fucking won't. It
fucking won't. It fucking won't. It fucking won't. It
fucking won't. It fucking won't. It fucking won't. It
fucking won't. It fucking won't. It fucking won't. It

fucking won't. It fucking won't. It fucking won't. It
fucking won't. It fucking won't. It fucking won't. It
fucking won't. It fucking won't. It fucking won't. It
fucking won't. It fucking won't. It fucking won't. It
fucking won't. It fucking won't. It fucking won't. It
fucking won't. It fucking won't. It fucking won't. It
fucking won't. It fucking won't. It fucking won't. It
fucking won't. It fucking won't. It fucking won't. It
fucking won't. It fucking won't. It fucking won't. It
fucking won't. It fucking won't. It fucking won't. It
fucking won't. It fucking won't. It fucking won't. It
fucking won't. It fucking won't. It fucking won't. It
fucking won't. It fucking won't. It fucking won't. It
fucking won't. It fucking won't. It fucking won't. It
fucking won't. It fucking won't. It fucking won't. It
fucking won't. It fucking won't. It fucking won't. It
fucking won't. It fucking won't. It fucking won't. It
fucking won't. It fucking won't. It fucking won't. It
fucking won't. It fucking won't. It fucking won't. It
fucking won't. It fucking won't. It fucking won't. It
fucking won't. It fucking won't. It fucking won't. It
fucking won't. It fucking won't. It fucking won't. It
fucking won't. It fucking won't. It fucking won't. It
fucking won't. It fucking won't. It fucking won't. It
fucking won't. It fucking won't. It fucking won't. It
fucking won't. It fucking won't. It fucking won't. It
fucking won't. It fucking won't. It fucking won't. It
fucking won't. It fucking won't. It fucking won't. It
fucking won't. It fucking won't. It fucking won't. It
fucking won't. It fucking won't. It fucking won't. It
fucking won't. It fucking won't. It fucking won't. It

fucking won't. It fucking won't. It fucking won't. It
fucking won't. It fucking won't. It fucking won't. It
fucking won't. It fucking won't. It fucking won't. It
fucking won't. It fucking won't. It fucking won't. It
fucking won't. It fucking won't. It fucking won't. It
fucking won't. It fucking won't. It fucking won't. It
fucking won't. It fucking won't. It fucking won't. It
fucking won't. It fucking won't. It fucking won't. It
fucking won't. It fucking won't. It fucking won't. It
fucking won't. It fucking won't. It fucking won't. It
fucking won't. It fucking won't. It fucking won't. It
fucking won't. It fucking won't. It fucking won't. It
fucking won't. It fucking won't. It fucking won't. It
fucking won't. It fucking won't. It fucking won't. It
fucking won't. It fucking won't. It fucking won't. It
fucking won't. It fucking won't. It fucking won't. It
fucking won't. It fucking won't. It fucking won't. It
fucking won't. It fucking won't. It fucking won't. It
fucking won't. It fucking won't. It fucking won't. It
fucking won't. It fucking won't. It fucking won't. It
fucking won't. It fucking won't. It fucking won't. It
fucking won't. It fucking won't. It fucking won't. It
fucking won't. It fucking won't. It fucking won't. It
fucking won't. It fucking won't. It fucking won't. It
fucking won't. It fucking won't. It fucking won't. It
fucking won't. It fucking won't. It fucking won't. It
fucking won't. It fucking won't. It fucking won't. It
fucking won't. It fucking won't. It fucking won't. It
fucking won't. It fucking won't. It fucking won't. It
fucking won't. It fucking won't. It fucking won't. It

fucking won't. It fucking won't. It fucking won't. It
fucking won't. It fucking won't. It fucking won't. It
fucking won't. It fucking won't. It fucking won't. It
fucking won't. It fucking won't. It fucking won't. It
fucking won't. It fucking won't. It fucking won't. It
fucking won't. It fucking won't. It fucking won't. It
fucking won't. It fucking won't. It fucking won't. It
fucking won't. It fucking won't. It fucking won't. It
fucking won't. It fucking won't. It fucking won't. It
fucking won't. It fucking won't. It fucking won't. It
fucking won't. It fucking won't. It fucking won't. It
fucking won't. It fucking won't. It fucking won't. It
fucking won't. It fucking won't. It fucking won't. It
fucking won't. It fucking won't. It fucking won't. It
fucking won't. It fucking won't. It fucking won't. It
fucking won't. It fucking won't. It fucking won't. It
fucking won't. It fucking won't. It fucking won't. It
fucking won't. It fucking won't. It fucking won't. It
fucking won't. It fucking won't. It fucking won't. It
fucking won't. It fucking won't. It fucking won't. It
fucking won't. It fucking won't. It fucking won't. It
fucking won't. It fucking won't. It fucking won't. It
fucking won't. It fucking won't. It fucking won't. It
fucking won't. It fucking won't. It fucking won't. It
fucking won't. It fucking won't. It fucking won't. It
fucking won't. It fucking won't. It fucking won't. It
fucking won't. It fucking won't. It fucking won't. It
fucking won't. It fucking won't. It fucking won't. It
fucking won't. It fucking won't. It fucking won't. It
fucking won't. It fucking won't. It fucking won't. It

fucking won't. It fucking won't. It fucking won't. It
fucking won't. It fucking won't. It fucking won't. It
fucking won't. It fucking won't. It fucking won't. It
fucking won't. It fucking won't. It fucking won't. It
fucking won't. It fucking won't. It fucking won't. It
fucking won't. It fucking won't. It fucking won't. It
fucking won't. It fucking won't. It fucking won't. It
fucking won't. It fucking won't. It fucking won't. It
fucking won't. It fucking won't. It fucking won't. It
fucking won't. It fucking won't. It fucking won't. It
fucking won't. It fucking won't. It fucking won't. It
fucking won't. It fucking won't. It fucking won't. It
fucking won't. It fucking won't. It fucking won't. It
fucking won't. It fucking won't. It fucking won't. It
fucking won't. It fucking won't. It fucking won't. It
fucking won't. It fucking won't. It fucking won't. It
fucking won't. It fucking won't. It fucking won't. It
fucking won't. It fucking won't. It fucking won't. It
fucking won't. It fucking won't. It fucking won't. It
fucking won't. It fucking won't. It fucking won't. It
fucking won't. It fucking won't. It fucking won't. It
fucking won't. It fucking won't. It fucking won't. It
fucking won't. It fucking won't. It fucking won't. It
fucking won't. It fucking won't. It fucking won't. It
fucking won't. It fucking won't. It fucking won't. It
fucking won't. It fucking won't. It fucking won't. It
fucking won't. It fucking won't. It fucking won't. It
fucking won't. It fucking won't. It fucking won't. It
fucking won't. It fucking won't. It fucking won't. It
fucking won't. It fucking won't. It fucking won't. It
fucking won't. It fucking won't. It fucking won't. It

fucking won't. It fucking won't. It fucking won't. It
fucking won't. It fucking won't. It fucking won't. It
fucking won't. It fucking won't. It fucking won't. It
fucking won't. It fucking won't. It fucking won't. It
fucking won't. It fucking won't. It fucking won't. It
fucking won't. It fucking won't. It fucking won't. It
fucking won't. It fucking won't. It fucking won't. It
fucking won't. It fucking won't. It fucking won't. It
fucking won't. It fucking won't. It fucking won't. It
fucking won't. It fucking won't. It fucking won't. It
fucking won't. It fucking won't. It fucking won't. It
fucking won't. It fucking won't. It fucking won't. It
fucking won't. It fucking won't. It fucking won't. It
fucking won't. It fucking won't. It fucking won't. It
fucking won't. It fucking won't. It fucking won't. It
fucking won't. It fucking won't. It fucking won't. It
fucking won't. It fucking won't. It fucking won't. It
fucking won't. It fucking won't. It fucking won't. It
fucking won't. It fucking won't. It fucking won't. It
fucking won't. It fucking won't. It fucking won't. It
fucking won't. It fucking won't. It fucking won't. It
fucking won't. It fucking won't. It fucking won't. It
fucking won't. It fucking won't. It fucking won't. It
fucking won't. It fucking won't. It fucking won't. It
fucking won't. It fucking won't. It fucking won't. It
fucking won't. It fucking won't. It fucking won't. It
fucking won't. It fucking won't. It fucking won't. It
fucking won't. It fucking won't. It fucking won't. It
fucking won't. It fucking won't. It fucking won't. It
fucking won't. It fucking won't. It fucking won't. It

fucking won't. It fucking won't. It fucking won't. It
fucking won't. It fucking won't. It fucking won't. It
fucking won't. It fucking won't. It fucking won't. It
fucking won't. It fucking won't. It fucking won't. It
fucking won't. It fucking won't. It fucking won't. It
fucking won't. It fucking won't. It fucking won't. It
fucking won't. It fucking won't. It fucking won't. It
fucking won't. It fucking won't. It fucking won't. It
fucking won't. It fucking won't. It fucking won't. It
fucking won't. It fucking won't. It fucking won't. It
fucking won't. It fucking won't. It fucking won't. It
fucking won't. It fucking won't. It fucking won't. It
fucking won't. It fucking won't. It fucking won't. It
fucking won't. It fucking won't. It fucking won't. It
fucking won't. It fucking won't. It fucking won't. It
fucking won't. It fucking won't. It fucking won't. It
fucking won't. It fucking won't. It fucking won't. It
fucking won't. It fucking won't. It fucking won't. It
fucking won't. It fucking won't. It fucking won't. It
fucking won't. It fucking won't. It fucking won't. It
fucking won't. It fucking won't. It fucking won't. It
fucking won't. It fucking won't. It fucking won't. It
fucking won't. It fucking won't. It fucking won't. It
fucking won't. It fucking won't. It fucking won't. It
fucking won't. It fucking won't. It fucking won't. It
fucking won't. It fucking won't. It fucking won't. It
fucking won't. It fucking won't. It fucking won't. It
fucking won't. It fucking won't. It fucking won't. It
fucking won't. It fucking won't. It fucking won't. It
fucking won't. It fucking won't. It fucking won't. It

fucking won't. It fucking won't. It fucking won't. It
fucking won't. It fucking won't. It fucking won't. It
fucking won't. It fucking won't. It fucking won't. It
fucking won't. It fucking won't. It fucking won't. It
fucking won't. It fucking won't. It fucking won't. It
fucking won't. It fucking won't. It fucking won't. It
fucking won't. It fucking won't. It fucking won't. It
fucking won't. It fucking won't. It fucking won't. It
fucking won't. It fucking won't. It fucking won't. It
fucking won't. It fucking won't. It fucking won't. It
fucking won't. It fucking won't. It fucking won't. It
fucking won't. It fucking won't. It fucking won't. It
fucking won't. It fucking won't. It fucking won't. It
fucking won't. It fucking won't. It fucking won't. It
fucking won't. It fucking won't. It fucking won't.

It fucking won't. It fucking won't. It fucking won't. It
fucking won't. It fucking won't. It fucking won't. It
fucking won't. It fucking won't. It fucking won't. It
fucking won't. It fucking won't. It fucking won't. It
fucking won't. It fucking won't. It fucking won't. It
fucking won't. It fucking won't. It fucking won't. It
fucking won't. It fucking won't. It fucking won't. It
fucking won't. It fucking won't. It fucking won't. It
fucking won't. It fucking won't. It fucking won't. It
fucking won't. It fucking won't. It fucking won't. It
fucking won't. It fucking won't. It fucking won't. It
fucking won't. It fucking won't. It fucking won't. It
fucking won't. It fucking won't. It fucking won't. It
fucking won't. It fucking won't. It fucking won't. It
fucking won't. It fucking won't. It fucking won't. It

fucking won't. It fucking won't. It fucking won't. It
fucking won't. It fucking won't. It fucking won't. It
fucking won't. It fucking won't. It fucking won't. It
fucking won't. It fucking won't. It fucking won't. It
fucking won't. It fucking won't. It fucking won't. It
fucking won't. It fucking won't. It fucking won't. It
fucking won't. It fucking won't. It fucking won't. It
fucking won't. It fucking won't. It fucking won't. It
fucking won't. It fucking won't. It fucking won't. It
fucking won't. It fucking won't. It fucking won't. It
fucking won't. It fucking won't. It fucking won't. It
fucking won't. It fucking won't. It fucking won't. It
fucking won't. It fucking won't. It fucking won't. It
fucking won't. It fucking won't. It fucking won't. It
fucking won't. It fucking won't. It fucking won't. It
fucking won't. It fucking won't. It fucking won't. It
fucking won't. It fucking won't. It fucking won't. It
fucking won't. It fucking won't. It fucking won't. It
fucking won't. It fucking won't. It fucking won't. It
fucking won't. It fucking won't. It fucking won't. It
fucking won't. It fucking won't. It fucking won't. It
fucking won't. It fucking won't. It fucking won't. It
fucking won't. It fucking won't. It fucking won't. It
fucking won't. It fucking won't. It fucking won't. It
fucking won't. It fucking won't. It fucking won't. It
fucking won't. It fucking won't. It fucking won't. It
fucking won't. It fucking won't. It fucking won't. It
fucking won't. It fucking won't. It fucking won't. It
fucking won't. It fucking won't. It fucking won't. It
fucking won't. It fucking won't. It fucking won't. It
fucking won't. It fucking won't. It fucking won't. It

fucking won't. It fucking won't. It fucking won't. It
fucking won't. It fucking won't. It fucking won't. It
fucking won't. It fucking won't. It fucking won't. It
fucking won't. It fucking won't. It fucking won't. It
fucking won't. It fucking won't. It fucking won't. It
fucking won't. It fucking won't. It fucking won't. It
fucking won't. It fucking won't. It fucking won't. It
fucking won't. It fucking won't. It fucking won't. It
fucking won't. It fucking won't. It fucking won't. It
fucking won't. It fucking won't. It fucking won't. It
fucking won't. It fucking won't. It fucking won't. It
fucking won't. It fucking won't. It fucking won't. It
fucking won't. It fucking won't. It fucking won't. It
fucking won't. It fucking won't. It fucking won't. It
fucking won't. It fucking won't. It fucking won't. It
fucking won't. It fucking won't. It fucking won't. It
fucking won't. It fucking won't. It fucking won't. It
fucking won't. It fucking won't. It fucking won't. It
fucking won't. It fucking won't. It fucking won't. It
fucking won't. It fucking won't. It fucking won't. It
fucking won't. It fucking won't. It fucking won't. It
fucking won't. It fucking won't. It fucking won't. It
fucking won't. It fucking won't. It fucking won't. It
fucking won't. It fucking won't. It fucking won't. It
fucking won't. It fucking won't. It fucking won't. It
fucking won't. It fucking won't. It fucking won't. It
fucking won't. It fucking won't. It fucking won't. It
fucking won't. It fucking won't. It fucking won't. It
fucking won't. It fucking won't. It fucking won't. It
fucking won't. It fucking won't. It fucking won't. It

fucking won't. It fucking won't. It fucking won't. It
fucking won't. It fucking won't. It fucking won't. It
fucking won't. It fucking won't. It fucking won't. It
fucking won't. It fucking won't. It fucking won't. It
fucking won't. It fucking won't. It fucking won't. It
fucking won't. It fucking won't. It fucking won't. It
fucking won't. It fucking won't. It fucking won't. It
fucking won't. It fucking won't. It fucking won't. It
fucking won't. It fucking won't. It fucking won't. It
fucking won't. It fucking won't. It fucking won't. It
fucking won't. It fucking won't. It fucking won't. It
fucking won't. It fucking won't. It fucking won't. It
fucking won't. It fucking won't. It fucking won't. It
fucking won't. It fucking won't. It fucking won't. It
fucking won't. It fucking won't. It fucking won't. It
fucking won't. It fucking won't. It fucking won't. It
fucking won't. It fucking won't. It fucking won't. It
fucking won't. It fucking won't. It fucking won't. It
fucking won't. It fucking won't. It fucking won't. It
fucking won't. It fucking won't. It fucking won't. It
fucking won't. It fucking won't. It fucking won't. It
fucking won't. It fucking won't. It fucking won't. It
fucking won't. It fucking won't. It fucking won't. It
fucking won't. It fucking won't. It fucking won't. It
fucking won't. It fucking won't. It fucking won't. It
fucking won't. It fucking won't. It fucking won't. It
fucking won't. It fucking won't. It fucking won't. It
fucking won't. It fucking won't. It fucking won't. It
fucking won't. It fucking won't. It fucking won't. It
fucking won't. It fucking won't. It fucking won't. It

fucking won't. It fucking won't. It fucking won't. It
fucking won't. It fucking won't. It fucking won't. It
fucking won't. It fucking won't. It fucking won't. It
fucking won't. It fucking won't. It fucking won't. It
fucking won't. It fucking won't. It fucking won't. It
fucking won't. It fucking won't. It fucking won't. It
fucking won't. It fucking won't. It fucking won't. It
fucking won't. It fucking won't. It fucking won't. It
fucking won't. It fucking won't. It fucking won't. It
fucking won't. It fucking won't. It fucking won't. It
fucking won't. It fucking won't. It fucking won't. It
fucking won't. It fucking won't. It fucking won't. It
fucking won't. It fucking won't. It fucking won't. It
fucking won't. It fucking won't. It fucking won't. It
fucking won't. It fucking won't. It fucking won't. It
fucking won't. It fucking won't. It fucking won't. It
fucking won't. It fucking won't. It fucking won't. It
fucking won't. It fucking won't. It fucking won't. It
fucking won't. It fucking won't. It fucking won't. It
fucking won't. It fucking won't. It fucking won't. It
fucking won't. It fucking won't. It fucking won't. It
fucking won't. It fucking won't. It fucking won't. It
fucking won't. It fucking won't. It fucking won't. It
fucking won't. It fucking won't. It fucking won't. It
fucking won't. It fucking won't. It fucking won't. It
fucking won't. It fucking won't. It fucking won't. It
fucking won't. It fucking won't. It fucking won't. It
fucking won't. It fucking won't. It fucking won't. It
fucking won't. It fucking won't. It fucking won't. It
fucking won't. It fucking won't. It fucking won't. It
fucking won't. It fucking won't. It fucking won't. It

fucking won't. It fucking won't. It fucking won't. It
fucking won't. It fucking won't. It fucking won't. It
fucking won't. It fucking won't. It fucking won't. It
fucking won't. It fucking won't. It fucking won't. It
fucking won't. It fucking won't. It fucking won't. It
fucking won't. It fucking won't. It fucking won't. It
fucking won't. It fucking won't. It fucking won't. It
fucking won't. It fucking won't. It fucking won't. It
fucking won't. It fucking won't. It fucking won't. It
fucking won't. It fucking won't. It fucking won't. It
fucking won't. It fucking won't. It fucking won't. It
fucking won't. It fucking won't. It fucking won't. It
fucking won't. It fucking won't. It fucking won't. It
fucking won't. It fucking won't. It fucking won't. It
fucking won't. It fucking won't. It fucking won't. It
fucking won't. It fucking won't. It fucking won't. It
fucking won't. It fucking won't. It fucking won't. It
fucking won't. It fucking won't. It fucking won't. It
fucking won't. It fucking won't. It fucking won't. It
fucking won't. It fucking won't. It fucking won't. It
fucking won't. It fucking won't. It fucking won't. It
fucking won't. It fucking won't. It fucking won't. It
fucking won't. It fucking won't. It fucking won't. It
fucking won't. It fucking won't. It fucking won't. It
fucking won't. It fucking won't. It fucking won't. It
fucking won't. It fucking won't. It fucking won't. It
fucking won't. It fucking won't. It fucking won't. It
fucking won't. It fucking won't. It fucking won't. It
fucking won't. It fucking won't. It fucking won't. It
fucking won't. It fucking won't. It fucking won't. It

fucking won't. It fucking won't. It fucking won't. It
fucking won't. It fucking won't. It fucking won't. It
fucking won't. It fucking won't. It fucking won't. It
fucking won't. It fucking won't. It fucking won't. It
fucking won't. It fucking won't. It fucking won't. It
fucking won't. It fucking won't. It fucking won't. It
fucking won't. It fucking won't. It fucking won't. It
fucking won't. It fucking won't. It fucking won't. It
fucking won't. It fucking won't. It fucking won't. It
fucking won't. It fucking won't. It fucking won't. It
fucking won't. It fucking won't. It fucking won't. It
fucking won't. It fucking won't. It fucking won't. It
fucking won't. It fucking won't. It fucking won't. It
fucking won't. It fucking won't. It fucking won't. It
fucking won't. It fucking won't. It fucking won't. It
fucking won't. It fucking won't. It fucking won't. It
fucking won't. It fucking won't. It fucking won't. It
fucking won't. It fucking won't. It fucking won't. It
fucking won't. It fucking won't. It fucking won't. It
fucking won't. It fucking won't. It fucking won't. It
fucking won't. It fucking won't. It fucking won't. It
fucking won't. It fucking won't. It fucking won't. It
fucking won't. It fucking won't. It fucking won't. It
fucking won't. It fucking won't. It fucking won't. It
fucking won't. It fucking won't. It fucking won't. It
fucking won't. It fucking won't. It fucking won't. It
fucking won't. It fucking won't. It fucking won't. It
fucking won't. It fucking won't. It fucking won't. It
fucking won't. It fucking won't. It fucking won't. It
fucking won't. It fucking won't. It fucking won't. It

fucking won't. It fucking won't. It fucking won't. It
fucking won't. It fucking won't. It fucking won't. It
fucking won't. It fucking won't. It fucking won't. It
fucking won't. It fucking won't. It fucking won't. It
fucking won't. It fucking won't. It fucking won't. It
fucking won't. It fucking won't. It fucking won't. It
fucking won't. It fucking won't. It fucking won't. It
fucking won't. It fucking won't. It fucking won't. It
fucking won't. It fucking won't. It fucking won't. It
fucking won't. It fucking won't. It fucking won't. It
fucking won't. It fucking won't. It fucking won't. It
fucking won't. It fucking won't. It fucking won't. It
fucking won't. It fucking won't. It fucking won't. It
fucking won't. It fucking won't. It fucking won't. It
fucking won't. It fucking won't. It fucking won't. It
fucking won't. It fucking won't. It fucking won't. It
fucking won't. It fucking won't. It fucking won't. It
fucking won't. It fucking won't. It fucking won't. It
fucking won't. It fucking won't. It fucking won't. It
fucking won't. It fucking won't. It fucking won't. It
fucking won't. It fucking won't. It fucking won't. It
fucking won't. It fucking won't. It fucking won't. It
fucking won't. It fucking won't. It fucking won't. It
fucking won't. It fucking won't. It fucking won't. It
fucking won't. It fucking won't. It fucking won't. It
fucking won't. It fucking won't. It fucking won't. It
fucking won't. It fucking won't. It fucking won't. It
fucking won't. It fucking won't. It fucking won't. It
fucking won't. It fucking won't. It fucking won't. It
fucking won't. It fucking won't. It fucking won't. It

fucking won't. It fucking won't. It fucking won't. It
fucking won't. It fucking won't. It fucking won't. It
fucking won't. It fucking won't. It fucking won't. It
fucking won't. It fucking won't. It fucking won't. It
fucking won't. It fucking won't. It fucking won't. It
fucking won't. It fucking won't. It fucking won't. It
fucking won't. It fucking won't. It fucking won't. It
fucking won't. It fucking won't. It fucking won't. It
fucking won't. It fucking won't. It fucking won't. It
fucking won't. It fucking won't. It fucking won't. It
fucking won't. It fucking won't. It fucking won't. It
fucking won't. It fucking won't. It fucking won't. It
fucking won't. It fucking won't. It fucking won't. It
fucking won't. It fucking won't. It fucking won't. It
fucking won't. It fucking won't. It fucking won't. It
fucking won't. It fucking won't. It fucking won't. It
fucking won't. It fucking won't. It fucking won't. It
fucking won't. It fucking won't. It fucking won't. It
fucking won't. It fucking won't. It fucking won't. It
fucking won't. It fucking won't. It fucking won't. It
fucking won't. It fucking won't. It fucking won't. It
fucking won't. It fucking won't. It fucking won't. It
fucking won't. It fucking won't. It fucking won't. It
fucking won't. It fucking won't. It fucking won't. It
fucking won't. It fucking won't. It fucking won't. It
fucking won't. It fucking won't. It fucking won't. It
fucking won't. It fucking won't. It fucking won't. It
fucking won't. It fucking won't. It fucking won't. It
fucking won't. It fucking won't. It fucking won't. It
fucking won't. It fucking won't. It fucking won't. It

fucking won't. It fucking won't. It fucking won't. It
fucking won't. It fucking won't. It fucking won't. It
fucking won't. It fucking won't. It fucking won't. It
fucking won't. It fucking won't. It fucking won't. It
fucking won't. It fucking won't. It fucking won't. It
fucking won't. It fucking won't. It fucking won't. It
fucking won't. It fucking won't. It fucking won't. It
fucking won't. It fucking won't. It fucking won't. It
fucking won't. It fucking won't. It fucking won't. It
fucking won't. It fucking won't. It fucking won't. It
fucking won't. It fucking won't. It fucking won't. It
fucking won't. It fucking won't. It fucking won't. It
fucking won't. It fucking won't. It fucking won't. It
fucking won't. It fucking won't. It fucking won't. It
fucking won't. It fucking won't. It fucking won't. It
fucking won't. It fucking won't. It fucking won't. It
fucking won't. It fucking won't. It fucking won't. It
fucking won't. It fucking won't. It fucking won't. It
fucking won't. It fucking won't. It fucking won't. It
fucking won't. It fucking won't. It fucking won't. It
fucking won't. It fucking won't. It fucking won't. It
fucking won't. It fucking won't. It fucking won't. It
fucking won't. It fucking won't. It fucking won't. It
fucking won't. It fucking won't. It fucking won't. It
fucking won't. It fucking won't. It fucking won't. It
fucking won't. It fucking won't. It fucking won't. It
fucking won't. It fucking won't. It fucking won't. It
fucking won't. It fucking won't. It fucking won't. It
fucking won't. It fucking won't. It fucking won't. It
fucking won't. It fucking won't. It fucking won't. It
fucking won't. It fucking won't. It fucking won't. It

fucking won't. It fucking won't. It fucking won't. It
fucking won't. It fucking won't. It fucking won't. It
fucking won't. It fucking won't. It fucking won't. It
fucking won't. It fucking won't. It fucking won't. It
fucking won't. It fucking won't. It fucking won't. It
fucking won't. It fucking won't. It fucking won't. It
fucking won't. It fucking won't. It fucking won't. It
fucking won't. It fucking won't. It fucking won't. It
fucking won't. It fucking won't. It fucking won't. It
fucking won't. It fucking won't. It fucking won't. It
fucking won't. It fucking won't. It fucking won't. It
fucking won't. It fucking won't. It fucking won't. It
fucking won't. It fucking won't. It fucking won't. It
fucking won't. It fucking won't. It fucking won't. It
fucking won't. It fucking won't. It fucking won't. It
fucking won't. It fucking won't. It fucking won't. It
fucking won't. It fucking won't. It fucking won't. It
fucking won't. It fucking won't. It fucking won't. It
fucking won't. It fucking won't. It fucking won't. It
fucking won't. It fucking won't. It fucking won't. It
fucking won't. It fucking won't. It fucking won't. It
fucking won't. It fucking won't. It fucking won't. It
fucking won't. It fucking won't. It fucking won't. It
fucking won't. It fucking won't. It fucking won't. It
fucking won't. It fucking won't. It fucking won't. It
fucking won't. It fucking won't. It fucking won't. It
fucking won't. It fucking won't. It fucking won't. It
fucking won't. It fucking won't. It fucking won't. It
fucking won't. It fucking won't. It fucking won't. It
fucking won't. It fucking won't. It fucking won't. It

fucking won't. It fucking won't. It fucking won't. It
fucking won't. It fucking won't. It fucking won't. It
fucking won't. It fucking won't. It fucking won't. It
fucking won't. It fucking won't. It fucking won't. It
fucking won't. It fucking won't. It fucking won't. It
fucking won't. It fucking won't. It fucking won't. It
fucking won't. It fucking won't. It fucking won't. It
fucking won't. It fucking won't. It fucking won't. It
fucking won't. It fucking won't. It fucking won't. It
fucking won't. It fucking won't. It fucking won't. It
fucking won't. It fucking won't. It fucking won't. It
fucking won't. It fucking won't. It fucking won't. It
fucking won't. It fucking won't. It fucking won't. It
fucking won't. It fucking won't. It fucking won't. It
fucking won't. It fucking won't. It fucking won't. It
fucking won't. It fucking won't. It fucking won't. It
fucking won't. It fucking won't. It fucking won't. It
fucking won't. It fucking won't. It fucking won't. It
fucking won't. It fucking won't. It fucking won't.

It fucking won't. It fucking won't. It fucking won't. It
fucking won't. It fucking won't. It fucking won't. It
fucking won't. It fucking won't. It fucking won't. It
fucking won't. It fucking won't. It fucking won't. It
fucking won't. It fucking won't. It fucking won't. It
fucking won't. It fucking won't. It fucking won't. It
fucking won't. It fucking won't. It fucking won't. It
fucking won't. It fucking won't. It fucking won't. It
fucking won't. It fucking won't. It fucking won't. It
fucking won't. It fucking won't. It fucking won't. It
fucking won't. It fucking won't. It fucking won't. It

fucking won't. It fucking won't. It fucking won't. It
fucking won't. It fucking won't. It fucking won't. It
fucking won't. It fucking won't. It fucking won't. It
fucking won't. It fucking won't. It fucking won't. It
fucking won't. It fucking won't. It fucking won't. It
fucking won't. It fucking won't. It fucking won't. It
fucking won't. It fucking won't. It fucking won't. It
fucking won't. It fucking won't. It fucking won't. It
fucking won't. It fucking won't. It fucking won't. It
fucking won't. It fucking won't. It fucking won't. It
fucking won't. It fucking won't. It fucking won't. It
fucking won't. It fucking won't. It fucking won't. It
fucking won't. It fucking won't. It fucking won't. It
fucking won't. It fucking won't. It fucking won't. It
fucking won't. It fucking won't. It fucking won't. It
fucking won't. It fucking won't. It fucking won't. It
fucking won't. It fucking won't. It fucking won't. It
fucking won't. It fucking won't. It fucking won't. It
fucking won't. It fucking won't. It fucking won't. It
fucking won't. It fucking won't. It fucking won't. It
fucking won't. It fucking won't. It fucking won't. It
fucking won't. It fucking won't. It fucking won't. It
fucking won't. It fucking won't. It fucking won't. It
fucking won't. It fucking won't. It fucking won't. It
fucking won't. It fucking won't. It fucking won't. It
fucking won't. It fucking won't. It fucking won't. It
fucking won't. It fucking won't. It fucking won't. It
fucking won't. It fucking won't. It fucking won't. It
fucking won't. It fucking won't. It fucking won't. It
fucking won't. It fucking won't. It fucking won't. It
fucking won't. It fucking won't. It fucking won't. It

fucking won't. It fucking won't. It fucking won't. It
fucking won't. It fucking won't. It fucking won't. It
fucking won't. It fucking won't. It fucking won't. It
fucking won't. It fucking won't. It fucking won't. It
fucking won't. It fucking won't. It fucking won't. It
fucking won't. It fucking won't. It fucking won't. It
fucking won't. It fucking won't. It fucking won't. It
fucking won't. It fucking won't. It fucking won't. It
fucking won't. It fucking won't. It fucking won't. It
fucking won't. It fucking won't. It fucking won't. It
fucking won't. It fucking won't. It fucking won't. It
fucking won't. It fucking won't. It fucking won't. It
fucking won't. It fucking won't. It fucking won't. It
fucking won't. It fucking won't. It fucking won't. It
fucking won't. It fucking won't. It fucking won't. It
fucking won't. It fucking won't. It fucking won't. It
fucking won't. It fucking won't. It fucking won't. It
fucking won't. It fucking won't. It fucking won't. It
fucking won't. It fucking won't. It fucking won't. It
fucking won't. It fucking won't. It fucking won't. It
fucking won't. It fucking won't. It fucking won't. It
fucking won't. It fucking won't. It fucking won't. It
fucking won't. It fucking won't. It fucking won't. It
fucking won't. It fucking won't. It fucking won't. It
fucking won't. It fucking won't. It fucking won't. It
fucking won't. It fucking won't. It fucking won't. It
fucking won't. It fucking won't. It fucking won't. It
fucking won't. It fucking won't. It fucking won't. It
fucking won't. It fucking won't. It fucking won't. It
fucking won't. It fucking won't. It fucking won't. It

fucking won't. It fucking won't. It fucking won't. It
fucking won't. It fucking won't. It fucking won't. It
fucking won't. It fucking won't. It fucking won't. It
fucking won't. It fucking won't. It fucking won't. It
fucking won't. It fucking won't. It fucking won't. It
fucking won't. It fucking won't. It fucking won't. It
fucking won't. It fucking won't. It fucking won't. It
fucking won't. It fucking won't. It fucking won't. It
fucking won't. It fucking won't. It fucking won't. It
fucking won't. It fucking won't. It fucking won't. It
fucking won't. It fucking won't. It fucking won't. It
fucking won't. It fucking won't. It fucking won't. It
fucking won't. It fucking won't. It fucking won't. It
fucking won't. It fucking won't. It fucking won't. It
fucking won't. It fucking won't. It fucking won't. It
fucking won't. It fucking won't. It fucking won't. It
fucking won't. It fucking won't. It fucking won't. It
fucking won't. It fucking won't. It fucking won't. It
fucking won't. It fucking won't. It fucking won't. It
fucking won't. It fucking won't. It fucking won't. It
fucking won't. It fucking won't. It fucking won't. It
fucking won't. It fucking won't. It fucking won't. It
fucking won't. It fucking won't. It fucking won't. It
fucking won't. It fucking won't. It fucking won't. It
fucking won't. It fucking won't. It fucking won't. It
fucking won't. It fucking won't. It fucking won't. It
fucking won't. It fucking won't. It fucking won't. It
fucking won't. It fucking won't. It fucking won't. It
fucking won't. It fucking won't. It fucking won't. It
fucking won't. It fucking won't. It fucking won't. It
fucking won't. It fucking won't. It fucking won't. It
fucking won't. It fucking won't. It fucking won't. It

103

fucking won't. It fucking won't. It fucking won't. It
fucking won't. It fucking won't. It fucking won't. It
fucking won't. It fucking won't. It fucking won't. It
fucking won't. It fucking won't. It fucking won't. It
fucking won't. It fucking won't. It fucking won't. It
fucking won't. It fucking won't. It fucking won't. It
fucking won't. It fucking won't. It fucking won't. It
fucking won't. It fucking won't. It fucking won't. It
fucking won't. It fucking won't. It fucking won't. It
fucking won't. It fucking won't. It fucking won't. It
fucking won't. It fucking won't. It fucking won't. It
fucking won't. It fucking won't. It fucking won't. It
fucking won't. It fucking won't. It fucking won't. It
fucking won't. It fucking won't. It fucking won't. It
fucking won't. It fucking won't. It fucking won't. It
fucking won't. It fucking won't. It fucking won't. It
fucking won't. It fucking won't. It fucking won't. It
fucking won't. It fucking won't. It fucking won't. It
fucking won't. It fucking won't. It fucking won't. It
fucking won't. It fucking won't. It fucking won't. It
fucking won't. It fucking won't. It fucking won't. It
fucking won't. It fucking won't. It fucking won't. It
fucking won't. It fucking won't. It fucking won't. It
fucking won't. It fucking won't. It fucking won't. It
fucking won't. It fucking won't. It fucking won't. It
fucking won't. It fucking won't. It fucking won't. It
fucking won't. It fucking won't. It fucking won't. It
fucking won't. It fucking won't. It fucking won't. It
fucking won't. It fucking won't. It fucking won't. It
fucking won't. It fucking won't. It fucking won't. It

fucking won't. It fucking won't. It fucking won't. It
fucking won't. It fucking won't. It fucking won't. It
fucking won't. It fucking won't. It fucking won't. It
fucking won't. It fucking won't. It fucking won't. It
fucking won't. It fucking won't. It fucking won't. It
fucking won't. It fucking won't. It fucking won't. It
fucking won't. It fucking won't. It fucking won't. It
fucking won't. It fucking won't. It fucking won't. It
fucking won't. It fucking won't. It fucking won't. It
fucking won't. It fucking won't. It fucking won't. It
fucking won't. It fucking won't. It fucking won't. It
fucking won't. It fucking won't. It fucking won't. It
fucking won't. It fucking won't. It fucking won't. It
fucking won't. It fucking won't. It fucking won't. It
fucking won't. It fucking won't. It fucking won't. It
fucking won't. It fucking won't. It fucking won't. It
fucking won't. It fucking won't. It fucking won't. It
fucking won't. It fucking won't. It fucking won't. It
fucking won't. It fucking won't. It fucking won't. It
fucking won't. It fucking won't. It fucking won't. It
fucking won't. It fucking won't. It fucking won't. It
fucking won't. It fucking won't. It fucking won't. It
fucking won't. It fucking won't. It fucking won't. It
fucking won't. It fucking won't. It fucking won't. It
fucking won't. It fucking won't. It fucking won't. It
fucking won't. It fucking won't. It fucking won't. It
fucking won't. It fucking won't. It fucking won't. It
fucking won't. It fucking won't. It fucking won't. It
fucking won't. It fucking won't. It fucking won't. It
fucking won't. It fucking won't. It fucking won't. It

fucking won't. It fucking won't. It fucking won't. It
fucking won't. It fucking won't. It fucking won't. It
fucking won't. It fucking won't. It fucking won't. It
fucking won't. It fucking won't. It fucking won't. It
fucking won't. It fucking won't. It fucking won't. It
fucking won't. It fucking won't. It fucking won't. It
fucking won't. It fucking won't. It fucking won't. It
fucking won't. It fucking won't. It fucking won't. It
fucking won't. It fucking won't. It fucking won't. It
fucking won't. It fucking won't. It fucking won't. It
fucking won't. It fucking won't. It fucking won't. It
fucking won't. It fucking won't. It fucking won't. It
fucking won't. It fucking won't. It fucking won't. It
fucking won't. It fucking won't. It fucking won't. It
fucking won't. It fucking won't. It fucking won't. It
fucking won't. It fucking won't. It fucking won't. It
fucking won't. It fucking won't. It fucking won't. It
fucking won't. It fucking won't. It fucking won't. It
fucking won't. It fucking won't. It fucking won't. It
fucking won't. It fucking won't. It fucking won't. It
fucking won't. It fucking won't. It fucking won't. It
fucking won't. It fucking won't. It fucking won't. It
fucking won't. It fucking won't. It fucking won't. It
fucking won't. It fucking won't. It fucking won't. It
fucking won't. It fucking won't. It fucking won't. It
fucking won't. It fucking won't. It fucking won't. It
fucking won't. It fucking won't. It fucking won't. It
fucking won't. It fucking won't. It fucking won't. It
fucking won't. It fucking won't. It fucking won't. It
fucking won't. It fucking won't. It fucking won't. It
fucking won't. It fucking won't. It fucking won't. It

fucking won't. It fucking won't. It fucking won't. It
fucking won't. It fucking won't. It fucking won't. It
fucking won't. It fucking won't. It fucking won't. It
fucking won't. It fucking won't. It fucking won't. It
fucking won't. It fucking won't. It fucking won't. It
fucking won't. It fucking won't. It fucking won't. It
fucking won't. It fucking won't. It fucking won't. It
fucking won't. It fucking won't. It fucking won't. It
fucking won't. It fucking won't. It fucking won't. It
fucking won't. It fucking won't. It fucking won't. It
fucking won't. It fucking won't. It fucking won't. It
fucking won't. It fucking won't. It fucking won't. It
fucking won't. It fucking won't. It fucking won't. It
fucking won't. It fucking won't. It fucking won't. It
fucking won't. It fucking won't. It fucking won't. It
fucking won't. It fucking won't. It fucking won't. It
fucking won't. It fucking won't. It fucking won't. It
fucking won't. It fucking won't. It fucking won't. It
fucking won't. It fucking won't. It fucking won't. It
fucking won't. It fucking won't. It fucking won't. It
fucking won't. It fucking won't. It fucking won't. It
fucking won't. It fucking won't. It fucking won't. It
fucking won't. It fucking won't. It fucking won't. It
fucking won't. It fucking won't. It fucking won't. It
fucking won't. It fucking won't. It fucking won't. It
fucking won't. It fucking won't. It fucking won't. It
fucking won't. It fucking won't. It fucking won't. It
fucking won't. It fucking won't. It fucking won't. It
fucking won't. It fucking won't. It fucking won't. It
fucking won't. It fucking won't. It fucking won't. It
fucking won't. It fucking won't. It fucking won't. It

fucking won't. It fucking won't. It fucking won't. It
fucking won't. It fucking won't. It fucking won't. It
fucking won't. It fucking won't. It fucking won't. It
fucking won't. It fucking won't. It fucking won't. It
fucking won't. It fucking won't. It fucking won't. It
fucking won't. It fucking won't. It fucking won't. It
fucking won't. It fucking won't. It fucking won't. It
fucking won't. It fucking won't. It fucking won't. It
fucking won't. It fucking won't. It fucking won't. It
fucking won't. It fucking won't. It fucking won't. It
fucking won't. It fucking won't. It fucking won't. It
fucking won't. It fucking won't. It fucking won't. It
fucking won't. It fucking won't. It fucking won't. It
fucking won't. It fucking won't. It fucking won't. It
fucking won't. It fucking won't. It fucking won't. It
fucking won't. It fucking won't. It fucking won't. It
fucking won't. It fucking won't. It fucking won't. It
fucking won't. It fucking won't. It fucking won't. It
fucking won't. It fucking won't. It fucking won't. It
fucking won't. It fucking won't. It fucking won't. It
fucking won't. It fucking won't. It fucking won't. It
fucking won't. It fucking won't. It fucking won't. It
fucking won't. It fucking won't. It fucking won't. It
fucking won't. It fucking won't. It fucking won't. It
fucking won't. It fucking won't. It fucking won't. It
fucking won't. It fucking won't. It fucking won't. It
fucking won't. It fucking won't. It fucking won't. It
fucking won't. It fucking won't. It fucking won't. It
fucking won't. It fucking won't. It fucking won't. It
fucking won't. It fucking won't. It fucking won't. It

fucking won't. It fucking won't. It fucking won't. It
fucking won't. It fucking won't. It fucking won't. It
fucking won't. It fucking won't. It fucking won't. It
fucking won't. It fucking won't. It fucking won't. It
fucking won't. It fucking won't. It fucking won't. It
fucking won't. It fucking won't. It fucking won't. It
fucking won't. It fucking won't. It fucking won't. It
fucking won't. It fucking won't. It fucking won't. It
fucking won't. It fucking won't. It fucking won't. It
fucking won't. It fucking won't. It fucking won't. It
fucking won't. It fucking won't. It fucking won't. It
fucking won't. It fucking won't. It fucking won't. It
fucking won't. It fucking won't. It fucking won't. It
fucking won't. It fucking won't. It fucking won't. It
fucking won't. It fucking won't. It fucking won't. It
fucking won't. It fucking won't. It fucking won't. It
fucking won't. It fucking won't. It fucking won't. It
fucking won't. It fucking won't. It fucking won't. It
fucking won't. It fucking won't. It fucking won't. It
fucking won't. It fucking won't. It fucking won't. It
fucking won't. It fucking won't. It fucking won't. It
fucking won't. It fucking won't. It fucking won't. It
fucking won't. It fucking won't. It fucking won't. It
fucking won't. It fucking won't. It fucking won't. It
fucking won't. It fucking won't. It fucking won't. It
fucking won't. It fucking won't. It fucking won't. It
fucking won't. It fucking won't. It fucking won't. It
fucking won't. It fucking won't. It fucking won't. It
fucking won't. It fucking won't. It fucking won't. It
fucking won't. It fucking won't. It fucking won't. It

fucking won't. It fucking won't. It fucking won't. It
fucking won't. It fucking won't. It fucking won't. It
fucking won't. It fucking won't. It fucking won't. It
fucking won't. It fucking won't. It fucking won't. It
fucking won't. It fucking won't. It fucking won't. It
fucking won't. It fucking won't. It fucking won't. It
fucking won't. It fucking won't. It fucking won't. It
fucking won't. It fucking won't. It fucking won't. It
fucking won't. It fucking won't. It fucking won't. It
fucking won't. It fucking won't. It fucking won't. It
fucking won't. It fucking won't. It fucking won't. It
fucking won't. It fucking won't. It fucking won't. It
fucking won't. It fucking won't. It fucking won't. It
fucking won't. It fucking won't. It fucking won't. It
fucking won't. It fucking won't. It fucking won't. It
fucking won't. It fucking won't. It fucking won't. It
fucking won't. It fucking won't. It fucking won't. It
fucking won't. It fucking won't. It fucking won't. It
fucking won't. It fucking won't. It fucking won't. It
fucking won't. It fucking won't. It fucking won't. It
fucking won't. It fucking won't. It fucking won't. It
fucking won't. It fucking won't. It fucking won't. It
fucking won't. It fucking won't. It fucking won't. It
fucking won't. It fucking won't. It fucking won't. It
fucking won't. It fucking won't. It fucking won't. It
fucking won't. It fucking won't. It fucking won't. It
fucking won't. It fucking won't. It fucking won't. It
fucking won't. It fucking won't. It fucking won't. It
fucking won't. It fucking won't. It fucking won't. It
fucking won't. It fucking won't. It fucking won't. It
fucking won't. It fucking won't. It fucking won't. It

fucking won't. It fucking won't. It fucking won't. It
fucking won't. It fucking won't. It fucking won't. It
fucking won't. It fucking won't. It fucking won't. It
fucking won't. It fucking won't. It fucking won't. It
fucking won't. It fucking won't. It fucking won't. It
fucking won't. It fucking won't. It fucking won't. It
fucking won't. It fucking won't. It fucking won't. It
fucking won't. It fucking won't. It fucking won't. It
fucking won't. It fucking won't. It fucking won't. It
fucking won't. It fucking won't. It fucking won't. It
fucking won't. It fucking won't. It fucking won't. It
fucking won't. It fucking won't. It fucking won't. It
fucking won't. It fucking won't. It fucking won't. It
fucking won't. It fucking won't. It fucking won't. It
fucking won't. It fucking won't. It fucking won't. It
fucking won't. It fucking won't. It fucking won't. It
fucking won't. It fucking won't. It fucking won't. It
fucking won't. It fucking won't. It fucking won't. It
fucking won't. It fucking won't. It fucking won't. It
fucking won't. It fucking won't. It fucking won't. It
fucking won't. It fucking won't. It fucking won't. It
fucking won't. It fucking won't. It fucking won't.

It fucking won't. It fucking won't. It fucking won't. It
fucking won't. It fucking won't. It fucking won't. It
fucking won't. It fucking won't. It fucking won't. It
fucking won't. It fucking won't. It fucking won't. It
fucking won't. It fucking won't. It fucking won't. It
fucking won't. It fucking won't. It fucking won't. It
fucking won't. It fucking won't. It fucking won't. It

fucking won't. It fucking won't. It fucking won't. It
fucking won't. It fucking won't. It fucking won't. It
fucking won't. It fucking won't. It fucking won't. It
fucking won't. It fucking won't. It fucking won't. It
fucking won't. It fucking won't. It fucking won't. It
fucking won't. It fucking won't. It fucking won't. It
fucking won't. It fucking won't. It fucking won't. It
fucking won't. It fucking won't. It fucking won't. It
fucking won't. It fucking won't. It fucking won't. It
fucking won't. It fucking won't. It fucking won't. It
fucking won't. It fucking won't. It fucking won't. It
fucking won't. It fucking won't. It fucking won't. It
fucking won't. It fucking won't. It fucking won't. It
fucking won't. It fucking won't. It fucking won't. It
fucking won't. It fucking won't. It fucking won't. It
fucking won't. It fucking won't. It fucking won't. It
fucking won't. It fucking won't. It fucking won't. It
fucking won't. It fucking won't. It fucking won't. It
fucking won't. It fucking won't. It fucking won't. It
fucking won't. It fucking won't. It fucking won't. It
fucking won't. It fucking won't. It fucking won't. It
fucking won't. It fucking won't. It fucking won't. It
fucking won't. It fucking won't. It fucking won't. It
fucking won't. It fucking won't. It fucking won't. It
fucking won't. It fucking won't. It fucking won't. It
fucking won't. It fucking won't. It fucking won't. It
fucking won't. It fucking won't. It fucking won't. It
fucking won't. It fucking won't. It fucking won't. It
fucking won't. It fucking won't. It fucking won't. It
fucking won't. It fucking won't. It fucking won't. It

fucking won't. It fucking won't. It fucking won't. It
fucking won't. It fucking won't. It fucking won't. It
fucking won't. It fucking won't. It fucking won't. It
fucking won't. It fucking won't. It fucking won't. It
fucking won't. It fucking won't. It fucking won't. It
fucking won't. It fucking won't. It fucking won't. It
fucking won't. It fucking won't. It fucking won't. It
fucking won't. It fucking won't. It fucking won't. It
fucking won't. It fucking won't. It fucking won't. It
fucking won't. It fucking won't. It fucking won't. It
fucking won't. It fucking won't. It fucking won't. It
fucking won't. It fucking won't. It fucking won't. It
fucking won't. It fucking won't. It fucking won't. It
fucking won't. It fucking won't. It fucking won't. It
fucking won't. It fucking won't. It fucking won't. It
fucking won't. It fucking won't. It fucking won't. It
fucking won't. It fucking won't. It fucking won't. It
fucking won't. It fucking won't. It fucking won't. It
fucking won't. It fucking won't. It fucking won't. It
fucking won't. It fucking won't. It fucking won't. It
fucking won't. It fucking won't. It fucking won't. It
fucking won't. It fucking won't. It fucking won't. It
fucking won't. It fucking won't. It fucking won't. It
fucking won't. It fucking won't. It fucking won't. It
fucking won't. It fucking won't. It fucking won't. It
fucking won't. It fucking won't. It fucking won't. It
fucking won't. It fucking won't. It fucking won't. It
fucking won't. It fucking won't. It fucking won't. It
fucking won't. It fucking won't. It fucking won't. It
fucking won't. It fucking won't. It fucking won't. It
fucking won't. It fucking won't. It fucking won't. It
fucking won't. It fucking won't. It fucking won't. It

fucking won't. It fucking won't. It fucking won't. It
fucking won't. It fucking won't. It fucking won't. It
fucking won't. It fucking won't. It fucking won't. It
fucking won't. It fucking won't. It fucking won't. It
fucking won't. It fucking won't. It fucking won't. It
fucking won't. It fucking won't. It fucking won't. It
fucking won't. It fucking won't. It fucking won't. It
fucking won't. It fucking won't. It fucking won't. It
fucking won't. It fucking won't. It fucking won't. It
fucking won't. It fucking won't. It fucking won't. It
fucking won't. It fucking won't. It fucking won't. It
fucking won't. It fucking won't. It fucking won't. It
fucking won't. It fucking won't. It fucking won't. It
fucking won't. It fucking won't. It fucking won't. It
fucking won't. It fucking won't. It fucking won't. It
fucking won't. It fucking won't. It fucking won't. It
fucking won't. It fucking won't. It fucking won't. It
fucking won't. It fucking won't. It fucking won't. It
fucking won't. It fucking won't. It fucking won't. It
fucking won't. It fucking won't. It fucking won't. It
fucking won't. It fucking won't. It fucking won't. It
fucking won't. It fucking won't. It fucking won't. It
fucking won't. It fucking won't. It fucking won't. It
fucking won't. It fucking won't. It fucking won't. It
fucking won't. It fucking won't. It fucking won't. It
fucking won't. It fucking won't. It fucking won't. It
fucking won't. It fucking won't. It fucking won't. It
fucking won't. It fucking won't. It fucking won't. It
fucking won't. It fucking won't. It fucking won't. It
fucking won't. It fucking won't. It fucking won't. It

fucking won't. It fucking won't. It fucking won't. It
fucking won't. It fucking won't. It fucking won't. It
fucking won't. It fucking won't. It fucking won't. It
fucking won't. It fucking won't. It fucking won't. It
fucking won't. It fucking won't. It fucking won't. It
fucking won't. It fucking won't. It fucking won't. It
fucking won't. It fucking won't. It fucking won't. It
fucking won't. It fucking won't. It fucking won't. It
fucking won't. It fucking won't. It fucking won't. It
fucking won't. It fucking won't. It fucking won't. It
fucking won't. It fucking won't. It fucking won't. It
fucking won't. It fucking won't. It fucking won't. It
fucking won't. It fucking won't. It fucking won't. It
fucking won't. It fucking won't. It fucking won't. It
fucking won't. It fucking won't. It fucking won't. It
fucking won't. It fucking won't. It fucking won't. It
fucking won't. It fucking won't. It fucking won't. It
fucking won't. It fucking won't. It fucking won't. It
fucking won't. It fucking won't. It fucking won't. It
fucking won't. It fucking won't. It fucking won't. It
fucking won't. It fucking won't. It fucking won't. It
fucking won't. It fucking won't. It fucking won't. It
fucking won't. It fucking won't. It fucking won't. It
fucking won't. It fucking won't. It fucking won't. It
fucking won't. It fucking won't. It fucking won't. It
fucking won't. It fucking won't. It fucking won't. It
fucking won't. It fucking won't. It fucking won't. It
fucking won't. It fucking won't. It fucking won't. It
fucking won't. It fucking won't. It fucking won't. It
fucking won't. It fucking won't. It fucking won't. It

fucking won't. It fucking won't. It fucking won't. It
fucking won't. It fucking won't. It fucking won't. It
fucking won't. It fucking won't. It fucking won't. It
fucking won't. It fucking won't. It fucking won't. It
fucking won't. It fucking won't. It fucking won't. It
fucking won't. It fucking won't. It fucking won't. It
fucking won't. It fucking won't. It fucking won't. It
fucking won't. It fucking won't. It fucking won't. It
fucking won't. It fucking won't. It fucking won't. It
fucking won't. It fucking won't. It fucking won't. It
fucking won't. It fucking won't. It fucking won't. It
fucking won't. It fucking won't. It fucking won't. It
fucking won't. It fucking won't. It fucking won't. It
fucking won't. It fucking won't. It fucking won't. It
fucking won't. It fucking won't. It fucking won't. It
fucking won't. It fucking won't. It fucking won't. It
fucking won't. It fucking won't. It fucking won't. It
fucking won't. It fucking won't. It fucking won't. It
fucking won't. It fucking won't. It fucking won't. It
fucking won't. It fucking won't. It fucking won't. It
fucking won't. It fucking won't. It fucking won't. It
fucking won't. It fucking won't. It fucking won't. It
fucking won't. It fucking won't. It fucking won't. It
fucking won't. It fucking won't. It fucking won't. It
fucking won't. It fucking won't. It fucking won't. It
fucking won't. It fucking won't. It fucking won't. It
fucking won't. It fucking won't. It fucking won't. It
fucking won't. It fucking won't. It fucking won't. It
fucking won't. It fucking won't. It fucking won't. It
fucking won't. It fucking won't. It fucking won't. It

fucking won't. It fucking won't. It fucking won't. It
fucking won't. It fucking won't. It fucking won't. It
fucking won't. It fucking won't. It fucking won't. It
fucking won't. It fucking won't. It fucking won't. It
fucking won't. It fucking won't. It fucking won't. It
fucking won't. It fucking won't. It fucking won't. It
fucking won't. It fucking won't. It fucking won't. It
fucking won't. It fucking won't. It fucking won't. It
fucking won't. It fucking won't. It fucking won't. It
fucking won't. It fucking won't. It fucking won't. It
fucking won't. It fucking won't. It fucking won't. It
fucking won't. It fucking won't. It fucking won't. It
fucking won't. It fucking won't. It fucking won't. It
fucking won't. It fucking won't. It fucking won't. It
fucking won't. It fucking won't. It fucking won't. It
fucking won't. It fucking won't. It fucking won't. It
fucking won't. It fucking won't. It fucking won't. It
fucking won't. It fucking won't. It fucking won't. It
fucking won't. It fucking won't. It fucking won't. It
fucking won't. It fucking won't. It fucking won't. It
fucking won't. It fucking won't. It fucking won't. It
fucking won't. It fucking won't. It fucking won't. It
fucking won't. It fucking won't. It fucking won't. It
fucking won't. It fucking won't. It fucking won't. It
fucking won't. It fucking won't. It fucking won't. It
fucking won't. It fucking won't. It fucking won't. It
fucking won't. It fucking won't. It fucking won't. It
fucking won't. It fucking won't. It fucking won't. It
fucking won't. It fucking won't. It fucking won't. It
fucking won't. It fucking won't. It fucking won't. It

fucking won't. It fucking won't. It fucking won't. It
fucking won't. It fucking won't. It fucking won't. It
fucking won't. It fucking won't. It fucking won't. It
fucking won't. It fucking won't. It fucking won't. It
fucking won't. It fucking won't. It fucking won't. It
fucking won't. It fucking won't. It fucking won't. It
fucking won't. It fucking won't. It fucking won't. It
fucking won't. It fucking won't. It fucking won't. It
fucking won't. It fucking won't. It fucking won't. It
fucking won't. It fucking won't. It fucking won't. It
fucking won't. It fucking won't. It fucking won't. It
fucking won't. It fucking won't. It fucking won't. It
fucking won't. It fucking won't. It fucking won't. It
fucking won't. It fucking won't. It fucking won't. It
fucking won't. It fucking won't. It fucking won't. It
fucking won't. It fucking won't. It fucking won't. It
fucking won't. It fucking won't. It fucking won't. It
fucking won't. It fucking won't. It fucking won't. It
fucking won't. It fucking won't. It fucking won't. It
fucking won't. It fucking won't. It fucking won't. It
fucking won't. It fucking won't. It fucking won't. It
fucking won't. It fucking won't. It fucking won't. It
fucking won't. It fucking won't. It fucking won't. It
fucking won't. It fucking won't. It fucking won't. It
fucking won't. It fucking won't. It fucking won't. It
fucking won't. It fucking won't. It fucking won't. It
fucking won't. It fucking won't. It fucking won't. It
fucking won't. It fucking won't. It fucking won't. It
fucking won't. It fucking won't. It fucking won't. It
fucking won't. It fucking won't. It fucking won't. It
fucking won't. It fucking won't. It fucking won't. It

fucking won't. It fucking won't. It fucking won't. It
fucking won't. It fucking won't. It fucking won't. It
fucking won't. It fucking won't. It fucking won't. It
fucking won't. It fucking won't. It fucking won't. It
fucking won't. It fucking won't. It fucking won't. It
fucking won't. It fucking won't. It fucking won't. It
fucking won't. It fucking won't. It fucking won't. It
fucking won't. It fucking won't. It fucking won't. It
fucking won't. It fucking won't. It fucking won't. It
fucking won't. It fucking won't. It fucking won't. It
fucking won't. It fucking won't. It fucking won't. It
fucking won't. It fucking won't. It fucking won't. It
fucking won't. It fucking won't. It fucking won't. It
fucking won't. It fucking won't. It fucking won't. It
fucking won't. It fucking won't. It fucking won't. It
fucking won't. It fucking won't. It fucking won't. It
fucking won't. It fucking won't. It fucking won't. It
fucking won't. It fucking won't. It fucking won't. It
fucking won't. It fucking won't. It fucking won't. It
fucking won't. It fucking won't. It fucking won't. It
fucking won't. It fucking won't. It fucking won't. It
fucking won't. It fucking won't. It fucking won't. It
fucking won't. It fucking won't. It fucking won't. It
fucking won't. It fucking won't. It fucking won't. It
fucking won't. It fucking won't. It fucking won't. It
fucking won't. It fucking won't. It fucking won't. It
fucking won't. It fucking won't. It fucking won't. It
fucking won't. It fucking won't. It fucking won't. It
fucking won't. It fucking won't. It fucking won't. It
fucking won't. It fucking won't. It fucking won't. It

119

fucking won't. It fucking won't. It fucking won't. It
fucking won't. It fucking won't. It fucking won't. It
fucking won't. It fucking won't. It fucking won't. It
fucking won't. It fucking won't. It fucking won't. It
fucking won't. It fucking won't. It fucking won't. It
fucking won't. It fucking won't. It fucking won't. It
fucking won't. It fucking won't. It fucking won't. It
fucking won't. It fucking won't. It fucking won't. It
fucking won't. It fucking won't. It fucking won't. It
fucking won't. It fucking won't. It fucking won't. It
fucking won't. It fucking won't. It fucking won't. It
fucking won't. It fucking won't. It fucking won't. It
fucking won't. It fucking won't. It fucking won't. It
fucking won't. It fucking won't. It fucking won't. It
fucking won't. It fucking won't. It fucking won't. It
fucking won't. It fucking won't. It fucking won't. It
fucking won't. It fucking won't. It fucking won't. It
fucking won't. It fucking won't. It fucking won't. It
fucking won't. It fucking won't. It fucking won't. It
fucking won't. It fucking won't. It fucking won't. It
fucking won't. It fucking won't. It fucking won't. It
fucking won't. It fucking won't. It fucking won't. It
fucking won't. It fucking won't. It fucking won't. It
fucking won't. It fucking won't. It fucking won't. It
fucking won't. It fucking won't. It fucking won't. It
fucking won't. It fucking won't. It fucking won't. It
fucking won't. It fucking won't. It fucking won't. It
fucking won't. It fucking won't. It fucking won't. It
fucking won't. It fucking won't. It fucking won't. It
fucking won't. It fucking won't. It fucking won't. It

fucking won't. It fucking won't. It fucking won't. It
fucking won't. It fucking won't. It fucking won't. It
fucking won't. It fucking won't. It fucking won't. It
fucking won't. It fucking won't. It fucking won't. It
fucking won't. It fucking won't. It fucking won't. It
fucking won't. It fucking won't. It fucking won't. It
fucking won't. It fucking won't. It fucking won't. It
fucking won't. It fucking won't. It fucking won't. It
fucking won't. It fucking won't. It fucking won't. It
fucking won't. It fucking won't. It fucking won't. It
fucking won't. It fucking won't. It fucking won't. It
fucking won't. It fucking won't. It fucking won't. It
fucking won't. It fucking won't. It fucking won't. It
fucking won't. It fucking won't. It fucking won't. It
fucking won't. It fucking won't. It fucking won't. It
fucking won't. It fucking won't. It fucking won't. It
fucking won't. It fucking won't. It fucking won't. It
fucking won't. It fucking won't. It fucking won't. It
fucking won't. It fucking won't. It fucking won't. It
fucking won't. It fucking won't. It fucking won't. It
fucking won't. It fucking won't. It fucking won't. It
fucking won't. It fucking won't. It fucking won't. It
fucking won't. It fucking won't. It fucking won't. It
fucking won't. It fucking won't. It fucking won't. It
fucking won't. It fucking won't. It fucking won't. It
fucking won't. It fucking won't. It fucking won't. It
fucking won't. It fucking won't. It fucking won't. It
fucking won't. It fucking won't. It fucking won't. It
fucking won't. It fucking won't. It fucking won't. It
fucking won't. It fucking won't. It fucking won't. It
fucking won't. It fucking won't. It fucking won't. It

fucking won't. It fucking won't. It fucking won't. It
fucking won't. It fucking won't. It fucking won't. It
fucking won't. It fucking won't. It fucking won't. It
fucking won't. It fucking won't. It fucking won't. It
fucking won't. It fucking won't. It fucking won't. It
fucking won't. It fucking won't. It fucking won't. It
fucking won't. It fucking won't. It fucking won't. It
fucking won't. It fucking won't. It fucking won't. It
fucking won't. It fucking won't. It fucking won't. It
fucking won't. It fucking won't. It fucking won't. It
fucking won't. It fucking won't. It fucking won't. It
fucking won't. It fucking won't. It fucking won't. It
fucking won't. It fucking won't. It fucking won't. It
fucking won't. It fucking won't. It fucking won't. It
fucking won't. It fucking won't. It fucking won't. It
fucking won't. It fucking won't. It fucking won't. It
fucking won't. It fucking won't. It fucking won't. It
fucking won't. It fucking won't. It fucking won't. It
fucking won't. It fucking won't. It fucking won't. It
fucking won't. It fucking won't. It fucking won't. It
fucking won't. It fucking won't. It fucking won't. It
fucking won't. It fucking won't. It fucking won't. It
fucking won't. It fucking won't. It fucking won't. It
fucking won't. It fucking won't. It fucking won't. It
fucking won't. It fucking won't. It fucking won't. It
fucking won't. It fucking won't. It fucking won't. It
fucking won't. It fucking won't. It fucking won't.

It fucking won't. It fucking won't. It fucking won't. It
fucking won't. It fucking won't. It fucking won't. It
fucking won't. It fucking won't. It fucking won't. It

fucking won't. It fucking won't. It fucking won't. It
fucking won't. It fucking won't. It fucking won't. It
fucking won't. It fucking won't. It fucking won't. It
fucking won't. It fucking won't. It fucking won't. It
fucking won't. It fucking won't. It fucking won't. It
fucking won't. It fucking won't. It fucking won't. It
fucking won't. It fucking won't. It fucking won't. It
fucking won't. It fucking won't. It fucking won't. It
fucking won't. It fucking won't. It fucking won't. It
fucking won't. It fucking won't. It fucking won't. It
fucking won't. It fucking won't. It fucking won't. It
fucking won't. It fucking won't. It fucking won't. It
fucking won't. It fucking won't. It fucking won't. It
fucking won't. It fucking won't. It fucking won't. It
fucking won't. It fucking won't. It fucking won't. It
fucking won't. It fucking won't. It fucking won't. It
fucking won't. It fucking won't. It fucking won't. It
fucking won't. It fucking won't. It fucking won't. It
fucking won't. It fucking won't. It fucking won't. It
fucking won't. It fucking won't. It fucking won't. It
fucking won't. It fucking won't. It fucking won't. It
fucking won't. It fucking won't. It fucking won't. It
fucking won't. It fucking won't. It fucking won't. It
fucking won't. It fucking won't. It fucking won't. It
fucking won't. It fucking won't. It fucking won't. It
fucking won't. It fucking won't. It fucking won't. It
fucking won't. It fucking won't. It fucking won't. It
fucking won't. It fucking won't. It fucking won't. It
fucking won't. It fucking won't. It fucking won't. It
fucking won't. It fucking won't. It fucking won't. It

fucking won't. It fucking won't. It fucking won't. It
fucking won't. It fucking won't. It fucking won't. It
fucking won't. It fucking won't. It fucking won't. It
fucking won't. It fucking won't. It fucking won't. It
fucking won't. It fucking won't. It fucking won't. It
fucking won't. It fucking won't. It fucking won't. It
fucking won't. It fucking won't. It fucking won't. It
fucking won't. It fucking won't. It fucking won't. It
fucking won't. It fucking won't. It fucking won't. It
fucking won't. It fucking won't. It fucking won't. It
fucking won't. It fucking won't. It fucking won't. It
fucking won't. It fucking won't. It fucking won't. It
fucking won't. It fucking won't. It fucking won't. It
fucking won't. It fucking won't. It fucking won't. It
fucking won't. It fucking won't. It fucking won't. It
fucking won't. It fucking won't. It fucking won't. It
fucking won't. It fucking won't. It fucking won't. It
fucking won't. It fucking won't. It fucking won't. It
fucking won't. It fucking won't. It fucking won't. It
fucking won't. It fucking won't. It fucking won't. It
fucking won't. It fucking won't. It fucking won't. It
fucking won't. It fucking won't. It fucking won't. It
fucking won't. It fucking won't. It fucking won't. It
fucking won't. It fucking won't. It fucking won't. It
fucking won't. It fucking won't. It fucking won't. It
fucking won't. It fucking won't. It fucking won't. It
fucking won't. It fucking won't. It fucking won't. It
fucking won't. It fucking won't. It fucking won't. It
fucking won't. It fucking won't. It fucking won't. It
fucking won't. It fucking won't. It fucking won't. It
fucking won't. It fucking won't. It fucking won't. It
fucking won't. It fucking won't. It fucking won't. It

fucking won't. It fucking won't. It fucking won't. It
fucking won't. It fucking won't. It fucking won't. It
fucking won't. It fucking won't. It fucking won't. It
fucking won't. It fucking won't. It fucking won't. It
fucking won't. It fucking won't. It fucking won't. It
fucking won't. It fucking won't. It fucking won't. It
fucking won't. It fucking won't. It fucking won't. It
fucking won't. It fucking won't. It fucking won't. It
fucking won't. It fucking won't. It fucking won't. It
fucking won't. It fucking won't. It fucking won't. It
fucking won't. It fucking won't. It fucking won't. It
fucking won't. It fucking won't. It fucking won't. It
fucking won't. It fucking won't. It fucking won't. It
fucking won't. It fucking won't. It fucking won't. It
fucking won't. It fucking won't. It fucking won't. It
fucking won't. It fucking won't. It fucking won't. It
fucking won't. It fucking won't. It fucking won't. It
fucking won't. It fucking won't. It fucking won't. It
fucking won't. It fucking won't. It fucking won't. It
fucking won't. It fucking won't. It fucking won't. It
fucking won't. It fucking won't. It fucking won't. It
fucking won't. It fucking won't. It fucking won't. It
fucking won't. It fucking won't. It fucking won't. It
fucking won't. It fucking won't. It fucking won't. It
fucking won't. It fucking won't. It fucking won't. It
fucking won't. It fucking won't. It fucking won't. It
fucking won't. It fucking won't. It fucking won't. It
fucking won't. It fucking won't. It fucking won't. It
fucking won't. It fucking won't. It fucking won't. It
fucking won't. It fucking won't. It fucking won't. It
fucking won't. It fucking won't. It fucking won't. It

fucking won't. It fucking won't. It fucking won't. It
fucking won't. It fucking won't. It fucking won't. It
fucking won't. It fucking won't. It fucking won't. It
fucking won't. It fucking won't. It fucking won't. It
fucking won't. It fucking won't. It fucking won't. It
fucking won't. It fucking won't. It fucking won't. It
fucking won't. It fucking won't. It fucking won't. It
fucking won't. It fucking won't. It fucking won't. It
fucking won't. It fucking won't. It fucking won't. It
fucking won't. It fucking won't. It fucking won't. It
fucking won't. It fucking won't. It fucking won't. It
fucking won't. It fucking won't. It fucking won't. It
fucking won't. It fucking won't. It fucking won't. It
fucking won't. It fucking won't. It fucking won't. It
fucking won't. It fucking won't. It fucking won't. It
fucking won't. It fucking won't. It fucking won't. It
fucking won't. It fucking won't. It fucking won't. It
fucking won't. It fucking won't. It fucking won't. It
fucking won't. It fucking won't. It fucking won't. It
fucking won't. It fucking won't. It fucking won't. It
fucking won't. It fucking won't. It fucking won't. It
fucking won't. It fucking won't. It fucking won't. It
fucking won't. It fucking won't. It fucking won't. It
fucking won't. It fucking won't. It fucking won't. It
fucking won't. It fucking won't. It fucking won't. It
fucking won't. It fucking won't. It fucking won't. It
fucking won't. It fucking won't. It fucking won't. It
fucking won't. It fucking won't. It fucking won't. It
fucking won't. It fucking won't. It fucking won't. It
fucking won't. It fucking won't. It fucking won't. It
fucking won't. It fucking won't. It fucking won't. It

fucking won't. It fucking won't. It fucking won't. It
fucking won't. It fucking won't. It fucking won't. It
fucking won't. It fucking won't. It fucking won't. It
fucking won't. It fucking won't. It fucking won't. It
fucking won't. It fucking won't. It fucking won't. It
fucking won't. It fucking won't. It fucking won't. It
fucking won't. It fucking won't. It fucking won't. It
fucking won't. It fucking won't. It fucking won't. It
fucking won't. It fucking won't. It fucking won't. It
fucking won't. It fucking won't. It fucking won't. It
fucking won't. It fucking won't. It fucking won't. It
fucking won't. It fucking won't. It fucking won't. It
fucking won't. It fucking won't. It fucking won't. It
fucking won't. It fucking won't. It fucking won't. It
fucking won't. It fucking won't. It fucking won't. It
fucking won't. It fucking won't. It fucking won't. It
fucking won't. It fucking won't. It fucking won't. It
fucking won't. It fucking won't. It fucking won't. It
fucking won't. It fucking won't. It fucking won't. It
fucking won't. It fucking won't. It fucking won't. It
fucking won't. It fucking won't. It fucking won't. It
fucking won't. It fucking won't. It fucking won't. It
fucking won't. It fucking won't. It fucking won't. It
fucking won't. It fucking won't. It fucking won't. It
fucking won't. It fucking won't. It fucking won't. It
fucking won't. It fucking won't. It fucking won't. It
fucking won't. It fucking won't. It fucking won't. It
fucking won't. It fucking won't. It fucking won't. It
fucking won't. It fucking won't. It fucking won't. It
fucking won't. It fucking won't. It fucking won't. It

127

fucking won't. It fucking won't. It fucking won't. It
fucking won't. It fucking won't. It fucking won't. It
fucking won't. It fucking won't. It fucking won't. It
fucking won't. It fucking won't. It fucking won't. It
fucking won't. It fucking won't. It fucking won't. It
fucking won't. It fucking won't. It fucking won't. It
fucking won't. It fucking won't. It fucking won't. It
fucking won't. It fucking won't. It fucking won't. It
fucking won't. It fucking won't. It fucking won't. It
fucking won't. It fucking won't. It fucking won't. It
fucking won't. It fucking won't. It fucking won't. It
fucking won't. It fucking won't. It fucking won't. It
fucking won't. It fucking won't. It fucking won't. It
fucking won't. It fucking won't. It fucking won't. It
fucking won't. It fucking won't. It fucking won't. It
fucking won't. It fucking won't. It fucking won't. It
fucking won't. It fucking won't. It fucking won't. It
fucking won't. It fucking won't. It fucking won't. It
fucking won't. It fucking won't. It fucking won't. It
fucking won't. It fucking won't. It fucking won't. It
fucking won't. It fucking won't. It fucking won't. It
fucking won't. It fucking won't. It fucking won't. It
fucking won't. It fucking won't. It fucking won't. It
fucking won't. It fucking won't. It fucking won't. It
fucking won't. It fucking won't. It fucking won't. It
fucking won't. It fucking won't. It fucking won't. It
fucking won't. It fucking won't. It fucking won't. It
fucking won't. It fucking won't. It fucking won't. It
fucking won't. It fucking won't. It fucking won't. It
fucking won't. It fucking won't. It fucking won't. It

fucking won't. It fucking won't. It fucking won't. It
fucking won't. It fucking won't. It fucking won't. It
fucking won't. It fucking won't. It fucking won't. It
fucking won't. It fucking won't. It fucking won't. It
fucking won't. It fucking won't. It fucking won't. It
fucking won't. It fucking won't. It fucking won't. It
fucking won't. It fucking won't. It fucking won't. It
fucking won't. It fucking won't. It fucking won't. It
fucking won't. It fucking won't. It fucking won't. It
fucking won't. It fucking won't. It fucking won't. It
fucking won't. It fucking won't. It fucking won't. It
fucking won't. It fucking won't. It fucking won't. It
fucking won't. It fucking won't. It fucking won't. It
fucking won't. It fucking won't. It fucking won't. It
fucking won't. It fucking won't. It fucking won't. It
fucking won't. It fucking won't. It fucking won't. It
fucking won't. It fucking won't. It fucking won't. It
fucking won't. It fucking won't. It fucking won't. It
fucking won't. It fucking won't. It fucking won't. It
fucking won't. It fucking won't. It fucking won't. It
fucking won't. It fucking won't. It fucking won't. It
fucking won't. It fucking won't. It fucking won't. It
fucking won't. It fucking won't. It fucking won't. It
fucking won't. It fucking won't. It fucking won't. It
fucking won't. It fucking won't. It fucking won't. It
fucking won't. It fucking won't. It fucking won't. It
fucking won't. It fucking won't. It fucking won't. It
fucking won't. It fucking won't. It fucking won't. It
fucking won't. It fucking won't. It fucking won't. It
fucking won't. It fucking won't. It fucking won't. It
fucking won't. It fucking won't. It fucking won't. It

fucking won't. It fucking won't. It fucking won't. It
fucking won't. It fucking won't. It fucking won't. It
fucking won't. It fucking won't. It fucking won't. It
fucking won't. It fucking won't. It fucking won't. It
fucking won't. It fucking won't. It fucking won't. It
fucking won't. It fucking won't. It fucking won't. It
fucking won't. It fucking won't. It fucking won't. It
fucking won't. It fucking won't. It fucking won't. It
fucking won't. It fucking won't. It fucking won't. It
fucking won't. It fucking won't. It fucking won't. It
fucking won't. It fucking won't. It fucking won't. It
fucking won't. It fucking won't. It fucking won't. It
fucking won't. It fucking won't. It fucking won't. It
fucking won't. It fucking won't. It fucking won't. It
fucking won't. It fucking won't. It fucking won't. It
fucking won't. It fucking won't. It fucking won't. It
fucking won't. It fucking won't. It fucking won't. It
fucking won't. It fucking won't. It fucking won't. It
fucking won't. It fucking won't. It fucking won't. It
fucking won't. It fucking won't. It fucking won't. It
fucking won't. It fucking won't. It fucking won't. It
fucking won't. It fucking won't. It fucking won't. It
fucking won't. It fucking won't. It fucking won't. It
fucking won't. It fucking won't. It fucking won't. It
fucking won't. It fucking won't. It fucking won't. It
fucking won't. It fucking won't. It fucking won't. It
fucking won't. It fucking won't. It fucking won't. It
fucking won't. It fucking won't. It fucking won't. It
fucking won't. It fucking won't. It fucking won't. It
fucking won't. It fucking won't. It fucking won't. It

fucking won't. It fucking won't. It fucking won't. It
fucking won't. It fucking won't. It fucking won't. It
fucking won't. It fucking won't. It fucking won't. It
fucking won't. It fucking won't. It fucking won't. It
fucking won't. It fucking won't. It fucking won't. It
fucking won't. It fucking won't. It fucking won't. It
fucking won't. It fucking won't. It fucking won't. It
fucking won't. It fucking won't. It fucking won't. It
fucking won't. It fucking won't. It fucking won't. It
fucking won't. It fucking won't. It fucking won't. It
fucking won't. It fucking won't. It fucking won't. It
fucking won't. It fucking won't. It fucking won't. It
fucking won't. It fucking won't. It fucking won't. It
fucking won't. It fucking won't. It fucking won't. It
fucking won't. It fucking won't. It fucking won't. It
fucking won't. It fucking won't. It fucking won't. It
fucking won't. It fucking won't. It fucking won't. It
fucking won't. It fucking won't. It fucking won't. It
fucking won't. It fucking won't. It fucking won't. It
fucking won't. It fucking won't. It fucking won't. It
fucking won't. It fucking won't. It fucking won't. It
fucking won't. It fucking won't. It fucking won't. It
fucking won't. It fucking won't. It fucking won't. It
fucking won't. It fucking won't. It fucking won't. It
fucking won't. It fucking won't. It fucking won't. It
fucking won't. It fucking won't. It fucking won't. It
fucking won't. It fucking won't. It fucking won't. It
fucking won't. It fucking won't. It fucking won't. It
fucking won't. It fucking won't. It fucking won't. It
fucking won't. It fucking won't. It fucking won't. It
fucking won't. It fucking won't. It fucking won't. It

fucking won't. It fucking won't. It fucking won't. It
fucking won't. It fucking won't. It fucking won't. It
fucking won't. It fucking won't. It fucking won't. It
fucking won't. It fucking won't. It fucking won't. It
fucking won't. It fucking won't. It fucking won't. It
fucking won't. It fucking won't. It fucking won't. It
fucking won't. It fucking won't. It fucking won't. It
fucking won't. It fucking won't. It fucking won't. It
fucking won't. It fucking won't. It fucking won't. It
fucking won't. It fucking won't. It fucking won't. It
fucking won't. It fucking won't. It fucking won't. It
fucking won't. It fucking won't. It fucking won't. It
fucking won't. It fucking won't. It fucking won't. It
fucking won't. It fucking won't. It fucking won't. It
fucking won't. It fucking won't. It fucking won't. It
fucking won't. It fucking won't. It fucking won't. It
fucking won't. It fucking won't. It fucking won't. It
fucking won't. It fucking won't. It fucking won't. It
fucking won't. It fucking won't. It fucking won't. It
fucking won't. It fucking won't. It fucking won't. It
fucking won't. It fucking won't. It fucking won't. It
fucking won't. It fucking won't. It fucking won't. It
fucking won't. It fucking won't. It fucking won't. It
fucking won't. It fucking won't. It fucking won't. It
fucking won't. It fucking won't. It fucking won't. It
fucking won't. It fucking won't. It fucking won't. It
fucking won't. It fucking won't. It fucking won't. It
fucking won't. It fucking won't. It fucking won't. It
fucking won't. It fucking won't. It fucking won't. It
fucking won't. It fucking won't. It fucking won't. It

fucking won't. It fucking won't. It fucking won't. It
fucking won't. It fucking won't. It fucking won't. It
fucking won't. It fucking won't. It fucking won't. It
fucking won't. It fucking won't. It fucking won't. It
fucking won't. It fucking won't. It fucking won't. It
fucking won't. It fucking won't. It fucking won't. It
fucking won't. It fucking won't. It fucking won't. It
fucking won't. It fucking won't. It fucking won't. It
fucking won't. It fucking won't. It fucking won't. It
fucking won't. It fucking won't. It fucking won't. It
fucking won't. It fucking won't. It fucking won't. It
fucking won't. It fucking won't. It fucking won't. It
fucking won't. It fucking won't. It fucking won't. It
fucking won't. It fucking won't. It fucking won't. It
fucking won't. It fucking won't. It fucking won't. It
fucking won't. It fucking won't. It fucking won't. It
fucking won't. It fucking won't. It fucking won't. It
fucking won't. It fucking won't. It fucking won't. It
fucking won't. It fucking won't. It fucking won't. It
fucking won't. It fucking won't. It fucking won't. It
fucking won't. It fucking won't. It fucking won't. It
fucking won't. It fucking won't. It fucking won't. It
fucking won't. It fucking won't. It fucking won't. It
fucking won't. It fucking won't. It fucking won't. It
fucking won't. It fucking won't. It fucking won't. It
fucking won't. It fucking won't. It fucking won't. It
fucking won't. It fucking won't. It fucking won't. It
fucking won't. It fucking won't. It fucking won't. It
fucking won't. It fucking won't. It fucking won't. It
fucking won't. It fucking won't. It fucking won't.

It fucking won't. It fucking won't. It fucking won't. It
fucking won't. It fucking won't. It fucking won't. It
fucking won't. It fucking won't. It fucking won't. It
fucking won't. It fucking won't. It fucking won't. It
fucking won't. It fucking won't. It fucking won't. It
fucking won't. It fucking won't. It fucking won't. It
fucking won't. It fucking won't. It fucking won't. It
fucking won't. It fucking won't. It fucking won't. It
fucking won't. It fucking won't. It fucking won't. It
fucking won't. It fucking won't. It fucking won't. It
fucking won't. It fucking won't. It fucking won't. It
fucking won't. It fucking won't. It fucking won't. It
fucking won't. It fucking won't. It fucking won't. It
fucking won't. It fucking won't. It fucking won't. It
fucking won't. It fucking won't. It fucking won't. It
fucking won't. It fucking won't. It fucking won't. It
fucking won't. It fucking won't. It fucking won't. It
fucking won't. It fucking won't. It fucking won't. It
fucking won't. It fucking won't. It fucking won't. It
fucking won't. It fucking won't. It fucking won't. It
fucking won't. It fucking won't. It fucking won't. It
fucking won't. It fucking won't. It fucking won't. It
fucking won't. It fucking won't. It fucking won't. It
fucking won't. It fucking won't. It fucking won't. It
fucking won't. It fucking won't. It fucking won't. It
fucking won't. It fucking won't. It fucking won't. It
fucking won't. It fucking won't. It fucking won't. It
fucking won't. It fucking won't. It fucking won't. It
fucking won't. It fucking won't. It fucking won't. It
fucking won't. It fucking won't. It fucking won't. It

fucking won't. It fucking won't. It fucking won't. It
fucking won't. It fucking won't. It fucking won't. It
fucking won't. It fucking won't. It fucking won't. It
fucking won't. It fucking won't. It fucking won't. It
fucking won't. It fucking won't. It fucking won't. It
fucking won't. It fucking won't. It fucking won't. It
fucking won't. It fucking won't. It fucking won't. It
fucking won't. It fucking won't. It fucking won't. It
fucking won't. It fucking won't. It fucking won't. It
fucking won't. It fucking won't. It fucking won't. It
fucking won't. It fucking won't. It fucking won't. It
fucking won't. It fucking won't. It fucking won't. It
fucking won't. It fucking won't. It fucking won't. It
fucking won't. It fucking won't. It fucking won't. It
fucking won't. It fucking won't. It fucking won't. It
fucking won't. It fucking won't. It fucking won't. It
fucking won't. It fucking won't. It fucking won't. It
fucking won't. It fucking won't. It fucking won't. It
fucking won't. It fucking won't. It fucking won't. It
fucking won't. It fucking won't. It fucking won't. It
fucking won't. It fucking won't. It fucking won't. It
fucking won't. It fucking won't. It fucking won't. It
fucking won't. It fucking won't. It fucking won't. It
fucking won't. It fucking won't. It fucking won't. It
fucking won't. It fucking won't. It fucking won't. It
fucking won't. It fucking won't. It fucking won't. It
fucking won't. It fucking won't. It fucking won't. It
fucking won't. It fucking won't. It fucking won't. It
fucking won't. It fucking won't. It fucking won't. It
fucking won't. It fucking won't. It fucking won't. It

fucking won't. It fucking won't. It fucking won't. It
fucking won't. It fucking won't. It fucking won't. It
fucking won't. It fucking won't. It fucking won't. It
fucking won't. It fucking won't. It fucking won't. It
fucking won't. It fucking won't. It fucking won't. It
fucking won't. It fucking won't. It fucking won't. It
fucking won't. It fucking won't. It fucking won't. It
fucking won't. It fucking won't. It fucking won't. It
fucking won't. It fucking won't. It fucking won't. It
fucking won't. It fucking won't. It fucking won't. It
fucking won't. It fucking won't. It fucking won't. It
fucking won't. It fucking won't. It fucking won't. It
fucking won't. It fucking won't. It fucking won't. It
fucking won't. It fucking won't. It fucking won't. It
fucking won't. It fucking won't. It fucking won't. It
fucking won't. It fucking won't. It fucking won't. It
fucking won't. It fucking won't. It fucking won't. It
fucking won't. It fucking won't. It fucking won't. It
fucking won't. It fucking won't. It fucking won't. It
fucking won't. It fucking won't. It fucking won't. It
fucking won't. It fucking won't. It fucking won't. It
fucking won't. It fucking won't. It fucking won't. It
fucking won't. It fucking won't. It fucking won't. It
fucking won't. It fucking won't. It fucking won't. It
fucking won't. It fucking won't. It fucking won't. It
fucking won't. It fucking won't. It fucking won't. It
fucking won't. It fucking won't. It fucking won't. It
fucking won't. It fucking won't. It fucking won't. It
fucking won't. It fucking won't. It fucking won't. It
fucking won't. It fucking won't. It fucking won't. It

fucking won't. It fucking won't. It fucking won't. It
fucking won't. It fucking won't. It fucking won't. It
fucking won't. It fucking won't. It fucking won't. It
fucking won't. It fucking won't. It fucking won't. It
fucking won't. It fucking won't. It fucking won't. It
fucking won't. It fucking won't. It fucking won't. It
fucking won't. It fucking won't. It fucking won't. It
fucking won't. It fucking won't. It fucking won't. It
fucking won't. It fucking won't. It fucking won't. It
fucking won't. It fucking won't. It fucking won't. It
fucking won't. It fucking won't. It fucking won't. It
fucking won't. It fucking won't. It fucking won't. It
fucking won't. It fucking won't. It fucking won't. It
fucking won't. It fucking won't. It fucking won't. It
fucking won't. It fucking won't. It fucking won't. It
fucking won't. It fucking won't. It fucking won't. It
fucking won't. It fucking won't. It fucking won't. It
fucking won't. It fucking won't. It fucking won't. It
fucking won't. It fucking won't. It fucking won't. It
fucking won't. It fucking won't. It fucking won't. It
fucking won't. It fucking won't. It fucking won't. It
fucking won't. It fucking won't. It fucking won't. It
fucking won't. It fucking won't. It fucking won't. It
fucking won't. It fucking won't. It fucking won't. It
fucking won't. It fucking won't. It fucking won't. It
fucking won't. It fucking won't. It fucking won't. It
fucking won't. It fucking won't. It fucking won't. It
fucking won't. It fucking won't. It fucking won't. It
fucking won't. It fucking won't. It fucking won't. It
fucking won't. It fucking won't. It fucking won't. It

fucking won't. It fucking won't. It fucking won't. It
fucking won't. It fucking won't. It fucking won't. It
fucking won't. It fucking won't. It fucking won't. It
fucking won't. It fucking won't. It fucking won't. It
fucking won't. It fucking won't. It fucking won't. It
fucking won't. It fucking won't. It fucking won't. It
fucking won't. It fucking won't. It fucking won't. It
fucking won't. It fucking won't. It fucking won't. It
fucking won't. It fucking won't. It fucking won't. It
fucking won't. It fucking won't. It fucking won't. It
fucking won't. It fucking won't. It fucking won't. It
fucking won't. It fucking won't. It fucking won't. It
fucking won't. It fucking won't. It fucking won't. It
fucking won't. It fucking won't. It fucking won't. It
fucking won't. It fucking won't. It fucking won't. It
fucking won't. It fucking won't. It fucking won't. It
fucking won't. It fucking won't. It fucking won't. It
fucking won't. It fucking won't. It fucking won't. It
fucking won't. It fucking won't. It fucking won't. It
fucking won't. It fucking won't. It fucking won't. It
fucking won't. It fucking won't. It fucking won't. It
fucking won't. It fucking won't. It fucking won't. It
fucking won't. It fucking won't. It fucking won't. It
fucking won't. It fucking won't. It fucking won't. It
fucking won't. It fucking won't. It fucking won't. It
fucking won't. It fucking won't. It fucking won't. It
fucking won't. It fucking won't. It fucking won't. It
fucking won't. It fucking won't. It fucking won't. It
fucking won't. It fucking won't. It fucking won't. It
fucking won't. It fucking won't. It fucking won't. It

fucking won't. It fucking won't. It fucking won't. It
fucking won't. It fucking won't. It fucking won't. It
fucking won't. It fucking won't. It fucking won't. It
fucking won't. It fucking won't. It fucking won't. It
fucking won't. It fucking won't. It fucking won't. It
fucking won't. It fucking won't. It fucking won't. It
fucking won't. It fucking won't. It fucking won't. It
fucking won't. It fucking won't. It fucking won't. It
fucking won't. It fucking won't. It fucking won't. It
fucking won't. It fucking won't. It fucking won't. It
fucking won't. It fucking won't. It fucking won't. It
fucking won't. It fucking won't. It fucking won't. It
fucking won't. It fucking won't. It fucking won't. It
fucking won't. It fucking won't. It fucking won't. It
fucking won't. It fucking won't. It fucking won't. It
fucking won't. It fucking won't. It fucking won't. It
fucking won't. It fucking won't. It fucking won't. It
fucking won't. It fucking won't. It fucking won't. It
fucking won't. It fucking won't. It fucking won't. It
fucking won't. It fucking won't. It fucking won't. It
fucking won't. It fucking won't. It fucking won't. It
fucking won't. It fucking won't. It fucking won't. It
fucking won't. It fucking won't. It fucking won't. It
fucking won't. It fucking won't. It fucking won't. It
fucking won't. It fucking won't. It fucking won't. It
fucking won't. It fucking won't. It fucking won't. It
fucking won't. It fucking won't. It fucking won't. It
fucking won't. It fucking won't. It fucking won't. It
fucking won't. It fucking won't. It fucking won't. It
fucking won't. It fucking won't. It fucking won't. It

fucking won't. It fucking won't. It fucking won't. It
fucking won't. It fucking won't. It fucking won't. It
fucking won't. It fucking won't. It fucking won't. It
fucking won't. It fucking won't. It fucking won't. It
fucking won't. It fucking won't. It fucking won't. It
fucking won't. It fucking won't. It fucking won't. It
fucking won't. It fucking won't. It fucking won't. It
fucking won't. It fucking won't. It fucking won't. It
fucking won't. It fucking won't. It fucking won't. It
fucking won't. It fucking won't. It fucking won't. It
fucking won't. It fucking won't. It fucking won't. It
fucking won't. It fucking won't. It fucking won't. It
fucking won't. It fucking won't. It fucking won't. It
fucking won't. It fucking won't. It fucking won't. It
fucking won't. It fucking won't. It fucking won't. It
fucking won't. It fucking won't. It fucking won't. It
fucking won't. It fucking won't. It fucking won't. It
fucking won't. It fucking won't. It fucking won't. It
fucking won't. It fucking won't. It fucking won't. It
fucking won't. It fucking won't. It fucking won't. It
fucking won't. It fucking won't. It fucking won't. It
fucking won't. It fucking won't. It fucking won't. It
fucking won't. It fucking won't. It fucking won't. It
fucking won't. It fucking won't. It fucking won't. It
fucking won't. It fucking won't. It fucking won't. It
fucking won't. It fucking won't. It fucking won't. It
fucking won't. It fucking won't. It fucking won't. It
fucking won't. It fucking won't. It fucking won't. It
fucking won't. It fucking won't. It fucking won't. It
fucking won't. It fucking won't. It fucking won't. It

fucking won't. It fucking won't. It fucking won't. It
fucking won't. It fucking won't. It fucking won't. It
fucking won't. It fucking won't. It fucking won't. It
fucking won't. It fucking won't. It fucking won't. It
fucking won't. It fucking won't. It fucking won't. It
fucking won't. It fucking won't. It fucking won't. It
fucking won't. It fucking won't. It fucking won't. It
fucking won't. It fucking won't. It fucking won't. It
fucking won't. It fucking won't. It fucking won't. It
fucking won't. It fucking won't. It fucking won't. It
fucking won't. It fucking won't. It fucking won't. It
fucking won't. It fucking won't. It fucking won't. It
fucking won't. It fucking won't. It fucking won't. It
fucking won't. It fucking won't. It fucking won't. It
fucking won't. It fucking won't. It fucking won't. It
fucking won't. It fucking won't. It fucking won't. It
fucking won't. It fucking won't. It fucking won't. It
fucking won't. It fucking won't. It fucking won't. It
fucking won't. It fucking won't. It fucking won't. It
fucking won't. It fucking won't. It fucking won't. It
fucking won't. It fucking won't. It fucking won't. It
fucking won't. It fucking won't. It fucking won't. It
fucking won't. It fucking won't. It fucking won't. It
fucking won't. It fucking won't. It fucking won't. It
fucking won't. It fucking won't. It fucking won't. It
fucking won't. It fucking won't. It fucking won't. It
fucking won't. It fucking won't. It fucking won't. It
fucking won't. It fucking won't. It fucking won't. It
fucking won't. It fucking won't. It fucking won't. It
fucking won't. It fucking won't. It fucking won't. It

fucking won't. It fucking won't. It fucking won't. It
fucking won't. It fucking won't. It fucking won't. It
fucking won't. It fucking won't. It fucking won't. It
fucking won't. It fucking won't. It fucking won't. It
fucking won't. It fucking won't. It fucking won't. It
fucking won't. It fucking won't. It fucking won't. It
fucking won't. It fucking won't. It fucking won't. It
fucking won't. It fucking won't. It fucking won't. It
fucking won't. It fucking won't. It fucking won't. It
fucking won't. It fucking won't. It fucking won't. It
fucking won't. It fucking won't. It fucking won't. It
fucking won't. It fucking won't. It fucking won't. It
fucking won't. It fucking won't. It fucking won't. It
fucking won't. It fucking won't. It fucking won't. It
fucking won't. It fucking won't. It fucking won't. It
fucking won't. It fucking won't. It fucking won't. It
fucking won't. It fucking won't. It fucking won't. It
fucking won't. It fucking won't. It fucking won't. It
fucking won't. It fucking won't. It fucking won't. It
fucking won't. It fucking won't. It fucking won't. It
fucking won't. It fucking won't. It fucking won't. It
fucking won't. It fucking won't. It fucking won't. It
fucking won't. It fucking won't. It fucking won't. It
fucking won't. It fucking won't. It fucking won't. It
fucking won't. It fucking won't. It fucking won't. It
fucking won't. It fucking won't. It fucking won't. It
fucking won't. It fucking won't. It fucking won't. It
fucking won't. It fucking won't. It fucking won't. It
fucking won't. It fucking won't. It fucking won't. It
fucking won't. It fucking won't. It fucking won't. It
fucking won't. It fucking won't. It fucking won't. It

fucking won't. It fucking won't. It fucking won't. It
fucking won't. It fucking won't. It fucking won't. It
fucking won't. It fucking won't. It fucking won't. It
fucking won't. It fucking won't. It fucking won't. It
fucking won't. It fucking won't. It fucking won't. It
fucking won't. It fucking won't. It fucking won't. It
fucking won't. It fucking won't. It fucking won't. It
fucking won't. It fucking won't. It fucking won't. It
fucking won't. It fucking won't. It fucking won't. It
fucking won't. It fucking won't. It fucking won't. It
fucking won't. It fucking won't. It fucking won't. It
fucking won't. It fucking won't. It fucking won't. It
fucking won't. It fucking won't. It fucking won't. It
fucking won't. It fucking won't. It fucking won't. It
fucking won't. It fucking won't. It fucking won't. It
fucking won't. It fucking won't. It fucking won't. It
fucking won't. It fucking won't. It fucking won't. It
fucking won't. It fucking won't. It fucking won't. It
fucking won't. It fucking won't. It fucking won't. It
fucking won't. It fucking won't. It fucking won't. It
fucking won't. It fucking won't. It fucking won't. It
fucking won't. It fucking won't. It fucking won't. It
fucking won't. It fucking won't. It fucking won't. It
fucking won't. It fucking won't. It fucking won't. It
fucking won't. It fucking won't. It fucking won't. It
fucking won't. It fucking won't. It fucking won't. It
fucking won't. It fucking won't. It fucking won't. It
fucking won't. It fucking won't. It fucking won't. It
fucking won't. It fucking won't. It fucking won't. It
fucking won't. It fucking won't. It fucking won't. It

fucking won't. It fucking won't. It fucking won't. It
fucking won't. It fucking won't. It fucking won't. It
fucking won't. It fucking won't. It fucking won't. It
fucking won't. It fucking won't. It fucking won't. It
fucking won't. It fucking won't. It fucking won't. It
fucking won't. It fucking won't. It fucking won't. It
fucking won't. It fucking won't. It fucking won't. It
fucking won't. It fucking won't. It fucking won't. It
fucking won't. It fucking won't. It fucking won't. It
fucking won't. It fucking won't. It fucking won't. It
fucking won't. It fucking won't. It fucking won't. It
fucking won't. It fucking won't. It fucking won't. It
fucking won't. It fucking won't. It fucking won't. It
fucking won't. It fucking won't. It fucking won't. It
fucking won't. It fucking won't. It fucking won't. It
fucking won't. It fucking won't. It fucking won't. It
fucking won't. It fucking won't. It fucking won't. It
fucking won't. It fucking won't. It fucking won't. It
fucking won't. It fucking won't. It fucking won't. It
fucking won't. It fucking won't. It fucking won't. It
fucking won't. It fucking won't. It fucking won't. It
fucking won't. It fucking won't. It fucking won't. It
fucking won't. It fucking won't. It fucking won't. It
fucking won't. It fucking won't. It fucking won't. It
fucking won't. It fucking won't. It fucking won't. It
fucking won't. It fucking won't. It fucking won't. It
fucking won't. It fucking won't. It fucking won't. It
fucking won't. It fucking won't. It fucking won't. It
fucking won't. It fucking won't. It fucking won't. It
fucking won't. It fucking won't. It fucking won't. It
fucking won't. It fucking won't. It fucking won't. It

fucking won't. It fucking won't. It fucking won't. It
fucking won't. It fucking won't. It fucking won't. It
fucking won't. It fucking won't. It fucking won't.

It fucking won't. It fucking won't. It fucking won't. It
fucking won't. It fucking won't. It fucking won't. It
fucking won't. It fucking won't. It fucking won't. It
fucking won't. It fucking won't. It fucking won't. It
fucking won't. It fucking won't. It fucking won't. It
fucking won't. It fucking won't. It fucking won't. It
fucking won't. It fucking won't. It fucking won't. It
fucking won't. It fucking won't. It fucking won't. It
fucking won't. It fucking won't. It fucking won't. It
fucking won't. It fucking won't. It fucking won't. It
fucking won't. It fucking won't. It fucking won't. It
fucking won't. It fucking won't. It fucking won't. It
fucking won't. It fucking won't. It fucking won't. It
fucking won't. It fucking won't. It fucking won't. It
fucking won't. It fucking won't. It fucking won't. It
fucking won't. It fucking won't. It fucking won't. It
fucking won't. It fucking won't. It fucking won't. It
fucking won't. It fucking won't. It fucking won't. It
fucking won't. It fucking won't. It fucking won't. It
fucking won't. It fucking won't. It fucking won't. It
fucking won't. It fucking won't. It fucking won't. It
fucking won't. It fucking won't. It fucking won't. It
fucking won't. It fucking won't. It fucking won't. It
fucking won't. It fucking won't. It fucking won't. It
fucking won't. It fucking won't. It fucking won't. It
fucking won't. It fucking won't. It fucking won't. It

fucking won't. It fucking won't. It fucking won't. It
fucking won't. It fucking won't. It fucking won't. It
fucking won't. It fucking won't. It fucking won't. It
fucking won't. It fucking won't. It fucking won't. It
fucking won't. It fucking won't. It fucking won't. It
fucking won't. It fucking won't. It fucking won't. It
fucking won't. It fucking won't. It fucking won't. It
fucking won't. It fucking won't. It fucking won't. It
fucking won't. It fucking won't. It fucking won't. It
fucking won't. It fucking won't. It fucking won't. It
fucking won't. It fucking won't. It fucking won't. It
fucking won't. It fucking won't. It fucking won't. It
fucking won't. It fucking won't. It fucking won't. It
fucking won't. It fucking won't. It fucking won't. It
fucking won't. It fucking won't. It fucking won't. It
fucking won't. It fucking won't. It fucking won't. It
fucking won't. It fucking won't. It fucking won't. It
fucking won't. It fucking won't. It fucking won't. It
fucking won't. It fucking won't. It fucking won't. It
fucking won't. It fucking won't. It fucking won't. It
fucking won't. It fucking won't. It fucking won't. It
fucking won't. It fucking won't. It fucking won't. It
fucking won't. It fucking won't. It fucking won't. It
fucking won't. It fucking won't. It fucking won't. It
fucking won't. It fucking won't. It fucking won't. It
fucking won't. It fucking won't. It fucking won't. It
fucking won't. It fucking won't. It fucking won't. It
fucking won't. It fucking won't. It fucking won't. It
fucking won't. It fucking won't. It fucking won't. It
fucking won't. It fucking won't. It fucking won't. It
fucking won't. It fucking won't. It fucking won't. It

fucking won't. It fucking won't. It fucking won't. It
fucking won't. It fucking won't. It fucking won't. It
fucking won't. It fucking won't. It fucking won't. It
fucking won't. It fucking won't. It fucking won't. It
fucking won't. It fucking won't. It fucking won't. It
fucking won't. It fucking won't. It fucking won't. It
fucking won't. It fucking won't. It fucking won't. It
fucking won't. It fucking won't. It fucking won't. It
fucking won't. It fucking won't. It fucking won't. It
fucking won't. It fucking won't. It fucking won't. It
fucking won't. It fucking won't. It fucking won't. It
fucking won't. It fucking won't. It fucking won't. It
fucking won't. It fucking won't. It fucking won't. It
fucking won't. It fucking won't. It fucking won't. It
fucking won't. It fucking won't. It fucking won't. It
fucking won't. It fucking won't. It fucking won't. It
fucking won't. It fucking won't. It fucking won't. It
fucking won't. It fucking won't. It fucking won't. It
fucking won't. It fucking won't. It fucking won't. It
fucking won't. It fucking won't. It fucking won't. It
fucking won't. It fucking won't. It fucking won't. It
fucking won't. It fucking won't. It fucking won't. It
fucking won't. It fucking won't. It fucking won't. It
fucking won't. It fucking won't. It fucking won't. It
fucking won't. It fucking won't. It fucking won't. It
fucking won't. It fucking won't. It fucking won't. It
fucking won't. It fucking won't. It fucking won't. It
fucking won't. It fucking won't. It fucking won't. It
fucking won't. It fucking won't. It fucking won't. It
fucking won't. It fucking won't. It fucking won't. It

147

fucking won't. It fucking won't. It fucking won't. It
fucking won't. It fucking won't. It fucking won't. It
fucking won't. It fucking won't. It fucking won't. It
fucking won't. It fucking won't. It fucking won't. It
fucking won't. It fucking won't. It fucking won't. It
fucking won't. It fucking won't. It fucking won't. It
fucking won't. It fucking won't. It fucking won't. It
fucking won't. It fucking won't. It fucking won't. It
fucking won't. It fucking won't. It fucking won't. It
fucking won't. It fucking won't. It fucking won't. It
fucking won't. It fucking won't. It fucking won't. It
fucking won't. It fucking won't. It fucking won't. It
fucking won't. It fucking won't. It fucking won't. It
fucking won't. It fucking won't. It fucking won't. It
fucking won't. It fucking won't. It fucking won't. It
fucking won't. It fucking won't. It fucking won't. It
fucking won't. It fucking won't. It fucking won't. It
fucking won't. It fucking won't. It fucking won't. It
fucking won't. It fucking won't. It fucking won't. It
fucking won't. It fucking won't. It fucking won't. It
fucking won't. It fucking won't. It fucking won't. It
fucking won't. It fucking won't. It fucking won't. It
fucking won't. It fucking won't. It fucking won't. It
fucking won't. It fucking won't. It fucking won't. It
fucking won't. It fucking won't. It fucking won't. It
fucking won't. It fucking won't. It fucking won't. It
fucking won't. It fucking won't. It fucking won't. It
fucking won't. It fucking won't. It fucking won't. It
fucking won't. It fucking won't. It fucking won't. It
fucking won't. It fucking won't. It fucking won't. It

fucking won't. It fucking won't. It fucking won't. It
fucking won't. It fucking won't. It fucking won't. It
fucking won't. It fucking won't. It fucking won't. It
fucking won't. It fucking won't. It fucking won't. It
fucking won't. It fucking won't. It fucking won't. It
fucking won't. It fucking won't. It fucking won't. It
fucking won't. It fucking won't. It fucking won't. It
fucking won't. It fucking won't. It fucking won't. It
fucking won't. It fucking won't. It fucking won't. It
fucking won't. It fucking won't. It fucking won't. It
fucking won't. It fucking won't. It fucking won't. It
fucking won't. It fucking won't. It fucking won't. It
fucking won't. It fucking won't. It fucking won't. It
fucking won't. It fucking won't. It fucking won't. It
fucking won't. It fucking won't. It fucking won't. It
fucking won't. It fucking won't. It fucking won't. It
fucking won't. It fucking won't. It fucking won't. It
fucking won't. It fucking won't. It fucking won't. It
fucking won't. It fucking won't. It fucking won't. It
fucking won't. It fucking won't. It fucking won't. It
fucking won't. It fucking won't. It fucking won't. It
fucking won't. It fucking won't. It fucking won't. It
fucking won't. It fucking won't. It fucking won't. It
fucking won't. It fucking won't. It fucking won't. It
fucking won't. It fucking won't. It fucking won't. It
fucking won't. It fucking won't. It fucking won't. It
fucking won't. It fucking won't. It fucking won't. It
fucking won't. It fucking won't. It fucking won't. It
fucking won't. It fucking won't. It fucking won't. It
fucking won't. It fucking won't. It fucking won't. It

fucking won't. It fucking won't. It fucking won't. It
fucking won't. It fucking won't. It fucking won't. It
fucking won't. It fucking won't. It fucking won't. It
fucking won't. It fucking won't. It fucking won't. It
fucking won't. It fucking won't. It fucking won't. It
fucking won't. It fucking won't. It fucking won't. It
fucking won't. It fucking won't. It fucking won't. It
fucking won't. It fucking won't. It fucking won't. It
fucking won't. It fucking won't. It fucking won't. It
fucking won't. It fucking won't. It fucking won't. It
fucking won't. It fucking won't. It fucking won't. It
fucking won't. It fucking won't. It fucking won't. It
fucking won't. It fucking won't. It fucking won't. It
fucking won't. It fucking won't. It fucking won't. It
fucking won't. It fucking won't. It fucking won't. It
fucking won't. It fucking won't. It fucking won't. It
fucking won't. It fucking won't. It fucking won't. It
fucking won't. It fucking won't. It fucking won't. It
fucking won't. It fucking won't. It fucking won't. It
fucking won't. It fucking won't. It fucking won't. It
fucking won't. It fucking won't. It fucking won't. It
fucking won't. It fucking won't. It fucking won't. It
fucking won't. It fucking won't. It fucking won't. It
fucking won't. It fucking won't. It fucking won't. It
fucking won't. It fucking won't. It fucking won't. It
fucking won't. It fucking won't. It fucking won't. It
fucking won't. It fucking won't. It fucking won't. It
fucking won't. It fucking won't. It fucking won't. It
fucking won't. It fucking won't. It fucking won't. It
fucking won't. It fucking won't. It fucking won't. It

fucking won't. It fucking won't. It fucking won't. It
fucking won't. It fucking won't. It fucking won't. It
fucking won't. It fucking won't. It fucking won't. It
fucking won't. It fucking won't. It fucking won't. It
fucking won't. It fucking won't. It fucking won't. It
fucking won't. It fucking won't. It fucking won't. It
fucking won't. It fucking won't. It fucking won't. It
fucking won't. It fucking won't. It fucking won't. It
fucking won't. It fucking won't. It fucking won't. It
fucking won't. It fucking won't. It fucking won't. It
fucking won't. It fucking won't. It fucking won't. It
fucking won't. It fucking won't. It fucking won't. It
fucking won't. It fucking won't. It fucking won't. It
fucking won't. It fucking won't. It fucking won't. It
fucking won't. It fucking won't. It fucking won't. It
fucking won't. It fucking won't. It fucking won't. It
fucking won't. It fucking won't. It fucking won't. It
fucking won't. It fucking won't. It fucking won't. It
fucking won't. It fucking won't. It fucking won't. It
fucking won't. It fucking won't. It fucking won't. It
fucking won't. It fucking won't. It fucking won't. It
fucking won't. It fucking won't. It fucking won't. It
fucking won't. It fucking won't. It fucking won't. It
fucking won't. It fucking won't. It fucking won't. It
fucking won't. It fucking won't. It fucking won't. It
fucking won't. It fucking won't. It fucking won't. It
fucking won't. It fucking won't. It fucking won't. It
fucking won't. It fucking won't. It fucking won't. It
fucking won't. It fucking won't. It fucking won't. It
fucking won't. It fucking won't. It fucking won't. It

fucking won't. It fucking won't. It fucking won't. It
fucking won't. It fucking won't. It fucking won't. It
fucking won't. It fucking won't. It fucking won't. It
fucking won't. It fucking won't. It fucking won't. It
fucking won't. It fucking won't. It fucking won't. It
fucking won't. It fucking won't. It fucking won't. It
fucking won't. It fucking won't. It fucking won't. It
fucking won't. It fucking won't. It fucking won't. It
fucking won't. It fucking won't. It fucking won't. It
fucking won't. It fucking won't. It fucking won't. It
fucking won't. It fucking won't. It fucking won't. It
fucking won't. It fucking won't. It fucking won't. It
fucking won't. It fucking won't. It fucking won't. It
fucking won't. It fucking won't. It fucking won't. It
fucking won't. It fucking won't. It fucking won't. It
fucking won't. It fucking won't. It fucking won't. It
fucking won't. It fucking won't. It fucking won't. It
fucking won't. It fucking won't. It fucking won't. It
fucking won't. It fucking won't. It fucking won't. It
fucking won't. It fucking won't. It fucking won't. It
fucking won't. It fucking won't. It fucking won't. It
fucking won't. It fucking won't. It fucking won't. It
fucking won't. It fucking won't. It fucking won't. It
fucking won't. It fucking won't. It fucking won't. It
fucking won't. It fucking won't. It fucking won't. It
fucking won't. It fucking won't. It fucking won't. It
fucking won't. It fucking won't. It fucking won't. It
fucking won't. It fucking won't. It fucking won't. It
fucking won't. It fucking won't. It fucking won't. It
fucking won't. It fucking won't. It fucking won't. It

fucking won't. It fucking won't. It fucking won't. It
fucking won't. It fucking won't. It fucking won't. It
fucking won't. It fucking won't. It fucking won't. It
fucking won't. It fucking won't. It fucking won't. It
fucking won't. It fucking won't. It fucking won't. It
fucking won't. It fucking won't. It fucking won't. It
fucking won't. It fucking won't. It fucking won't. It
fucking won't. It fucking won't. It fucking won't. It
fucking won't. It fucking won't. It fucking won't. It
fucking won't. It fucking won't. It fucking won't. It
fucking won't. It fucking won't. It fucking won't. It
fucking won't. It fucking won't. It fucking won't. It
fucking won't. It fucking won't. It fucking won't. It
fucking won't. It fucking won't. It fucking won't. It
fucking won't. It fucking won't. It fucking won't. It
fucking won't. It fucking won't. It fucking won't. It
fucking won't. It fucking won't. It fucking won't. It
fucking won't. It fucking won't. It fucking won't. It
fucking won't. It fucking won't. It fucking won't. It
fucking won't. It fucking won't. It fucking won't. It
fucking won't. It fucking won't. It fucking won't. It
fucking won't. It fucking won't. It fucking won't. It
fucking won't. It fucking won't. It fucking won't. It
fucking won't. It fucking won't. It fucking won't. It
fucking won't. It fucking won't. It fucking won't. It
fucking won't. It fucking won't. It fucking won't. It
fucking won't. It fucking won't. It fucking won't. It
fucking won't. It fucking won't. It fucking won't. It
fucking won't. It fucking won't. It fucking won't. It
fucking won't. It fucking won't. It fucking won't. It

153

fucking won't. It fucking won't. It fucking won't. It
fucking won't. It fucking won't. It fucking won't. It
fucking won't. It fucking won't. It fucking won't. It
fucking won't. It fucking won't. It fucking won't. It
fucking won't. It fucking won't. It fucking won't. It
fucking won't. It fucking won't. It fucking won't. It
fucking won't. It fucking won't. It fucking won't. It
fucking won't. It fucking won't. It fucking won't. It
fucking won't. It fucking won't. It fucking won't. It
fucking won't. It fucking won't. It fucking won't. It
fucking won't. It fucking won't. It fucking won't. It
fucking won't. It fucking won't. It fucking won't. It
fucking won't. It fucking won't. It fucking won't. It
fucking won't. It fucking won't. It fucking won't. It
fucking won't. It fucking won't. It fucking won't. It
fucking won't. It fucking won't. It fucking won't. It
fucking won't. It fucking won't. It fucking won't. It
fucking won't. It fucking won't. It fucking won't. It
fucking won't. It fucking won't. It fucking won't. It
fucking won't. It fucking won't. It fucking won't. It
fucking won't. It fucking won't. It fucking won't. It
fucking won't. It fucking won't. It fucking won't. It
fucking won't. It fucking won't. It fucking won't. It
fucking won't. It fucking won't. It fucking won't. It
fucking won't. It fucking won't. It fucking won't. It
fucking won't. It fucking won't. It fucking won't. It
fucking won't. It fucking won't. It fucking won't. It
fucking won't. It fucking won't. It fucking won't. It
fucking won't. It fucking won't. It fucking won't. It
fucking won't. It fucking won't. It fucking won't. It

fucking won't. It fucking won't. It fucking won't. It
fucking won't. It fucking won't. It fucking won't. It
fucking won't. It fucking won't. It fucking won't. It
fucking won't. It fucking won't. It fucking won't. It
fucking won't. It fucking won't. It fucking won't. It
fucking won't. It fucking won't. It fucking won't. It
fucking won't. It fucking won't. It fucking won't. It
fucking won't. It fucking won't. It fucking won't. It
fucking won't. It fucking won't. It fucking won't. It
fucking won't. It fucking won't. It fucking won't. It
fucking won't. It fucking won't. It fucking won't. It
fucking won't. It fucking won't. It fucking won't. It
fucking won't. It fucking won't. It fucking won't. It
fucking won't. It fucking won't. It fucking won't. It
fucking won't. It fucking won't. It fucking won't. It
fucking won't. It fucking won't. It fucking won't. It
fucking won't. It fucking won't. It fucking won't. It
fucking won't. It fucking won't. It fucking won't. It
fucking won't. It fucking won't. It fucking won't. It
fucking won't. It fucking won't. It fucking won't. It
fucking won't. It fucking won't. It fucking won't. It
fucking won't. It fucking won't. It fucking won't. It
fucking won't. It fucking won't. It fucking won't. It
fucking won't. It fucking won't. It fucking won't. It
fucking won't. It fucking won't. It fucking won't. It
fucking won't. It fucking won't. It fucking won't. It
fucking won't. It fucking won't. It fucking won't. It
fucking won't. It fucking won't. It fucking won't. It
fucking won't. It fucking won't. It fucking won't. It
fucking won't. It fucking won't. It fucking won't. It
fucking won't. It fucking won't. It fucking won't. It
fucking won't. It fucking won't. It fucking won't. It

fucking won't. It fucking won't. It fucking won't. It
fucking won't. It fucking won't. It fucking won't. It
fucking won't. It fucking won't. It fucking won't. It
fucking won't. It fucking won't. It fucking won't. It
fucking won't. It fucking won't. It fucking won't. It
fucking won't. It fucking won't. It fucking won't. It
fucking won't. It fucking won't. It fucking won't.

It fucking won't. It fucking won't. It fucking won't. It
fucking won't. It fucking won't. It fucking won't. It
fucking won't. It fucking won't. It fucking won't. It
fucking won't. It fucking won't. It fucking won't. It
fucking won't. It fucking won't. It fucking won't. It
fucking won't. It fucking won't. It fucking won't. It
fucking won't. It fucking won't. It fucking won't. It
fucking won't. It fucking won't. It fucking won't. It
fucking won't. It fucking won't. It fucking won't. It
fucking won't. It fucking won't. It fucking won't. It
fucking won't. It fucking won't. It fucking won't. It
fucking won't. It fucking won't. It fucking won't. It
fucking won't. It fucking won't. It fucking won't. It
fucking won't. It fucking won't. It fucking won't. It
fucking won't. It fucking won't. It fucking won't. It
fucking won't. It fucking won't. It fucking won't. It
fucking won't. It fucking won't. It fucking won't. It
fucking won't. It fucking won't. It fucking won't. It
fucking won't. It fucking won't. It fucking won't. It
fucking won't. It fucking won't. It fucking won't. It
fucking won't. It fucking won't. It fucking won't. It

fucking won't. It fucking won't. It fucking won't. It
fucking won't. It fucking won't. It fucking won't. It
fucking won't. It fucking won't. It fucking won't. It
fucking won't. It fucking won't. It fucking won't. It
fucking won't. It fucking won't. It fucking won't. It
fucking won't. It fucking won't. It fucking won't. It
fucking won't. It fucking won't. It fucking won't. It
fucking won't. It fucking won't. It fucking won't. It
fucking won't. It fucking won't. It fucking won't. It
fucking won't. It fucking won't. It fucking won't. It
fucking won't. It fucking won't. It fucking won't. It
fucking won't. It fucking won't. It fucking won't. It
fucking won't. It fucking won't. It fucking won't. It
fucking won't. It fucking won't. It fucking won't. It
fucking won't. It fucking won't. It fucking won't. It
fucking won't. It fucking won't. It fucking won't. It
fucking won't. It fucking won't. It fucking won't. It
fucking won't. It fucking won't. It fucking won't. It
fucking won't. It fucking won't. It fucking won't. It
fucking won't. It fucking won't. It fucking won't. It
fucking won't. It fucking won't. It fucking won't. It
fucking won't. It fucking won't. It fucking won't. It
fucking won't. It fucking won't. It fucking won't. It
fucking won't. It fucking won't. It fucking won't. It
fucking won't. It fucking won't. It fucking won't. It
fucking won't. It fucking won't. It fucking won't. It
fucking won't. It fucking won't. It fucking won't. It
fucking won't. It fucking won't. It fucking won't. It
fucking won't. It fucking won't. It fucking won't. It
fucking won't. It fucking won't. It fucking won't. It

fucking won't. It fucking won't. It fucking won't. It
fucking won't. It fucking won't. It fucking won't. It
fucking won't. It fucking won't. It fucking won't. It
fucking won't. It fucking won't. It fucking won't. It
fucking won't. It fucking won't. It fucking won't. It
fucking won't. It fucking won't. It fucking won't. It
fucking won't. It fucking won't. It fucking won't. It
fucking won't. It fucking won't. It fucking won't. It
fucking won't. It fucking won't. It fucking won't. It
fucking won't. It fucking won't. It fucking won't. It
fucking won't. It fucking won't. It fucking won't. It
fucking won't. It fucking won't. It fucking won't. It
fucking won't. It fucking won't. It fucking won't. It
fucking won't. It fucking won't. It fucking won't. It
fucking won't. It fucking won't. It fucking won't. It
fucking won't. It fucking won't. It fucking won't. It
fucking won't. It fucking won't. It fucking won't. It
fucking won't. It fucking won't. It fucking won't. It
fucking won't. It fucking won't. It fucking won't. It
fucking won't. It fucking won't. It fucking won't. It
fucking won't. It fucking won't. It fucking won't. It
fucking won't. It fucking won't. It fucking won't. It
fucking won't. It fucking won't. It fucking won't. It
fucking won't. It fucking won't. It fucking won't. It
fucking won't. It fucking won't. It fucking won't. It
fucking won't. It fucking won't. It fucking won't. It
fucking won't. It fucking won't. It fucking won't. It
fucking won't. It fucking won't. It fucking won't. It
fucking won't. It fucking won't. It fucking won't. It
fucking won't. It fucking won't. It fucking won't. It

fucking won't. It fucking won't. It fucking won't. It
fucking won't. It fucking won't. It fucking won't. It
fucking won't. It fucking won't. It fucking won't. It
fucking won't. It fucking won't. It fucking won't. It
fucking won't. It fucking won't. It fucking won't. It
fucking won't. It fucking won't. It fucking won't. It
fucking won't. It fucking won't. It fucking won't. It
fucking won't. It fucking won't. It fucking won't. It
fucking won't. It fucking won't. It fucking won't. It
fucking won't. It fucking won't. It fucking won't. It
fucking won't. It fucking won't. It fucking won't. It
fucking won't. It fucking won't. It fucking won't. It
fucking won't. It fucking won't. It fucking won't. It
fucking won't. It fucking won't. It fucking won't. It
fucking won't. It fucking won't. It fucking won't. It
fucking won't. It fucking won't. It fucking won't. It
fucking won't. It fucking won't. It fucking won't. It
fucking won't. It fucking won't. It fucking won't. It
fucking won't. It fucking won't. It fucking won't. It
fucking won't. It fucking won't. It fucking won't. It
fucking won't. It fucking won't. It fucking won't. It
fucking won't. It fucking won't. It fucking won't. It
fucking won't. It fucking won't. It fucking won't. It
fucking won't. It fucking won't. It fucking won't. It
fucking won't. It fucking won't. It fucking won't. It
fucking won't. It fucking won't. It fucking won't. It
fucking won't. It fucking won't. It fucking won't. It
fucking won't. It fucking won't. It fucking won't. It
fucking won't. It fucking won't. It fucking won't. It
fucking won't. It fucking won't. It fucking won't. It

fucking won't. It fucking won't. It fucking won't. It
fucking won't. It fucking won't. It fucking won't. It
fucking won't. It fucking won't. It fucking won't. It
fucking won't. It fucking won't. It fucking won't. It
fucking won't. It fucking won't. It fucking won't. It
fucking won't. It fucking won't. It fucking won't. It
fucking won't. It fucking won't. It fucking won't. It
fucking won't. It fucking won't. It fucking won't. It
fucking won't. It fucking won't. It fucking won't. It
fucking won't. It fucking won't. It fucking won't. It
fucking won't. It fucking won't. It fucking won't. It
fucking won't. It fucking won't. It fucking won't. It
fucking won't. It fucking won't. It fucking won't. It
fucking won't. It fucking won't. It fucking won't. It
fucking won't. It fucking won't. It fucking won't. It
fucking won't. It fucking won't. It fucking won't. It
fucking won't. It fucking won't. It fucking won't. It
fucking won't. It fucking won't. It fucking won't. It
fucking won't. It fucking won't. It fucking won't. It
fucking won't. It fucking won't. It fucking won't. It
fucking won't. It fucking won't. It fucking won't. It
fucking won't. It fucking won't. It fucking won't. It
fucking won't. It fucking won't. It fucking won't. It
fucking won't. It fucking won't. It fucking won't. It
fucking won't. It fucking won't. It fucking won't. It
fucking won't. It fucking won't. It fucking won't. It
fucking won't. It fucking won't. It fucking won't. It
fucking won't. It fucking won't. It fucking won't. It
fucking won't. It fucking won't. It fucking won't. It
fucking won't. It fucking won't. It fucking won't. It

fucking won't. It fucking won't. It fucking won't. It
fucking won't. It fucking won't. It fucking won't. It
fucking won't. It fucking won't. It fucking won't. It
fucking won't. It fucking won't. It fucking won't. It
fucking won't. It fucking won't. It fucking won't. It
fucking won't. It fucking won't. It fucking won't. It
fucking won't. It fucking won't. It fucking won't. It
fucking won't. It fucking won't. It fucking won't. It
fucking won't. It fucking won't. It fucking won't. It
fucking won't. It fucking won't. It fucking won't. It
fucking won't. It fucking won't. It fucking won't. It
fucking won't. It fucking won't. It fucking won't. It
fucking won't. It fucking won't. It fucking won't. It
fucking won't. It fucking won't. It fucking won't. It
fucking won't. It fucking won't. It fucking won't. It
fucking won't. It fucking won't. It fucking won't. It
fucking won't. It fucking won't. It fucking won't. It
fucking won't. It fucking won't. It fucking won't. It
fucking won't. It fucking won't. It fucking won't. It
fucking won't. It fucking won't. It fucking won't. It
fucking won't. It fucking won't. It fucking won't. It
fucking won't. It fucking won't. It fucking won't. It
fucking won't. It fucking won't. It fucking won't. It
fucking won't. It fucking won't. It fucking won't. It
fucking won't. It fucking won't. It fucking won't. It
fucking won't. It fucking won't. It fucking won't. It
fucking won't. It fucking won't. It fucking won't. It
fucking won't. It fucking won't. It fucking won't. It
fucking won't. It fucking won't. It fucking won't. It
fucking won't. It fucking won't. It fucking won't. It
fucking won't. It fucking won't. It fucking won't. It

fucking won't. It fucking won't. It fucking won't. It
fucking won't. It fucking won't. It fucking won't. It
fucking won't. It fucking won't. It fucking won't. It
fucking won't. It fucking won't. It fucking won't. It
fucking won't. It fucking won't. It fucking won't. It
fucking won't. It fucking won't. It fucking won't. It
fucking won't. It fucking won't. It fucking won't. It
fucking won't. It fucking won't. It fucking won't. It
fucking won't. It fucking won't. It fucking won't. It
fucking won't. It fucking won't. It fucking won't. It
fucking won't. It fucking won't. It fucking won't. It
fucking won't. It fucking won't. It fucking won't. It
fucking won't. It fucking won't. It fucking won't. It
fucking won't. It fucking won't. It fucking won't. It
fucking won't. It fucking won't. It fucking won't. It
fucking won't. It fucking won't. It fucking won't. It
fucking won't. It fucking won't. It fucking won't. It
fucking won't. It fucking won't. It fucking won't. It
fucking won't. It fucking won't. It fucking won't. It
fucking won't. It fucking won't. It fucking won't. It
fucking won't. It fucking won't. It fucking won't. It
fucking won't. It fucking won't. It fucking won't. It
fucking won't. It fucking won't. It fucking won't. It
fucking won't. It fucking won't. It fucking won't. It
fucking won't. It fucking won't. It fucking won't. It
fucking won't. It fucking won't. It fucking won't. It
fucking won't. It fucking won't. It fucking won't. It
fucking won't. It fucking won't. It fucking won't. It
fucking won't. It fucking won't. It fucking won't. It
fucking won't. It fucking won't. It fucking won't. It

fucking won't. It fucking won't. It fucking won't. It
fucking won't. It fucking won't. It fucking won't. It
fucking won't. It fucking won't. It fucking won't. It
fucking won't. It fucking won't. It fucking won't. It
fucking won't. It fucking won't. It fucking won't. It
fucking won't. It fucking won't. It fucking won't. It
fucking won't. It fucking won't. It fucking won't. It
fucking won't. It fucking won't. It fucking won't. It
fucking won't. It fucking won't. It fucking won't. It
fucking won't. It fucking won't. It fucking won't. It
fucking won't. It fucking won't. It fucking won't. It
fucking won't. It fucking won't. It fucking won't. It
fucking won't. It fucking won't. It fucking won't. It
fucking won't. It fucking won't. It fucking won't. It
fucking won't. It fucking won't. It fucking won't. It
fucking won't. It fucking won't. It fucking won't. It
fucking won't. It fucking won't. It fucking won't. It
fucking won't. It fucking won't. It fucking won't. It
fucking won't. It fucking won't. It fucking won't. It
fucking won't. It fucking won't. It fucking won't. It
fucking won't. It fucking won't. It fucking won't. It
fucking won't. It fucking won't. It fucking won't. It
fucking won't. It fucking won't. It fucking won't. It
fucking won't. It fucking won't. It fucking won't. It
fucking won't. It fucking won't. It fucking won't. It
fucking won't. It fucking won't. It fucking won't. It
fucking won't. It fucking won't. It fucking won't. It
fucking won't. It fucking won't. It fucking won't. It
fucking won't. It fucking won't. It fucking won't. It
fucking won't. It fucking won't. It fucking won't. It

fucking won't. It fucking won't. It fucking won't. It
fucking won't. It fucking won't. It fucking won't. It
fucking won't. It fucking won't. It fucking won't. It
fucking won't. It fucking won't. It fucking won't. It
fucking won't. It fucking won't. It fucking won't. It
fucking won't. It fucking won't. It fucking won't. It
fucking won't. It fucking won't. It fucking won't. It
fucking won't. It fucking won't. It fucking won't. It
fucking won't. It fucking won't. It fucking won't. It
fucking won't. It fucking won't. It fucking won't. It
fucking won't. It fucking won't. It fucking won't. It
fucking won't. It fucking won't. It fucking won't. It
fucking won't. It fucking won't. It fucking won't. It
fucking won't. It fucking won't. It fucking won't. It
fucking won't. It fucking won't. It fucking won't. It
fucking won't. It fucking won't. It fucking won't. It
fucking won't. It fucking won't. It fucking won't. It
fucking won't. It fucking won't. It fucking won't. It
fucking won't. It fucking won't. It fucking won't. It
fucking won't. It fucking won't. It fucking won't. It
fucking won't. It fucking won't. It fucking won't. It
fucking won't. It fucking won't. It fucking won't. It
fucking won't. It fucking won't. It fucking won't. It
fucking won't. It fucking won't. It fucking won't. It
fucking won't. It fucking won't. It fucking won't. It
fucking won't. It fucking won't. It fucking won't. It
fucking won't. It fucking won't. It fucking won't. It
fucking won't. It fucking won't. It fucking won't. It
fucking won't. It fucking won't. It fucking won't. It
fucking won't. It fucking won't. It fucking won't. It

fucking won't. It fucking won't. It fucking won't. It
fucking won't. It fucking won't. It fucking won't. It
fucking won't. It fucking won't. It fucking won't. It
fucking won't. It fucking won't. It fucking won't. It
fucking won't. It fucking won't. It fucking won't. It
fucking won't. It fucking won't. It fucking won't. It
fucking won't. It fucking won't. It fucking won't. It
fucking won't. It fucking won't. It fucking won't. It
fucking won't. It fucking won't. It fucking won't. It
fucking won't. It fucking won't. It fucking won't. It
fucking won't. It fucking won't. It fucking won't. It
fucking won't. It fucking won't. It fucking won't. It
fucking won't. It fucking won't. It fucking won't. It
fucking won't. It fucking won't. It fucking won't. It
fucking won't. It fucking won't. It fucking won't. It
fucking won't. It fucking won't. It fucking won't. It
fucking won't. It fucking won't. It fucking won't. It
fucking won't. It fucking won't. It fucking won't. It
fucking won't. It fucking won't. It fucking won't. It
fucking won't. It fucking won't. It fucking won't. It
fucking won't. It fucking won't. It fucking won't. It
fucking won't. It fucking won't. It fucking won't. It
fucking won't. It fucking won't. It fucking won't. It
fucking won't. It fucking won't. It fucking won't. It
fucking won't. It fucking won't. It fucking won't. It
fucking won't. It fucking won't. It fucking won't. It
fucking won't. It fucking won't. It fucking won't. It
fucking won't. It fucking won't. It fucking won't. It
fucking won't. It fucking won't. It fucking won't. It
fucking won't. It fucking won't. It fucking won't. It
fucking won't. It fucking won't. It fucking won't. It

fucking won't. It fucking won't. It fucking won't. It
fucking won't. It fucking won't. It fucking won't. It
fucking won't. It fucking won't. It fucking won't. It
fucking won't. It fucking won't. It fucking won't. It
fucking won't. It fucking won't. It fucking won't. It
fucking won't. It fucking won't. It fucking won't. It
fucking won't. It fucking won't. It fucking won't. It
fucking won't. It fucking won't. It fucking won't. It
fucking won't. It fucking won't. It fucking won't. It
fucking won't. It fucking won't. It fucking won't. It
fucking won't. It fucking won't. It fucking won't. It
fucking won't. It fucking won't. It fucking won't. It
fucking won't. It fucking won't. It fucking won't. It
fucking won't. It fucking won't. It fucking won't. It
fucking won't. It fucking won't. It fucking won't. It
fucking won't. It fucking won't. It fucking won't. It
fucking won't. It fucking won't. It fucking won't. It
fucking won't. It fucking won't. It fucking won't. It
fucking won't. It fucking won't. It fucking won't. It
fucking won't. It fucking won't. It fucking won't. It
fucking won't. It fucking won't. It fucking won't. It
fucking won't. It fucking won't. It fucking won't. It
fucking won't. It fucking won't. It fucking won't. It
fucking won't. It fucking won't. It fucking won't. It
fucking won't. It fucking won't. It fucking won't. It
fucking won't. It fucking won't. It fucking won't. It
fucking won't. It fucking won't. It fucking won't. It
fucking won't. It fucking won't. It fucking won't. It
fucking won't. It fucking won't. It fucking won't. It

fucking won't. It fucking won't.

It fucking won't. It

fucking won't. It fucking won't. It fucking won't. It
fucking won't. It fucking won't. It fucking won't. It
fucking won't. It fucking won't. It fucking won't. It
fucking won't. It fucking won't. It fucking won't. It
fucking won't. It fucking won't. It fucking won't. It
fucking won't. It fucking won't. It fucking won't. It
fucking won't. It fucking won't. It fucking won't. It
fucking won't. It fucking won't. It fucking won't. It
fucking won't. It fucking won't. It fucking won't. It
fucking won't. It fucking won't. It fucking won't. It
fucking won't. It fucking won't. It fucking won't. It
fucking won't. It fucking won't. It fucking won't. It
fucking won't. It fucking won't. It fucking won't. It
fucking won't. It fucking won't. It fucking won't. It
fucking won't. It fucking won't. It fucking won't. It
fucking won't. It fucking won't. It fucking won't. It
fucking won't. It fucking won't. It fucking won't. It
fucking won't. It fucking won't. It fucking won't. It
fucking won't. It fucking won't. It fucking won't. It
fucking won't. It fucking won't. It fucking won't. It
fucking won't. It fucking won't. It fucking won't. It
fucking won't. It fucking won't. It fucking won't. It
fucking won't. It fucking won't. It fucking won't. It
fucking won't. It fucking won't. It fucking won't. It
fucking won't. It fucking won't. It fucking won't. It
fucking won't. It fucking won't. It fucking won't. It
fucking won't. It fucking won't. It fucking won't. It
fucking won't. It fucking won't. It fucking won't. It
fucking won't. It fucking won't. It fucking won't. It
fucking won't. It fucking won't. It fucking won't. It

fucking won't. It fucking won't. It fucking won't. It
fucking won't. It fucking won't. It fucking won't. It
fucking won't. It fucking won't. It fucking won't. It
fucking won't. It fucking won't. It fucking won't. It
fucking won't. It fucking won't. It fucking won't. It
fucking won't. It fucking won't. It fucking won't. It
fucking won't. It fucking won't. It fucking won't. It
fucking won't. It fucking won't. It fucking won't. It
fucking won't. It fucking won't. It fucking won't. It
fucking won't. It fucking won't. It fucking won't. It
fucking won't. It fucking won't. It fucking won't. It
fucking won't. It fucking won't. It fucking won't. It
fucking won't. It fucking won't. It fucking won't. It
fucking won't. It fucking won't. It fucking won't. It
fucking won't. It fucking won't. It fucking won't. It
fucking won't. It fucking won't. It fucking won't. It
fucking won't. It fucking won't. It fucking won't. It
fucking won't. It fucking won't. It fucking won't. It
fucking won't. It fucking won't. It fucking won't. It
fucking won't. It fucking won't. It fucking won't. It
fucking won't. It fucking won't. It fucking won't. It
fucking won't. It fucking won't. It fucking won't. It
fucking won't. It fucking won't. It fucking won't. It
fucking won't. It fucking won't. It fucking won't. It
fucking won't. It fucking won't. It fucking won't. It
fucking won't. It fucking won't. It fucking won't. It
fucking won't. It fucking won't. It fucking won't. It
fucking won't. It fucking won't. It fucking won't. It
fucking won't. It fucking won't. It fucking won't. It
fucking won't. It fucking won't. It fucking won't. It

fucking won't. It fucking won't. It fucking won't. It
fucking won't. It fucking won't. It fucking won't. It
fucking won't. It fucking won't. It fucking won't. It
fucking won't. It fucking won't. It fucking won't. It
fucking won't. It fucking won't. It fucking won't. It
fucking won't. It fucking won't. It fucking won't. It
fucking won't. It fucking won't. It fucking won't. It
fucking won't. It fucking won't. It fucking won't. It
fucking won't. It fucking won't. It fucking won't. It
fucking won't. It fucking won't. It fucking won't. It
fucking won't. It fucking won't. It fucking won't. It
fucking won't. It fucking won't. It fucking won't. It
fucking won't. It fucking won't. It fucking won't. It
fucking won't. It fucking won't. It fucking won't. It
fucking won't. It fucking won't. It fucking won't. It
fucking won't. It fucking won't. It fucking won't. It
fucking won't. It fucking won't. It fucking won't. It
fucking won't. It fucking won't. It fucking won't. It
fucking won't. It fucking won't. It fucking won't. It
fucking won't. It fucking won't. It fucking won't. It
fucking won't. It fucking won't. It fucking won't. It
fucking won't. It fucking won't. It fucking won't. It
fucking won't. It fucking won't. It fucking won't. It
fucking won't. It fucking won't. It fucking won't. It
fucking won't. It fucking won't. It fucking won't. It
fucking won't. It fucking won't. It fucking won't. It
fucking won't. It fucking won't. It fucking won't. It
fucking won't. It fucking won't. It fucking won't. It
fucking won't. It fucking won't. It fucking won't. It
fucking won't. It fucking won't. It fucking won't. It

fucking won't. It fucking won't. It fucking won't. It
fucking won't. It fucking won't. It fucking won't. It
fucking won't. It fucking won't. It fucking won't. It
fucking won't. It fucking won't. It fucking won't. It
fucking won't. It fucking won't. It fucking won't. It
fucking won't. It fucking won't. It fucking won't. It
fucking won't. It fucking won't. It fucking won't. It
fucking won't. It fucking won't. It fucking won't. It
fucking won't. It fucking won't. It fucking won't. It
fucking won't. It fucking won't. It fucking won't. It
fucking won't. It fucking won't. It fucking won't. It
fucking won't. It fucking won't. It fucking won't. It
fucking won't. It fucking won't. It fucking won't. It
fucking won't. It fucking won't. It fucking won't. It
fucking won't. It fucking won't. It fucking won't. It
fucking won't. It fucking won't. It fucking won't. It
fucking won't. It fucking won't. It fucking won't. It
fucking won't. It fucking won't. It fucking won't. It
fucking won't. It fucking won't. It fucking won't. It
fucking won't. It fucking won't. It fucking won't. It
fucking won't. It fucking won't. It fucking won't. It
fucking won't. It fucking won't. It fucking won't. It
fucking won't. It fucking won't. It fucking won't. It
fucking won't. It fucking won't. It fucking won't. It
fucking won't. It fucking won't. It fucking won't. It
fucking won't. It fucking won't. It fucking won't. It
fucking won't. It fucking won't. It fucking won't. It
fucking won't. It fucking won't. It fucking won't. It
fucking won't. It fucking won't. It fucking won't. It
fucking won't. It fucking won't. It fucking won't. It

fucking won't. It fucking won't. It fucking won't. It
fucking won't. It fucking won't. It fucking won't. It
fucking won't. It fucking won't. It fucking won't. It
fucking won't. It fucking won't. It fucking won't. It
fucking won't. It fucking won't. It fucking won't. It
fucking won't. It fucking won't. It fucking won't. It
fucking won't. It fucking won't. It fucking won't. It
fucking won't. It fucking won't. It fucking won't. It
fucking won't. It fucking won't. It fucking won't. It
fucking won't. It fucking won't. It fucking won't. It
fucking won't. It fucking won't. It fucking won't. It
fucking won't. It fucking won't. It fucking won't. It
fucking won't. It fucking won't. It fucking won't. It
fucking won't. It fucking won't. It fucking won't. It
fucking won't. It fucking won't. It fucking won't. It
fucking won't. It fucking won't. It fucking won't. It
fucking won't. It fucking won't. It fucking won't. It
fucking won't. It fucking won't. It fucking won't. It
fucking won't. It fucking won't. It fucking won't. It
fucking won't. It fucking won't. It fucking won't. It
fucking won't. It fucking won't. It fucking won't. It
fucking won't. It fucking won't. It fucking won't. It
fucking won't. It fucking won't. It fucking won't. It
fucking won't. It fucking won't. It fucking won't. It
fucking won't. It fucking won't. It fucking won't. It
fucking won't. It fucking won't. It fucking won't. It
fucking won't. It fucking won't. It fucking won't. It
fucking won't. It fucking won't. It fucking won't. It
fucking won't. It fucking won't. It fucking won't. It
fucking won't. It fucking won't. It fucking won't. It

fucking won't. It fucking won't. It fucking won't. It
fucking won't. It fucking won't. It fucking won't. It
fucking won't. It fucking won't. It fucking won't. It
fucking won't. It fucking won't. It fucking won't. It
fucking won't. It fucking won't. It fucking won't. It
fucking won't. It fucking won't. It fucking won't. It
fucking won't. It fucking won't. It fucking won't. It
fucking won't. It fucking won't. It fucking won't. It
fucking won't. It fucking won't. It fucking won't. It
fucking won't. It fucking won't. It fucking won't. It
fucking won't. It fucking won't. It fucking won't. It
fucking won't. It fucking won't. It fucking won't. It
fucking won't. It fucking won't. It fucking won't. It
fucking won't. It fucking won't. It fucking won't. It
fucking won't. It fucking won't. It fucking won't. It
fucking won't. It fucking won't. It fucking won't. It
fucking won't. It fucking won't. It fucking won't. It
fucking won't. It fucking won't. It fucking won't. It
fucking won't. It fucking won't. It fucking won't. It
fucking won't. It fucking won't. It fucking won't. It
fucking won't. It fucking won't. It fucking won't. It
fucking won't. It fucking won't. It fucking won't. It
fucking won't. It fucking won't. It fucking won't. It
fucking won't. It fucking won't. It fucking won't. It
fucking won't. It fucking won't. It fucking won't. It
fucking won't. It fucking won't. It fucking won't. It
fucking won't. It fucking won't. It fucking won't. It
fucking won't. It fucking won't. It fucking won't. It
fucking won't. It fucking won't. It fucking won't. It
fucking won't. It fucking won't. It fucking won't. It

fucking won't. It fucking won't. It fucking won't. It
fucking won't. It fucking won't. It fucking won't. It
fucking won't. It fucking won't. It fucking won't. It
fucking won't. It fucking won't. It fucking won't. It
fucking won't. It fucking won't. It fucking won't. It
fucking won't. It fucking won't. It fucking won't. It
fucking won't. It fucking won't. It fucking won't. It
fucking won't. It fucking won't. It fucking won't. It
fucking won't. It fucking won't. It fucking won't. It
fucking won't. It fucking won't. It fucking won't. It
fucking won't. It fucking won't. It fucking won't. It
fucking won't. It fucking won't. It fucking won't. It
fucking won't. It fucking won't. It fucking won't. It
fucking won't. It fucking won't. It fucking won't. It
fucking won't. It fucking won't. It fucking won't. It
fucking won't. It fucking won't. It fucking won't. It
fucking won't. It fucking won't. It fucking won't. It
fucking won't. It fucking won't. It fucking won't. It
fucking won't. It fucking won't. It fucking won't. It
fucking won't. It fucking won't. It fucking won't. It
fucking won't. It fucking won't. It fucking won't. It
fucking won't. It fucking won't. It fucking won't. It
fucking won't. It fucking won't. It fucking won't. It
fucking won't. It fucking won't. It fucking won't. It
fucking won't. It fucking won't. It fucking won't. It
fucking won't. It fucking won't. It fucking won't. It
fucking won't. It fucking won't. It fucking won't. It
fucking won't. It fucking won't. It fucking won't. It
fucking won't. It fucking won't. It fucking won't. It
fucking won't. It fucking won't. It fucking won't. It

fucking won't. It fucking won't. It fucking won't. It
fucking won't. It fucking won't. It fucking won't. It
fucking won't. It fucking won't. It fucking won't. It
fucking won't. It fucking won't. It fucking won't. It
fucking won't. It fucking won't. It fucking won't. It
fucking won't. It fucking won't. It fucking won't. It
fucking won't. It fucking won't. It fucking won't. It
fucking won't. It fucking won't. It fucking won't. It
fucking won't. It fucking won't. It fucking won't. It
fucking won't. It fucking won't. It fucking won't. It
fucking won't. It fucking won't. It fucking won't. It
fucking won't. It fucking won't. It fucking won't. It
fucking won't. It fucking won't. It fucking won't. It
fucking won't. It fucking won't. It fucking won't. It
fucking won't. It fucking won't. It fucking won't. It
fucking won't. It fucking won't. It fucking won't. It
fucking won't. It fucking won't. It fucking won't. It
fucking won't. It fucking won't. It fucking won't. It
fucking won't. It fucking won't. It fucking won't. It
fucking won't. It fucking won't. It fucking won't. It
fucking won't. It fucking won't. It fucking won't. It
fucking won't. It fucking won't. It fucking won't. It
fucking won't. It fucking won't. It fucking won't. It
fucking won't. It fucking won't. It fucking won't. It
fucking won't. It fucking won't. It fucking won't. It
fucking won't. It fucking won't. It fucking won't. It
fucking won't. It fucking won't. It fucking won't. It
fucking won't. It fucking won't. It fucking won't. It
fucking won't. It fucking won't. It fucking won't. It
fucking won't. It fucking won't. It fucking won't. It

175

fucking won't. It fucking won't. It fucking won't. It
fucking won't. It fucking won't. It fucking won't. It
fucking won't. It fucking won't. It fucking won't. It
fucking won't. It fucking won't. It fucking won't. It
fucking won't. It fucking won't. It fucking won't. It
fucking won't. It fucking won't. It fucking won't. It
fucking won't. It fucking won't. It fucking won't. It
fucking won't. It fucking won't. It fucking won't. It
fucking won't. It fucking won't. It fucking won't. It
fucking won't. It fucking won't. It fucking won't. It
fucking won't. It fucking won't. It fucking won't. It
fucking won't. It fucking won't. It fucking won't. It
fucking won't. It fucking won't. It fucking won't. It
fucking won't. It fucking won't. It fucking won't. It
fucking won't. It fucking won't. It fucking won't. It
fucking won't. It fucking won't. It fucking won't. It
fucking won't. It fucking won't. It fucking won't. It
fucking won't. It fucking won't. It fucking won't. It
fucking won't. It fucking won't. It fucking won't. It
fucking won't. It fucking won't. It fucking won't. It
fucking won't. It fucking won't. It fucking won't. It
fucking won't. It fucking won't. It fucking won't. It
fucking won't. It fucking won't. It fucking won't. It
fucking won't. It fucking won't. It fucking won't. It
fucking won't. It fucking won't. It fucking won't. It
fucking won't. It fucking won't. It fucking won't. It
fucking won't. It fucking won't. It fucking won't. It
fucking won't. It fucking won't. It fucking won't. It
fucking won't. It fucking won't. It fucking won't. It
fucking won't. It fucking won't. It fucking won't. It
fucking won't. It fucking won't. It fucking won't. It

fucking won't. It fucking won't. It fucking won't. It
fucking won't. It fucking won't. It fucking won't. It
fucking won't. It fucking won't. It fucking won't. It
fucking won't. It fucking won't. It fucking won't. It
fucking won't. It fucking won't. It fucking won't. It
fucking won't. It fucking won't. It fucking won't. It
fucking won't. It fucking won't. It fucking won't. It
fucking won't. It fucking won't. It fucking won't. It
fucking won't. It fucking won't. It fucking won't. It
fucking won't. It fucking won't. It fucking won't. It
fucking won't. It fucking won't. It fucking won't. It
fucking won't. It fucking won't. It fucking won't. It
fucking won't. It fucking won't. It fucking won't. It
fucking won't. It fucking won't. It fucking won't. It
fucking won't. It fucking won't. It fucking won't. It
fucking won't. It fucking won't. It fucking won't. It
fucking won't. It fucking won't. It fucking won't. It
fucking won't. It fucking won't. It fucking won't. It
fucking won't. It fucking won't. It fucking won't. It
fucking won't. It fucking won't. It fucking won't. It
fucking won't. It fucking won't. It fucking won't. It
fucking won't. It fucking won't. It fucking won't. It
fucking won't. It fucking won't. It fucking won't. It
fucking won't. It fucking won't. It fucking won't. It
fucking won't. It fucking won't. It fucking won't. It
fucking won't. It fucking won't. It fucking won't. It
fucking won't. It fucking won't. It fucking won't. It
fucking won't. It fucking won't. It fucking won't. It
fucking won't. It fucking won't. It fucking won't. It
fucking won't. It fucking won't. It fucking won't. It

fucking won't. It fucking won't. It fucking won't. It
fucking won't. It fucking won't. It fucking won't. It
fucking won't. It fucking won't. It fucking won't. It
fucking won't. It fucking won't. It fucking won't. It
fucking won't. It fucking won't. It fucking won't. It
fucking won't. It fucking won't. It fucking won't. It
fucking won't. It fucking won't. It fucking won't. It
fucking won't. It fucking won't. It fucking won't. It
fucking won't. It fucking won't. It fucking won't. It
fucking won't. It fucking won't. It fucking won't. It
fucking won't. It fucking won't. It fucking won't. It
fucking won't. It fucking won't. It fucking won't. It
fucking won't. It fucking won't. It fucking won't. It
fucking won't. It fucking won't. It fucking won't. It
fucking won't. It fucking won't. It fucking won't.

It fucking won't. It fucking won't. It fucking won't. It
fucking won't. It fucking won't. It fucking won't. It
fucking won't. It fucking won't. It fucking won't. It
fucking won't. It fucking won't. It fucking won't. It
fucking won't. It fucking won't. It fucking won't. It
fucking won't. It fucking won't. It fucking won't. It
fucking won't. It fucking won't. It fucking won't. It
fucking won't. It fucking won't. It fucking won't. It
fucking won't. It fucking won't. It fucking won't. It
fucking won't. It fucking won't. It fucking won't. It
fucking won't. It fucking won't. It fucking won't. It
fucking won't. It fucking won't. It fucking won't. It
fucking won't. It fucking won't. It fucking won't. It
fucking won't. It fucking won't. It fucking won't. It
fucking won't. It fucking won't. It fucking won't. It

fucking won't. It fucking won't. It fucking won't. It
fucking won't. It fucking won't. It fucking won't. It
fucking won't. It fucking won't. It fucking won't. It
fucking won't. It fucking won't. It fucking won't. It
fucking won't. It fucking won't. It fucking won't. It
fucking won't. It fucking won't. It fucking won't. It
fucking won't. It fucking won't. It fucking won't. It
fucking won't. It fucking won't. It fucking won't. It
fucking won't. It fucking won't. It fucking won't. It
fucking won't. It fucking won't. It fucking won't. It
fucking won't. It fucking won't. It fucking won't. It
fucking won't. It fucking won't. It fucking won't. It
fucking won't. It fucking won't. It fucking won't. It
fucking won't. It fucking won't. It fucking won't. It
fucking won't. It fucking won't. It fucking won't. It
fucking won't. It fucking won't. It fucking won't. It
fucking won't. It fucking won't. It fucking won't. It
fucking won't. It fucking won't. It fucking won't. It
fucking won't. It fucking won't. It fucking won't. It
fucking won't. It fucking won't. It fucking won't. It
fucking won't. It fucking won't. It fucking won't. It
fucking won't. It fucking won't. It fucking won't. It
fucking won't. It fucking won't. It fucking won't. It
fucking won't. It fucking won't. It fucking won't. It
fucking won't. It fucking won't. It fucking won't. It
fucking won't. It fucking won't. It fucking won't. It
fucking won't. It fucking won't. It fucking won't. It
fucking won't. It fucking won't. It fucking won't. It
fucking won't. It fucking won't. It fucking won't. It
fucking won't. It fucking won't. It fucking won't. It

fucking won't. It fucking won't. It fucking won't. It
fucking won't. It fucking won't. It fucking won't. It
fucking won't. It fucking won't. It fucking won't. It
fucking won't. It fucking won't. It fucking won't. It
fucking won't. It fucking won't. It fucking won't. It
fucking won't. It fucking won't. It fucking won't. It
fucking won't. It fucking won't. It fucking won't. It
fucking won't. It fucking won't. It fucking won't. It
fucking won't. It fucking won't. It fucking won't. It
fucking won't. It fucking won't. It fucking won't. It
fucking won't. It fucking won't. It fucking won't. It
fucking won't. It fucking won't. It fucking won't. It
fucking won't. It fucking won't. It fucking won't. It
fucking won't. It fucking won't. It fucking won't. It
fucking won't. It fucking won't. It fucking won't. It
fucking won't. It fucking won't. It fucking won't. It
fucking won't. It fucking won't. It fucking won't. It
fucking won't. It fucking won't. It fucking won't. It
fucking won't. It fucking won't. It fucking won't. It
fucking won't. It fucking won't. It fucking won't. It
fucking won't. It fucking won't. It fucking won't. It
fucking won't. It fucking won't. It fucking won't. It
fucking won't. It fucking won't. It fucking won't. It
fucking won't. It fucking won't. It fucking won't. It
fucking won't. It fucking won't. It fucking won't. It
fucking won't. It fucking won't. It fucking won't. It
fucking won't. It fucking won't. It fucking won't. It
fucking won't. It fucking won't. It fucking won't. It
fucking won't. It fucking won't. It fucking won't. It
fucking won't. It fucking won't. It fucking won't. It
fucking won't. It fucking won't. It fucking won't. It

fucking won't. It fucking won't. It fucking won't. It
fucking won't. It fucking won't. It fucking won't. It
fucking won't. It fucking won't. It fucking won't. It
fucking won't. It fucking won't. It fucking won't. It
fucking won't. It fucking won't. It fucking won't. It
fucking won't. It fucking won't. It fucking won't. It
fucking won't. It fucking won't. It fucking won't. It
fucking won't. It fucking won't. It fucking won't. It
fucking won't. It fucking won't. It fucking won't. It
fucking won't. It fucking won't. It fucking won't. It
fucking won't. It fucking won't. It fucking won't. It
fucking won't. It fucking won't. It fucking won't. It
fucking won't. It fucking won't. It fucking won't. It
fucking won't. It fucking won't. It fucking won't. It
fucking won't. It fucking won't. It fucking won't. It
fucking won't. It fucking won't. It fucking won't. It
fucking won't. It fucking won't. It fucking won't. It
fucking won't. It fucking won't. It fucking won't. It
fucking won't. It fucking won't. It fucking won't. It
fucking won't. It fucking won't. It fucking won't. It
fucking won't. It fucking won't. It fucking won't. It
fucking won't. It fucking won't. It fucking won't. It
fucking won't. It fucking won't. It fucking won't. It
fucking won't. It fucking won't. It fucking won't. It
fucking won't. It fucking won't. It fucking won't. It
fucking won't. It fucking won't. It fucking won't. It
fucking won't. It fucking won't. It fucking won't. It
fucking won't. It fucking won't. It fucking won't. It
fucking won't. It fucking won't. It fucking won't. It
fucking won't. It fucking won't. It fucking won't. It

fucking won't. It fucking won't. It fucking won't. It
fucking won't. It fucking won't. It fucking won't. It
fucking won't. It fucking won't. It fucking won't. It
fucking won't. It fucking won't. It fucking won't. It
fucking won't. It fucking won't. It fucking won't. It
fucking won't. It fucking won't. It fucking won't. It
fucking won't. It fucking won't. It fucking won't. It
fucking won't. It fucking won't. It fucking won't. It
fucking won't. It fucking won't. It fucking won't. It
fucking won't. It fucking won't. It fucking won't. It
fucking won't. It fucking won't. It fucking won't. It
fucking won't. It fucking won't. It fucking won't. It
fucking won't. It fucking won't. It fucking won't. It
fucking won't. It fucking won't. It fucking won't. It
fucking won't. It fucking won't. It fucking won't. It
fucking won't. It fucking won't. It fucking won't. It
fucking won't. It fucking won't. It fucking won't. It
fucking won't. It fucking won't. It fucking won't. It
fucking won't. It fucking won't. It fucking won't. It
fucking won't. It fucking won't. It fucking won't. It
fucking won't. It fucking won't. It fucking won't. It
fucking won't. It fucking won't. It fucking won't. It
fucking won't. It fucking won't. It fucking won't. It
fucking won't. It fucking won't. It fucking won't. It
fucking won't. It fucking won't. It fucking won't. It
fucking won't. It fucking won't. It fucking won't. It
fucking won't. It fucking won't. It fucking won't. It
fucking won't. It fucking won't. It fucking won't. It
fucking won't. It fucking won't. It fucking won't. It
fucking won't. It fucking won't. It fucking won't. It

fucking won't. It fucking won't. It fucking won't. It
fucking won't. It fucking won't. It fucking won't. It
fucking won't. It fucking won't. It fucking won't. It
fucking won't. It fucking won't. It fucking won't. It
fucking won't. It fucking won't. It fucking won't. It
fucking won't. It fucking won't. It fucking won't. It
fucking won't. It fucking won't. It fucking won't. It
fucking won't. It fucking won't. It fucking won't. It
fucking won't. It fucking won't. It fucking won't. It
fucking won't. It fucking won't. It fucking won't. It
fucking won't. It fucking won't. It fucking won't. It
fucking won't. It fucking won't. It fucking won't. It
fucking won't. It fucking won't. It fucking won't. It
fucking won't. It fucking won't. It fucking won't. It
fucking won't. It fucking won't. It fucking won't. It
fucking won't. It fucking won't. It fucking won't. It
fucking won't. It fucking won't. It fucking won't. It
fucking won't. It fucking won't. It fucking won't. It
fucking won't. It fucking won't. It fucking won't. It
fucking won't. It fucking won't. It fucking won't. It
fucking won't. It fucking won't. It fucking won't. It
fucking won't. It fucking won't. It fucking won't. It
fucking won't. It fucking won't. It fucking won't. It
fucking won't. It fucking won't. It fucking won't. It
fucking won't. It fucking won't. It fucking won't. It
fucking won't. It fucking won't. It fucking won't. It
fucking won't. It fucking won't. It fucking won't. It
fucking won't. It fucking won't. It fucking won't. It
fucking won't. It fucking won't. It fucking won't. It
fucking won't. It fucking won't. It fucking won't. It

fucking won't. It fucking won't. It fucking won't. It
fucking won't. It fucking won't. It fucking won't. It
fucking won't. It fucking won't. It fucking won't. It
fucking won't. It fucking won't. It fucking won't. It
fucking won't. It fucking won't. It fucking won't. It
fucking won't. It fucking won't. It fucking won't. It
fucking won't. It fucking won't. It fucking won't. It
fucking won't. It fucking won't. It fucking won't. It
fucking won't. It fucking won't. It fucking won't. It
fucking won't. It fucking won't. It fucking won't. It
fucking won't. It fucking won't. It fucking won't. It
fucking won't. It fucking won't. It fucking won't. It
fucking won't. It fucking won't. It fucking won't. It
fucking won't. It fucking won't. It fucking won't. It
fucking won't. It fucking won't. It fucking won't. It
fucking won't. It fucking won't. It fucking won't. It
fucking won't. It fucking won't. It fucking won't. It
fucking won't. It fucking won't. It fucking won't. It
fucking won't. It fucking won't. It fucking won't. It
fucking won't. It fucking won't. It fucking won't. It
fucking won't. It fucking won't. It fucking won't. It
fucking won't. It fucking won't. It fucking won't. It
fucking won't. It fucking won't. It fucking won't. It
fucking won't. It fucking won't. It fucking won't. It
fucking won't. It fucking won't. It fucking won't. It
fucking won't. It fucking won't. It fucking won't. It
fucking won't. It fucking won't. It fucking won't. It
fucking won't. It fucking won't. It fucking won't. It
fucking won't. It fucking won't. It fucking won't. It
fucking won't. It fucking won't. It fucking won't. It
fucking won't. It fucking won't. It fucking won't. It

fucking won't. It fucking won't. It fucking won't. It
fucking won't. It fucking won't. It fucking won't. It
fucking won't. It fucking won't. It fucking won't. It
fucking won't. It fucking won't. It fucking won't. It
fucking won't. It fucking won't. It fucking won't. It
fucking won't. It fucking won't. It fucking won't. It
fucking won't. It fucking won't. It fucking won't. It
fucking won't. It fucking won't. It fucking won't. It
fucking won't. It fucking won't. It fucking won't. It
fucking won't. It fucking won't. It fucking won't. It
fucking won't. It fucking won't. It fucking won't. It
fucking won't. It fucking won't. It fucking won't. It
fucking won't. It fucking won't. It fucking won't. It
fucking won't. It fucking won't. It fucking won't. It
fucking won't. It fucking won't. It fucking won't. It
fucking won't. It fucking won't. It fucking won't. It
fucking won't. It fucking won't. It fucking won't. It
fucking won't. It fucking won't. It fucking won't. It
fucking won't. It fucking won't. It fucking won't. It
fucking won't. It fucking won't. It fucking won't. It
fucking won't. It fucking won't. It fucking won't. It
fucking won't. It fucking won't. It fucking won't. It
fucking won't. It fucking won't. It fucking won't. It
fucking won't. It fucking won't. It fucking won't. It
fucking won't. It fucking won't. It fucking won't. It
fucking won't. It fucking won't. It fucking won't. It
fucking won't. It fucking won't. It fucking won't. It
fucking won't. It fucking won't. It fucking won't. It
fucking won't. It fucking won't. It fucking won't. It
fucking won't. It fucking won't. It fucking won't. It

fucking won't. It fucking won't. It fucking won't. It
fucking won't. It fucking won't. It fucking won't. It
fucking won't. It fucking won't. It fucking won't. It
fucking won't. It fucking won't. It fucking won't. It
fucking won't. It fucking won't. It fucking won't. It
fucking won't. It fucking won't. It fucking won't. It
fucking won't. It fucking won't. It fucking won't. It
fucking won't. It fucking won't. It fucking won't. It
fucking won't. It fucking won't. It fucking won't. It
fucking won't. It fucking won't. It fucking won't. It
fucking won't. It fucking won't. It fucking won't. It
fucking won't. It fucking won't. It fucking won't. It
fucking won't. It fucking won't. It fucking won't. It
fucking won't. It fucking won't. It fucking won't. It
fucking won't. It fucking won't. It fucking won't. It
fucking won't. It fucking won't. It fucking won't. It
fucking won't. It fucking won't. It fucking won't. It
fucking won't. It fucking won't. It fucking won't. It
fucking won't. It fucking won't. It fucking won't. It
fucking won't. It fucking won't. It fucking won't. It
fucking won't. It fucking won't. It fucking won't. It
fucking won't. It fucking won't. It fucking won't. It
fucking won't. It fucking won't. It fucking won't. It
fucking won't. It fucking won't. It fucking won't. It
fucking won't. It fucking won't. It fucking won't. It
fucking won't. It fucking won't. It fucking won't. It
fucking won't. It fucking won't. It fucking won't. It
fucking won't. It fucking won't. It fucking won't. It
fucking won't. It fucking won't. It fucking won't. It
fucking won't. It fucking won't. It fucking won't. It

fucking won't. It fucking won't. It fucking won't. It
fucking won't. It fucking won't. It fucking won't. It
fucking won't. It fucking won't. It fucking won't. It
fucking won't. It fucking won't. It fucking won't. It
fucking won't. It fucking won't. It fucking won't. It
fucking won't. It fucking won't. It fucking won't. It
fucking won't. It fucking won't. It fucking won't. It
fucking won't. It fucking won't. It fucking won't. It
fucking won't. It fucking won't. It fucking won't. It
fucking won't. It fucking won't. It fucking won't. It
fucking won't. It fucking won't. It fucking won't. It
fucking won't. It fucking won't. It fucking won't. It
fucking won't. It fucking won't. It fucking won't. It
fucking won't. It fucking won't. It fucking won't. It
fucking won't. It fucking won't. It fucking won't. It
fucking won't. It fucking won't. It fucking won't. It
fucking won't. It fucking won't. It fucking won't. It
fucking won't. It fucking won't. It fucking won't. It
fucking won't. It fucking won't. It fucking won't. It
fucking won't. It fucking won't. It fucking won't. It
fucking won't. It fucking won't. It fucking won't. It
fucking won't. It fucking won't. It fucking won't. It
fucking won't. It fucking won't. It fucking won't. It
fucking won't. It fucking won't. It fucking won't. It
fucking won't. It fucking won't. It fucking won't. It
fucking won't. It fucking won't. It fucking won't. It
fucking won't. It fucking won't. It fucking won't. It
fucking won't. It fucking won't. It fucking won't. It
fucking won't. It fucking won't. It fucking won't. It
fucking won't. It fucking won't. It fucking won't. It

fucking won't. It fucking won't. It fucking won't. It
fucking won't. It fucking won't. It fucking won't. It
fucking won't. It fucking won't. It fucking won't. It
fucking won't. It fucking won't. It fucking won't. It
fucking won't. It fucking won't. It fucking won't. It
fucking won't. It fucking won't. It fucking won't. It
fucking won't. It fucking won't. It fucking won't. It
fucking won't. It fucking won't. It fucking won't. It
fucking won't. It fucking won't. It fucking won't. It
fucking won't. It fucking won't. It fucking won't. It
fucking won't. It fucking won't. It fucking won't. It
fucking won't. It fucking won't. It fucking won't. It
fucking won't. It fucking won't. It fucking won't. It
fucking won't. It fucking won't. It fucking won't. It
fucking won't. It fucking won't. It fucking won't. It
fucking won't. It fucking won't. It fucking won't. It
fucking won't. It fucking won't. It fucking won't. It
fucking won't. It fucking won't. It fucking won't. It
fucking won't. It fucking won't. It fucking won't. It
fucking won't. It fucking won't. It fucking won't. It
fucking won't. It fucking won't. It fucking won't. It
fucking won't. It fucking won't. It fucking won't. It
fucking won't. It fucking won't. It fucking won't. It
fucking won't. It fucking won't. It fucking won't. It
fucking won't. It fucking won't. It fucking won't. It
fucking won't. It fucking won't. It fucking won't. It
fucking won't. It fucking won't. It fucking won't. It
fucking won't. It fucking won't. It fucking won't. It
fucking won't. It fucking won't. It fucking won't. It
fucking won't. It fucking won't. It fucking won't. It
fucking won't. It fucking won't. It fucking won't. It

fucking won't. It fucking won't. It fucking won't. It
fucking won't. It fucking won't. It fucking won't. It
fucking won't. It fucking won't. It fucking won't. It
fucking won't. It fucking won't. It fucking won't. It
fucking won't. It fucking won't. It fucking won't. It
fucking won't. It fucking won't. It fucking won't. It
fucking won't. It fucking won't. It fucking won't. It
fucking won't. It fucking won't. It fucking won't. It
fucking won't. It fucking won't. It fucking won't. It
fucking won't. It fucking won't. It fucking won't. It
fucking won't. It fucking won't. It fucking won't. It
fucking won't. It fucking won't. It fucking won't. It
fucking won't. It fucking won't. It fucking won't. It
fucking won't. It fucking won't. It fucking won't. It
fucking won't. It fucking won't. It fucking won't. It
fucking won't. It fucking won't. It fucking won't. It
fucking won't. It fucking won't. It fucking won't. It
fucking won't. It fucking won't. It fucking won't. It
fucking won't. It fucking won't. It fucking won't.

It fucking won't. It fucking won't. It fucking won't. It
fucking won't. It fucking won't. It fucking won't. It
fucking won't. It fucking won't. It fucking won't. It
fucking won't. It fucking won't. It fucking won't. It
fucking won't. It fucking won't. It fucking won't. It
fucking won't. It fucking won't. It fucking won't. It
fucking won't. It fucking won't. It fucking won't. It
fucking won't. It fucking won't. It fucking won't. It
fucking won't. It fucking won't. It fucking won't. It
fucking won't. It fucking won't. It fucking won't. It
fucking won't. It fucking won't. It fucking won't. It

fucking won't. It fucking won't. It fucking won't. It
fucking won't. It fucking won't. It fucking won't. It
fucking won't. It fucking won't. It fucking won't. It
fucking won't. It fucking won't. It fucking won't. It
fucking won't. It fucking won't. It fucking won't. It
fucking won't. It fucking won't. It fucking won't. It
fucking won't. It fucking won't. It fucking won't. It
fucking won't. It fucking won't. It fucking won't. It
fucking won't. It fucking won't. It fucking won't. It
fucking won't. It fucking won't. It fucking won't. It
fucking won't. It fucking won't. It fucking won't. It
fucking won't. It fucking won't. It fucking won't. It
fucking won't. It fucking won't. It fucking won't. It
fucking won't. It fucking won't. It fucking won't. It
fucking won't. It fucking won't. It fucking won't. It
fucking won't. It fucking won't. It fucking won't. It
fucking won't. It fucking won't. It fucking won't. It
fucking won't. It fucking won't. It fucking won't. It
fucking won't. It fucking won't. It fucking won't. It
fucking won't. It fucking won't. It fucking won't. It
fucking won't. It fucking won't. It fucking won't. It
fucking won't. It fucking won't. It fucking won't. It
fucking won't. It fucking won't. It fucking won't. It
fucking won't. It fucking won't. It fucking won't. It
fucking won't. It fucking won't. It fucking won't. It
fucking won't. It fucking won't. It fucking won't. It
fucking won't. It fucking won't. It fucking won't. It
fucking won't. It fucking won't. It fucking won't. It
fucking won't. It fucking won't. It fucking won't. It
fucking won't. It fucking won't. It fucking won't. It
fucking won't. It fucking won't. It fucking won't. It

fucking won't. It fucking won't. It fucking won't. It
fucking won't. It fucking won't. It fucking won't. It
fucking won't. It fucking won't. It fucking won't. It
fucking won't. It fucking won't. It fucking won't. It
fucking won't. It fucking won't. It fucking won't. It
fucking won't. It fucking won't. It fucking won't. It
fucking won't. It fucking won't. It fucking won't. It
fucking won't. It fucking won't. It fucking won't. It
fucking won't. It fucking won't. It fucking won't. It
fucking won't. It fucking won't. It fucking won't. It
fucking won't. It fucking won't. It fucking won't. It
fucking won't. It fucking won't. It fucking won't. It
fucking won't. It fucking won't. It fucking won't. It
fucking won't. It fucking won't. It fucking won't. It
fucking won't. It fucking won't. It fucking won't. It
fucking won't. It fucking won't. It fucking won't. It
fucking won't. It fucking won't. It fucking won't. It
fucking won't. It fucking won't. It fucking won't. It
fucking won't. It fucking won't. It fucking won't. It
fucking won't. It fucking won't. It fucking won't. It
fucking won't. It fucking won't. It fucking won't. It
fucking won't. It fucking won't. It fucking won't. It
fucking won't. It fucking won't. It fucking won't. It
fucking won't. It fucking won't. It fucking won't. It
fucking won't. It fucking won't. It fucking won't. It
fucking won't. It fucking won't. It fucking won't. It
fucking won't. It fucking won't. It fucking won't. It
fucking won't. It fucking won't. It fucking won't. It
fucking won't. It fucking won't. It fucking won't. It
fucking won't. It fucking won't. It fucking won't. It

fucking won't. It fucking won't. It fucking won't. It
fucking won't. It fucking won't. It fucking won't. It
fucking won't. It fucking won't. It fucking won't. It
fucking won't. It fucking won't. It fucking won't. It
fucking won't. It fucking won't. It fucking won't. It
fucking won't. It fucking won't. It fucking won't. It
fucking won't. It fucking won't. It fucking won't. It
fucking won't. It fucking won't. It fucking won't. It
fucking won't. It fucking won't. It fucking won't. It
fucking won't. It fucking won't. It fucking won't. It
fucking won't. It fucking won't. It fucking won't. It
fucking won't. It fucking won't. It fucking won't. It
fucking won't. It fucking won't. It fucking won't. It
fucking won't. It fucking won't. It fucking won't. It
fucking won't. It fucking won't. It fucking won't. It
fucking won't. It fucking won't. It fucking won't. It
fucking won't. It fucking won't. It fucking won't. It
fucking won't. It fucking won't. It fucking won't. It
fucking won't. It fucking won't. It fucking won't. It
fucking won't. It fucking won't. It fucking won't. It
fucking won't. It fucking won't. It fucking won't. It
fucking won't. It fucking won't. It fucking won't. It
fucking won't. It fucking won't. It fucking won't. It
fucking won't. It fucking won't. It fucking won't. It
fucking won't. It fucking won't. It fucking won't. It
fucking won't. It fucking won't. It fucking won't. It
fucking won't. It fucking won't. It fucking won't. It
fucking won't. It fucking won't. It fucking won't. It
fucking won't. It fucking won't. It fucking won't. It
fucking won't. It fucking won't. It fucking won't. It
fucking won't. It fucking won't. It fucking won't. It

fucking won't. It fucking won't. It fucking won't. It
fucking won't. It fucking won't. It fucking won't. It
fucking won't. It fucking won't. It fucking won't. It
fucking won't. It fucking won't. It fucking won't. It
fucking won't. It fucking won't. It fucking won't. It
fucking won't. It fucking won't. It fucking won't. It
fucking won't. It fucking won't. It fucking won't. It
fucking won't. It fucking won't. It fucking won't. It
fucking won't. It fucking won't. It fucking won't. It
fucking won't. It fucking won't. It fucking won't. It
fucking won't. It fucking won't. It fucking won't. It
fucking won't. It fucking won't. It fucking won't. It
fucking won't. It fucking won't. It fucking won't. It
fucking won't. It fucking won't. It fucking won't. It
fucking won't. It fucking won't. It fucking won't. It
fucking won't. It fucking won't. It fucking won't. It
fucking won't. It fucking won't. It fucking won't. It
fucking won't. It fucking won't. It fucking won't. It
fucking won't. It fucking won't. It fucking won't. It
fucking won't. It fucking won't. It fucking won't. It
fucking won't. It fucking won't. It fucking won't. It
fucking won't. It fucking won't. It fucking won't. It
fucking won't. It fucking won't. It fucking won't. It
fucking won't. It fucking won't. It fucking won't. It
fucking won't. It fucking won't. It fucking won't. It
fucking won't. It fucking won't. It fucking won't. It
fucking won't. It fucking won't. It fucking won't. It
fucking won't. It fucking won't. It fucking won't. It
fucking won't. It fucking won't. It fucking won't. It
fucking won't. It fucking won't. It fucking won't. It

fucking won't. It fucking won't. It fucking won't. It
fucking won't. It fucking won't. It fucking won't. It
fucking won't. It fucking won't. It fucking won't. It
fucking won't. It fucking won't. It fucking won't. It
fucking won't. It fucking won't. It fucking won't. It
fucking won't. It fucking won't. It fucking won't. It
fucking won't. It fucking won't. It fucking won't. It
fucking won't. It fucking won't. It fucking won't. It
fucking won't. It fucking won't. It fucking won't. It
fucking won't. It fucking won't. It fucking won't. It
fucking won't. It fucking won't. It fucking won't. It
fucking won't. It fucking won't. It fucking won't. It
fucking won't. It fucking won't. It fucking won't. It
fucking won't. It fucking won't. It fucking won't. It
fucking won't. It fucking won't. It fucking won't. It
fucking won't. It fucking won't. It fucking won't. It
fucking won't. It fucking won't. It fucking won't. It
fucking won't. It fucking won't. It fucking won't. It
fucking won't. It fucking won't. It fucking won't. It
fucking won't. It fucking won't. It fucking won't. It
fucking won't. It fucking won't. It fucking won't. It
fucking won't. It fucking won't. It fucking won't. It
fucking won't. It fucking won't. It fucking won't. It
fucking won't. It fucking won't. It fucking won't. It
fucking won't. It fucking won't. It fucking won't. It
fucking won't. It fucking won't. It fucking won't. It
fucking won't. It fucking won't. It fucking won't. It
fucking won't. It fucking won't. It fucking won't. It
fucking won't. It fucking won't. It fucking won't. It
fucking won't. It fucking won't. It fucking won't. It

fucking won't. It fucking won't. It fucking won't. It
fucking won't. It fucking won't. It fucking won't. It
fucking won't. It fucking won't. It fucking won't. It
fucking won't. It fucking won't. It fucking won't. It
fucking won't. It fucking won't. It fucking won't. It
fucking won't. It fucking won't. It fucking won't. It
fucking won't. It fucking won't. It fucking won't. It
fucking won't. It fucking won't. It fucking won't. It
fucking won't. It fucking won't. It fucking won't. It
fucking won't. It fucking won't. It fucking won't. It
fucking won't. It fucking won't. It fucking won't. It
fucking won't. It fucking won't. It fucking won't. It
fucking won't. It fucking won't. It fucking won't. It
fucking won't. It fucking won't. It fucking won't. It
fucking won't. It fucking won't. It fucking won't. It
fucking won't. It fucking won't. It fucking won't. It
fucking won't. It fucking won't. It fucking won't. It
fucking won't. It fucking won't. It fucking won't. It
fucking won't. It fucking won't. It fucking won't. It
fucking won't. It fucking won't. It fucking won't. It
fucking won't. It fucking won't. It fucking won't. It
fucking won't. It fucking won't. It fucking won't. It
fucking won't. It fucking won't. It fucking won't. It
fucking won't. It fucking won't. It fucking won't. It
fucking won't. It fucking won't. It fucking won't. It
fucking won't. It fucking won't. It fucking won't. It
fucking won't. It fucking won't. It fucking won't. It
fucking won't. It fucking won't. It fucking won't. It
fucking won't. It fucking won't. It fucking won't. It
fucking won't. It fucking won't. It fucking won't. It
fucking won't. It fucking won't. It fucking won't. It

195

fucking won't. It fucking won't. It fucking won't. It
fucking won't. It fucking won't. It fucking won't. It
fucking won't. It fucking won't. It fucking won't. It
fucking won't. It fucking won't. It fucking won't. It
fucking won't. It fucking won't. It fucking won't. It
fucking won't. It fucking won't. It fucking won't. It
fucking won't. It fucking won't. It fucking won't. It
fucking won't. It fucking won't. It fucking won't. It
fucking won't. It fucking won't. It fucking won't. It
fucking won't. It fucking won't. It fucking won't. It
fucking won't. It fucking won't. It fucking won't. It
fucking won't. It fucking won't. It fucking won't. It
fucking won't. It fucking won't. It fucking won't. It
fucking won't. It fucking won't. It fucking won't. It
fucking won't. It fucking won't. It fucking won't. It
fucking won't. It fucking won't. It fucking won't. It
fucking won't. It fucking won't. It fucking won't. It
fucking won't. It fucking won't. It fucking won't. It
fucking won't. It fucking won't. It fucking won't. It
fucking won't. It fucking won't. It fucking won't. It
fucking won't. It fucking won't. It fucking won't. It
fucking won't. It fucking won't. It fucking won't. It
fucking won't. It fucking won't. It fucking won't. It
fucking won't. It fucking won't. It fucking won't. It
fucking won't. It fucking won't. It fucking won't. It
fucking won't. It fucking won't. It fucking won't. It
fucking won't. It fucking won't. It fucking won't. It
fucking won't. It fucking won't. It fucking won't. It
fucking won't. It fucking won't. It fucking won't. It
fucking won't. It fucking won't. It fucking won't. It
fucking won't. It fucking won't. It fucking won't. It

fucking won't. It fucking won't. It fucking won't. It
fucking won't. It fucking won't. It fucking won't. It
fucking won't. It fucking won't. It fucking won't. It
fucking won't. It fucking won't. It fucking won't. It
fucking won't. It fucking won't. It fucking won't. It
fucking won't. It fucking won't. It fucking won't. It
fucking won't. It fucking won't. It fucking won't. It
fucking won't. It fucking won't. It fucking won't. It
fucking won't. It fucking won't. It fucking won't. It
fucking won't. It fucking won't. It fucking won't. It
fucking won't. It fucking won't. It fucking won't. It
fucking won't. It fucking won't. It fucking won't. It
fucking won't. It fucking won't. It fucking won't. It
fucking won't. It fucking won't. It fucking won't. It
fucking won't. It fucking won't. It fucking won't. It
fucking won't. It fucking won't. It fucking won't. It
fucking won't. It fucking won't. It fucking won't. It
fucking won't. It fucking won't. It fucking won't. It
fucking won't. It fucking won't. It fucking won't. It
fucking won't. It fucking won't. It fucking won't. It
fucking won't. It fucking won't. It fucking won't. It
fucking won't. It fucking won't. It fucking won't. It
fucking won't. It fucking won't. It fucking won't. It
fucking won't. It fucking won't. It fucking won't. It
fucking won't. It fucking won't. It fucking won't. It
fucking won't. It fucking won't. It fucking won't. It
fucking won't. It fucking won't. It fucking won't. It
fucking won't. It fucking won't. It fucking won't. It
fucking won't. It fucking won't. It fucking won't. It
fucking won't. It fucking won't. It fucking won't. It

fucking won't. It fucking won't. It fucking won't. It
fucking won't. It fucking won't. It fucking won't. It
fucking won't. It fucking won't. It fucking won't. It
fucking won't. It fucking won't. It fucking won't. It
fucking won't. It fucking won't. It fucking won't. It
fucking won't. It fucking won't. It fucking won't. It
fucking won't. It fucking won't. It fucking won't. It
fucking won't. It fucking won't. It fucking won't. It
fucking won't. It fucking won't. It fucking won't. It
fucking won't. It fucking won't. It fucking won't. It
fucking won't. It fucking won't. It fucking won't. It
fucking won't. It fucking won't. It fucking won't. It
fucking won't. It fucking won't. It fucking won't. It
fucking won't. It fucking won't. It fucking won't. It
fucking won't. It fucking won't. It fucking won't. It
fucking won't. It fucking won't. It fucking won't. It
fucking won't. It fucking won't. It fucking won't. It
fucking won't. It fucking won't. It fucking won't. It
fucking won't. It fucking won't. It fucking won't. It
fucking won't. It fucking won't. It fucking won't. It
fucking won't. It fucking won't. It fucking won't. It
fucking won't. It fucking won't. It fucking won't. It
fucking won't. It fucking won't. It fucking won't. It
fucking won't. It fucking won't. It fucking won't. It
fucking won't. It fucking won't. It fucking won't. It
fucking won't. It fucking won't. It fucking won't. It
fucking won't. It fucking won't. It fucking won't. It
fucking won't. It fucking won't. It fucking won't. It
fucking won't. It fucking won't. It fucking won't. It
fucking won't. It fucking won't. It fucking won't. It

fucking won't. It fucking won't. It fucking won't. It
fucking won't. It fucking won't. It fucking won't. It
fucking won't. It fucking won't. It fucking won't. It
fucking won't. It fucking won't. It fucking won't. It
fucking won't. It fucking won't. It fucking won't. It
fucking won't. It fucking won't. It fucking won't. It
fucking won't. It fucking won't. It fucking won't. It
fucking won't. It fucking won't. It fucking won't. It
fucking won't. It fucking won't. It fucking won't. It
fucking won't. It fucking won't. It fucking won't. It
fucking won't. It fucking won't. It fucking won't. It
fucking won't. It fucking won't. It fucking won't. It
fucking won't. It fucking won't. It fucking won't. It
fucking won't. It fucking won't. It fucking won't. It
fucking won't. It fucking won't. It fucking won't. It
fucking won't. It fucking won't. It fucking won't. It
fucking won't. It fucking won't. It fucking won't. It
fucking won't. It fucking won't. It fucking won't. It
fucking won't. It fucking won't. It fucking won't. It
fucking won't. It fucking won't. It fucking won't. It
fucking won't. It fucking won't. It fucking won't. It
fucking won't. It fucking won't. It fucking won't. It
fucking won't. It fucking won't. It fucking won't. It
fucking won't. It fucking won't. It fucking won't. It
fucking won't. It fucking won't. It fucking won't. It
fucking won't. It fucking won't. It fucking won't. It
fucking won't. It fucking won't. It fucking won't. It
fucking won't. It fucking won't. It fucking won't. It
fucking won't. It fucking won't. It fucking won't. It

fucking won't. It fucking won't. It fucking won't. It
fucking won't. It fucking won't. It fucking won't. It
fucking won't. It fucking won't. It fucking won't. It
fucking won't. It fucking won't. It fucking won't. It
fucking won't. It fucking won't. It fucking won't. It
fucking won't. It fucking won't. It fucking won't. It
fucking won't. It fucking won't. It fucking won't. It
fucking won't. It fucking won't. It fucking won't. It
fucking won't. It fucking won't. It fucking won't. It
fucking won't. It fucking won't. It fucking won't. It
fucking won't. It fucking won't. It fucking won't. It
fucking won't. It fucking won't. It fucking won't. It
fucking won't. It fucking won't. It fucking won't. It
fucking won't. It fucking won't. It fucking won't. It
fucking won't. It fucking won't. It fucking won't. It
fucking won't. It fucking won't. It fucking won't. It
fucking won't. It fucking won't. It fucking won't. It
fucking won't. It fucking won't. It fucking won't. It
fucking won't. It fucking won't. It fucking won't. It
fucking won't. It fucking won't. It fucking won't. It
fucking won't. It fucking won't. It fucking won't. It
fucking won't. It fucking won't. It fucking won't. It
fucking won't. It fucking won't. It fucking won't.

It fucking won't. It fucking won't. It fucking won't. It
fucking won't. It fucking won't. It fucking won't. It
fucking won't. It fucking won't. It fucking won't. It
fucking won't. It fucking won't. It fucking won't. It
fucking won't. It fucking won't. It fucking won't. It
fucking won't. It fucking won't. It fucking won't. It
fucking won't. It fucking won't. It fucking won't. It

fucking won't. It fucking won't. It fucking won't. It
fucking won't. It fucking won't. It fucking won't. It
fucking won't. It fucking won't. It fucking won't. It
fucking won't. It fucking won't. It fucking won't. It
fucking won't. It fucking won't. It fucking won't. It
fucking won't. It fucking won't. It fucking won't. It
fucking won't. It fucking won't. It fucking won't. It
fucking won't. It fucking won't. It fucking won't. It
fucking won't. It fucking won't. It fucking won't. It
fucking won't. It fucking won't. It fucking won't. It
fucking won't. It fucking won't. It fucking won't. It
fucking won't. It fucking won't. It fucking won't. It
fucking won't. It fucking won't. It fucking won't. It
fucking won't. It fucking won't. It fucking won't. It
fucking won't. It fucking won't. It fucking won't. It
fucking won't. It fucking won't. It fucking won't. It
fucking won't. It fucking won't. It fucking won't. It
fucking won't. It fucking won't. It fucking won't. It
fucking won't. It fucking won't. It fucking won't. It
fucking won't. It fucking won't. It fucking won't. It
fucking won't. It fucking won't. It fucking won't. It
fucking won't. It fucking won't. It fucking won't. It
fucking won't. It fucking won't. It fucking won't. It
fucking won't. It fucking won't. It fucking won't. It
fucking won't. It fucking won't. It fucking won't. It
fucking won't. It fucking won't. It fucking won't. It
fucking won't. It fucking won't. It fucking won't. It
fucking won't. It fucking won't. It fucking won't. It
fucking won't. It fucking won't. It fucking won't. It
fucking won't. It fucking won't. It fucking won't. It

fucking won't. It fucking won't. It fucking won't. It
fucking won't. It fucking won't. It fucking won't. It
fucking won't. It fucking won't. It fucking won't. It
fucking won't. It fucking won't. It fucking won't. It
fucking won't. It fucking won't. It fucking won't. It
fucking won't. It fucking won't. It fucking won't. It
fucking won't. It fucking won't. It fucking won't. It
fucking won't. It fucking won't. It fucking won't. It
fucking won't. It fucking won't. It fucking won't. It
fucking won't. It fucking won't. It fucking won't. It
fucking won't. It fucking won't. It fucking won't. It
fucking won't. It fucking won't. It fucking won't. It
fucking won't. It fucking won't. It fucking won't. It
fucking won't. It fucking won't. It fucking won't. It
fucking won't. It fucking won't. It fucking won't. It
fucking won't. It fucking won't. It fucking won't. It
fucking won't. It fucking won't. It fucking won't. It
fucking won't. It fucking won't. It fucking won't. It
fucking won't. It fucking won't. It fucking won't. It
fucking won't. It fucking won't. It fucking won't. It
fucking won't. It fucking won't. It fucking won't. It
fucking won't. It fucking won't. It fucking won't. It
fucking won't. It fucking won't. It fucking won't. It
fucking won't. It fucking won't. It fucking won't. It
fucking won't. It fucking won't. It fucking won't. It
fucking won't. It fucking won't. It fucking won't. It
fucking won't. It fucking won't. It fucking won't. It
fucking won't. It fucking won't. It fucking won't. It
fucking won't. It fucking won't. It fucking won't. It
fucking won't. It fucking won't. It fucking won't. It

fucking won't. It fucking won't. It fucking won't. It
fucking won't. It fucking won't. It fucking won't. It
fucking won't. It fucking won't. It fucking won't. It
fucking won't. It fucking won't. It fucking won't. It
fucking won't. It fucking won't. It fucking won't. It
fucking won't. It fucking won't. It fucking won't. It
fucking won't. It fucking won't. It fucking won't. It
fucking won't. It fucking won't. It fucking won't. It
fucking won't. It fucking won't. It fucking won't. It
fucking won't. It fucking won't. It fucking won't. It
fucking won't. It fucking won't. It fucking won't. It
fucking won't. It fucking won't. It fucking won't. It
fucking won't. It fucking won't. It fucking won't. It
fucking won't. It fucking won't. It fucking won't. It
fucking won't. It fucking won't. It fucking won't. It
fucking won't. It fucking won't. It fucking won't. It
fucking won't. It fucking won't. It fucking won't. It
fucking won't. It fucking won't. It fucking won't. It
fucking won't. It fucking won't. It fucking won't. It
fucking won't. It fucking won't. It fucking won't. It
fucking won't. It fucking won't. It fucking won't. It
fucking won't. It fucking won't. It fucking won't. It
fucking won't. It fucking won't. It fucking won't. It
fucking won't. It fucking won't. It fucking won't. It
fucking won't. It fucking won't. It fucking won't. It
fucking won't. It fucking won't. It fucking won't. It
fucking won't. It fucking won't. It fucking won't. It
fucking won't. It fucking won't. It fucking won't. It
fucking won't. It fucking won't. It fucking won't. It
fucking won't. It fucking won't. It fucking won't. It
fucking won't. It fucking won't. It fucking won't. It

fucking won't. It fucking won't. It fucking won't. It
fucking won't. It fucking won't. It fucking won't. It
fucking won't. It fucking won't. It fucking won't. It
fucking won't. It fucking won't. It fucking won't. It
fucking won't. It fucking won't. It fucking won't. It
fucking won't. It fucking won't. It fucking won't. It
fucking won't. It fucking won't. It fucking won't. It
fucking won't. It fucking won't. It fucking won't. It
fucking won't. It fucking won't. It fucking won't. It
fucking won't. It fucking won't. It fucking won't. It
fucking won't. It fucking won't. It fucking won't. It
fucking won't. It fucking won't. It fucking won't. It
fucking won't. It fucking won't. It fucking won't. It
fucking won't. It fucking won't. It fucking won't. It
fucking won't. It fucking won't. It fucking won't. It
fucking won't. It fucking won't. It fucking won't. It
fucking won't. It fucking won't. It fucking won't. It
fucking won't. It fucking won't. It fucking won't. It
fucking won't. It fucking won't. It fucking won't. It
fucking won't. It fucking won't. It fucking won't. It
fucking won't. It fucking won't. It fucking won't. It
fucking won't. It fucking won't. It fucking won't. It
fucking won't. It fucking won't. It fucking won't. It
fucking won't. It fucking won't. It fucking won't. It
fucking won't. It fucking won't. It fucking won't. It
fucking won't. It fucking won't. It fucking won't. It
fucking won't. It fucking won't. It fucking won't. It
fucking won't. It fucking won't. It fucking won't. It
fucking won't. It fucking won't. It fucking won't. It

fucking won't. It fucking won't. It fucking won't. It
fucking won't. It fucking won't. It fucking won't. It
fucking won't. It fucking won't. It fucking won't. It
fucking won't. It fucking won't. It fucking won't. It
fucking won't. It fucking won't. It fucking won't. It
fucking won't. It fucking won't. It fucking won't. It
fucking won't. It fucking won't. It fucking won't. It
fucking won't. It fucking won't. It fucking won't. It
fucking won't. It fucking won't. It fucking won't. It
fucking won't. It fucking won't. It fucking won't. It
fucking won't. It fucking won't. It fucking won't. It
fucking won't. It fucking won't. It fucking won't. It
fucking won't. It fucking won't. It fucking won't. It
fucking won't. It fucking won't. It fucking won't. It
fucking won't. It fucking won't. It fucking won't. It
fucking won't. It fucking won't. It fucking won't. It
fucking won't. It fucking won't. It fucking won't. It
fucking won't. It fucking won't. It fucking won't. It
fucking won't. It fucking won't. It fucking won't. It
fucking won't. It fucking won't. It fucking won't. It
fucking won't. It fucking won't. It fucking won't. It
fucking won't. It fucking won't. It fucking won't. It
fucking won't. It fucking won't. It fucking won't. It
fucking won't. It fucking won't. It fucking won't. It
fucking won't. It fucking won't. It fucking won't. It
fucking won't. It fucking won't. It fucking won't. It
fucking won't. It fucking won't. It fucking won't. It
fucking won't. It fucking won't. It fucking won't. It
fucking won't. It fucking won't. It fucking won't. It
fucking won't. It fucking won't. It fucking won't. It

fucking won't. It fucking won't. It fucking won't. It
fucking won't. It fucking won't. It fucking won't. It
fucking won't. It fucking won't. It fucking won't. It
fucking won't. It fucking won't. It fucking won't. It
fucking won't. It fucking won't. It fucking won't. It
fucking won't. It fucking won't. It fucking won't. It
fucking won't. It fucking won't. It fucking won't. It
fucking won't. It fucking won't. It fucking won't. It
fucking won't. It fucking won't. It fucking won't. It
fucking won't. It fucking won't. It fucking won't. It
fucking won't. It fucking won't. It fucking won't. It
fucking won't. It fucking won't. It fucking won't. It
fucking won't. It fucking won't. It fucking won't. It
fucking won't. It fucking won't. It fucking won't. It
fucking won't. It fucking won't. It fucking won't. It
fucking won't. It fucking won't. It fucking won't. It
fucking won't. It fucking won't. It fucking won't. It
fucking won't. It fucking won't. It fucking won't. It
fucking won't. It fucking won't. It fucking won't. It
fucking won't. It fucking won't. It fucking won't. It
fucking won't. It fucking won't. It fucking won't. It
fucking won't. It fucking won't. It fucking won't. It
fucking won't. It fucking won't. It fucking won't. It
fucking won't. It fucking won't. It fucking won't. It
fucking won't. It fucking won't. It fucking won't. It
fucking won't. It fucking won't. It fucking won't. It
fucking won't. It fucking won't. It fucking won't. It
fucking won't. It fucking won't. It fucking won't. It
fucking won't. It fucking won't. It fucking won't. It
fucking won't. It fucking won't. It fucking won't. It

fucking won't. It fucking won't. It fucking won't. It
fucking won't. It fucking won't. It fucking won't. It
fucking won't. It fucking won't. It fucking won't. It
fucking won't. It fucking won't. It fucking won't. It
fucking won't. It fucking won't. It fucking won't. It
fucking won't. It fucking won't. It fucking won't. It
fucking won't. It fucking won't. It fucking won't. It
fucking won't. It fucking won't. It fucking won't. It
fucking won't. It fucking won't. It fucking won't. It
fucking won't. It fucking won't. It fucking won't. It
fucking won't. It fucking won't. It fucking won't. It
fucking won't. It fucking won't. It fucking won't. It
fucking won't. It fucking won't. It fucking won't. It
fucking won't. It fucking won't. It fucking won't. It
fucking won't. It fucking won't. It fucking won't. It
fucking won't. It fucking won't. It fucking won't. It
fucking won't. It fucking won't. It fucking won't. It
fucking won't. It fucking won't. It fucking won't. It
fucking won't. It fucking won't. It fucking won't. It
fucking won't. It fucking won't. It fucking won't. It
fucking won't. It fucking won't. It fucking won't. It
fucking won't. It fucking won't. It fucking won't. It
fucking won't. It fucking won't. It fucking won't. It
fucking won't. It fucking won't. It fucking won't. It
fucking won't. It fucking won't. It fucking won't. It
fucking won't. It fucking won't. It fucking won't. It
fucking won't. It fucking won't. It fucking won't. It
fucking won't. It fucking won't. It fucking won't. It
fucking won't. It fucking won't. It fucking won't. It

fucking won't. It fucking won't. It fucking won't. It
fucking won't. It fucking won't. It fucking won't. It
fucking won't. It fucking won't. It fucking won't. It
fucking won't. It fucking won't. It fucking won't. It
fucking won't. It fucking won't. It fucking won't. It
fucking won't. It fucking won't. It fucking won't. It
fucking won't. It fucking won't. It fucking won't. It
fucking won't. It fucking won't. It fucking won't. It
fucking won't. It fucking won't. It fucking won't. It
fucking won't. It fucking won't. It fucking won't. It
fucking won't. It fucking won't. It fucking won't. It
fucking won't. It fucking won't. It fucking won't. It
fucking won't. It fucking won't. It fucking won't. It
fucking won't. It fucking won't. It fucking won't. It
fucking won't. It fucking won't. It fucking won't. It
fucking won't. It fucking won't. It fucking won't. It
fucking won't. It fucking won't. It fucking won't. It
fucking won't. It fucking won't. It fucking won't. It
fucking won't. It fucking won't. It fucking won't. It
fucking won't. It fucking won't. It fucking won't. It
fucking won't. It fucking won't. It fucking won't. It
fucking won't. It fucking won't. It fucking won't. It
fucking won't. It fucking won't. It fucking won't. It
fucking won't. It fucking won't. It fucking won't. It
fucking won't. It fucking won't. It fucking won't. It
fucking won't. It fucking won't. It fucking won't. It
fucking won't. It fucking won't. It fucking won't. It
fucking won't. It fucking won't. It fucking won't. It
fucking won't. It fucking won't. It fucking won't. It
fucking won't. It fucking won't. It fucking won't. It

fucking won't. It fucking won't. It fucking won't. It
fucking won't. It fucking won't. It fucking won't. It
fucking won't. It fucking won't. It fucking won't. It
fucking won't. It fucking won't. It fucking won't. It
fucking won't. It fucking won't. It fucking won't. It
fucking won't. It fucking won't. It fucking won't. It
fucking won't. It fucking won't. It fucking won't. It
fucking won't. It fucking won't. It fucking won't. It
fucking won't. It fucking won't. It fucking won't. It
fucking won't. It fucking won't. It fucking won't. It
fucking won't. It fucking won't. It fucking won't. It
fucking won't. It fucking won't. It fucking won't. It
fucking won't. It fucking won't. It fucking won't. It
fucking won't. It fucking won't. It fucking won't. It
fucking won't. It fucking won't. It fucking won't. It
fucking won't. It fucking won't. It fucking won't. It
fucking won't. It fucking won't. It fucking won't. It
fucking won't. It fucking won't. It fucking won't. It
fucking won't. It fucking won't. It fucking won't. It
fucking won't. It fucking won't. It fucking won't. It
fucking won't. It fucking won't. It fucking won't. It
fucking won't. It fucking won't. It fucking won't. It
fucking won't. It fucking won't. It fucking won't. It
fucking won't. It fucking won't. It fucking won't. It
fucking won't. It fucking won't. It fucking won't. It
fucking won't. It fucking won't. It fucking won't. It
fucking won't. It fucking won't. It fucking won't. It
fucking won't. It fucking won't. It fucking won't. It
fucking won't. It fucking won't. It fucking won't. It

fucking won't. It fucking won't. It fucking won't. It
fucking won't. It fucking won't. It fucking won't. It
fucking won't. It fucking won't. It fucking won't. It
fucking won't. It fucking won't. It fucking won't. It
fucking won't. It fucking won't. It fucking won't. It
fucking won't. It fucking won't. It fucking won't. It
fucking won't. It fucking won't. It fucking won't. It
fucking won't. It fucking won't. It fucking won't. It
fucking won't. It fucking won't. It fucking won't. It
fucking won't. It fucking won't. It fucking won't. It
fucking won't. It fucking won't. It fucking won't. It
fucking won't. It fucking won't. It fucking won't. It
fucking won't. It fucking won't. It fucking won't. It
fucking won't. It fucking won't. It fucking won't. It
fucking won't. It fucking won't. It fucking won't. It
fucking won't. It fucking won't. It fucking won't. It
fucking won't. It fucking won't. It fucking won't. It
fucking won't. It fucking won't. It fucking won't. It
fucking won't. It fucking won't. It fucking won't. It
fucking won't. It fucking won't. It fucking won't. It
fucking won't. It fucking won't. It fucking won't. It
fucking won't. It fucking won't. It fucking won't. It
fucking won't. It fucking won't. It fucking won't. It
fucking won't. It fucking won't. It fucking won't. It
fucking won't. It fucking won't. It fucking won't. It
fucking won't. It fucking won't. It fucking won't. It
fucking won't. It fucking won't. It fucking won't. It
fucking won't. It fucking won't. It fucking won't. It
fucking won't. It fucking won't. It fucking won't. It
fucking won't. It fucking won't. It fucking won't. It

fucking won't. It fucking won't. It fucking won't. It
fucking won't. It fucking won't. It fucking won't. It
fucking won't. It fucking won't. It fucking won't. It
fucking won't. It fucking won't. It fucking won't. It
fucking won't. It fucking won't. It fucking won't. It
fucking won't. It fucking won't. It fucking won't. It
fucking won't. It fucking won't. It fucking won't. It
fucking won't. It fucking won't. It fucking won't. It
fucking won't. It fucking won't. It fucking won't. It
fucking won't. It fucking won't. It fucking won't. It
fucking won't. It fucking won't. It fucking won't. It
fucking won't. It fucking won't. It fucking won't. It
fucking won't. It fucking won't. It fucking won't. It
fucking won't. It fucking won't. It fucking won't. It
fucking won't. It fucking won't. It fucking won't. It
fucking won't. It fucking won't. It fucking won't. It
fucking won't. It fucking won't. It fucking won't. It
fucking won't. It fucking won't. It fucking won't. It
fucking won't. It fucking won't. It fucking won't. It
fucking won't. It fucking won't. It fucking won't. It
fucking won't. It fucking won't. It fucking won't. It
fucking won't. It fucking won't. It fucking won't. It
fucking won't. It fucking won't. It fucking won't. It
fucking won't. It fucking won't. It fucking won't. It
fucking won't. It fucking won't. It fucking won't. It
fucking won't. It fucking won't. It fucking won't. It
fucking won't. It fucking won't. It fucking won't.

It fucking won't. It fucking won't. It fucking won't. It
fucking won't. It fucking won't. It fucking won't. It
fucking won't. It fucking won't. It fucking won't. It

fucking won't. It fucking won't. It fucking won't. It
fucking won't. It fucking won't. It fucking won't. It
fucking won't. It fucking won't. It fucking won't. It
fucking won't. It fucking won't. It fucking won't. It
fucking won't. It fucking won't. It fucking won't. It
fucking won't. It fucking won't. It fucking won't. It
fucking won't. It fucking won't. It fucking won't. It
fucking won't. It fucking won't. It fucking won't. It
fucking won't. It fucking won't. It fucking won't. It
fucking won't. It fucking won't. It fucking won't. It
fucking won't. It fucking won't. It fucking won't. It
fucking won't. It fucking won't. It fucking won't. It
fucking won't. It fucking won't. It fucking won't. It
fucking won't. It fucking won't. It fucking won't. It
fucking won't. It fucking won't. It fucking won't. It
fucking won't. It fucking won't. It fucking won't. It
fucking won't. It fucking won't. It fucking won't. It
fucking won't. It fucking won't. It fucking won't. It
fucking won't. It fucking won't. It fucking won't. It
fucking won't. It fucking won't. It fucking won't. It
fucking won't. It fucking won't. It fucking won't. It
fucking won't. It fucking won't. It fucking won't. It
fucking won't. It fucking won't. It fucking won't. It
fucking won't. It fucking won't. It fucking won't. It
fucking won't. It fucking won't. It fucking won't. It
fucking won't. It fucking won't. It fucking won't. It
fucking won't. It fucking won't. It fucking won't. It
fucking won't. It fucking won't. It fucking won't. It
fucking won't. It fucking won't. It fucking won't. It
fucking won't. It fucking won't. It fucking won't. It

fucking won't. It fucking won't. It fucking won't. It
fucking won't. It fucking won't. It fucking won't. It
fucking won't. It fucking won't. It fucking won't. It
fucking won't. It fucking won't. It fucking won't. It
fucking won't. It fucking won't. It fucking won't. It
fucking won't. It fucking won't. It fucking won't. It
fucking won't. It fucking won't. It fucking won't. It
fucking won't. It fucking won't. It fucking won't. It
fucking won't. It fucking won't. It fucking won't. It
fucking won't. It fucking won't. It fucking won't. It
fucking won't. It fucking won't. It fucking won't. It
fucking won't. It fucking won't. It fucking won't. It
fucking won't. It fucking won't. It fucking won't. It
fucking won't. It fucking won't. It fucking won't. It
fucking won't. It fucking won't. It fucking won't. It
fucking won't. It fucking won't. It fucking won't. It
fucking won't. It fucking won't. It fucking won't. It
fucking won't. It fucking won't. It fucking won't. It
fucking won't. It fucking won't. It fucking won't. It
fucking won't. It fucking won't. It fucking won't. It
fucking won't. It fucking won't. It fucking won't. It
fucking won't. It fucking won't. It fucking won't. It
fucking won't. It fucking won't. It fucking won't. It
fucking won't. It fucking won't. It fucking won't. It
fucking won't. It fucking won't. It fucking won't. It
fucking won't. It fucking won't. It fucking won't. It
fucking won't. It fucking won't. It fucking won't. It
fucking won't. It fucking won't. It fucking won't. It
fucking won't. It fucking won't. It fucking won't. It
fucking won't. It fucking won't. It fucking won't. It

fucking won't. It fucking won't. It fucking won't. It
fucking won't. It fucking won't. It fucking won't. It
fucking won't. It fucking won't. It fucking won't. It
fucking won't. It fucking won't. It fucking won't. It
fucking won't. It fucking won't. It fucking won't. It
fucking won't. It fucking won't. It fucking won't. It
fucking won't. It fucking won't. It fucking won't. It
fucking won't. It fucking won't. It fucking won't. It
fucking won't. It fucking won't. It fucking won't. It
fucking won't. It fucking won't. It fucking won't. It
fucking won't. It fucking won't. It fucking won't. It
fucking won't. It fucking won't. It fucking won't. It
fucking won't. It fucking won't. It fucking won't. It
fucking won't. It fucking won't. It fucking won't. It
fucking won't. It fucking won't. It fucking won't. It
fucking won't. It fucking won't. It fucking won't. It
fucking won't. It fucking won't. It fucking won't. It
fucking won't. It fucking won't. It fucking won't. It
fucking won't. It fucking won't. It fucking won't. It
fucking won't. It fucking won't. It fucking won't. It
fucking won't. It fucking won't. It fucking won't. It
fucking won't. It fucking won't. It fucking won't. It
fucking won't. It fucking won't. It fucking won't. It
fucking won't. It fucking won't. It fucking won't. It
fucking won't. It fucking won't. It fucking won't. It
fucking won't. It fucking won't. It fucking won't. It
fucking won't. It fucking won't. It fucking won't. It
fucking won't. It fucking won't. It fucking won't. It
fucking won't. It fucking won't. It fucking won't. It
fucking won't. It fucking won't. It fucking won't. It
fucking won't. It fucking won't. It fucking won't. It

fucking won't. It fucking won't. It fucking won't. It
fucking won't. It fucking won't. It fucking won't. It
fucking won't. It fucking won't. It fucking won't. It
fucking won't. It fucking won't. It fucking won't. It
fucking won't. It fucking won't. It fucking won't. It
fucking won't. It fucking won't. It fucking won't. It
fucking won't. It fucking won't. It fucking won't. It
fucking won't. It fucking won't. It fucking won't. It
fucking won't. It fucking won't. It fucking won't. It
fucking won't. It fucking won't. It fucking won't. It
fucking won't. It fucking won't. It fucking won't. It
fucking won't. It fucking won't. It fucking won't. It
fucking won't. It fucking won't. It fucking won't. It
fucking won't. It fucking won't. It fucking won't. It
fucking won't. It fucking won't. It fucking won't. It
fucking won't. It fucking won't. It fucking won't. It
fucking won't. It fucking won't. It fucking won't. It
fucking won't. It fucking won't. It fucking won't. It
fucking won't. It fucking won't. It fucking won't. It
fucking won't. It fucking won't. It fucking won't. It
fucking won't. It fucking won't. It fucking won't. It
fucking won't. It fucking won't. It fucking won't. It
fucking won't. It fucking won't. It fucking won't. It
fucking won't. It fucking won't. It fucking won't. It
fucking won't. It fucking won't. It fucking won't. It
fucking won't. It fucking won't. It fucking won't. It
fucking won't. It fucking won't. It fucking won't. It
fucking won't. It fucking won't. It fucking won't. It
fucking won't. It fucking won't. It fucking won't. It

fucking won't. It fucking won't. It fucking won't. It
fucking won't. It fucking won't. It fucking won't. It
fucking won't. It fucking won't. It fucking won't. It
fucking won't. It fucking won't. It fucking won't. It
fucking won't. It fucking won't. It fucking won't. It
fucking won't. It fucking won't. It fucking won't. It
fucking won't. It fucking won't. It fucking won't. It
fucking won't. It fucking won't. It fucking won't. It
fucking won't. It fucking won't. It fucking won't. It
fucking won't. It fucking won't. It fucking won't. It
fucking won't. It fucking won't. It fucking won't. It
fucking won't. It fucking won't. It fucking won't. It
fucking won't. It fucking won't. It fucking won't. It
fucking won't. It fucking won't. It fucking won't. It
fucking won't. It fucking won't. It fucking won't. It
fucking won't. It fucking won't. It fucking won't. It
fucking won't. It fucking won't. It fucking won't. It
fucking won't. It fucking won't. It fucking won't. It
fucking won't. It fucking won't. It fucking won't. It
fucking won't. It fucking won't. It fucking won't. It
fucking won't. It fucking won't. It fucking won't. It
fucking won't. It fucking won't. It fucking won't. It
fucking won't. It fucking won't. It fucking won't. It
fucking won't. It fucking won't. It fucking won't. It
fucking won't. It fucking won't. It fucking won't. It
fucking won't. It fucking won't. It fucking won't. It
fucking won't. It fucking won't. It fucking won't. It
fucking won't. It fucking won't. It fucking won't. It
fucking won't. It fucking won't. It fucking won't. It
fucking won't. It fucking won't. It fucking won't. It

fucking won't. It fucking won't. It fucking won't. It
fucking won't. It fucking won't. It fucking won't. It
fucking won't. It fucking won't. It fucking won't. It
fucking won't. It fucking won't. It fucking won't. It
fucking won't. It fucking won't. It fucking won't. It
fucking won't. It fucking won't. It fucking won't. It
fucking won't. It fucking won't. It fucking won't. It
fucking won't. It fucking won't. It fucking won't. It
fucking won't. It fucking won't. It fucking won't. It
fucking won't. It fucking won't. It fucking won't. It
fucking won't. It fucking won't. It fucking won't. It
fucking won't. It fucking won't. It fucking won't. It
fucking won't. It fucking won't. It fucking won't. It
fucking won't. It fucking won't. It fucking won't. It
fucking won't. It fucking won't. It fucking won't. It
fucking won't. It fucking won't. It fucking won't. It
fucking won't. It fucking won't. It fucking won't. It
fucking won't. It fucking won't. It fucking won't. It
fucking won't. It fucking won't. It fucking won't. It
fucking won't. It fucking won't. It fucking won't. It
fucking won't. It fucking won't. It fucking won't. It
fucking won't. It fucking won't. It fucking won't. It
fucking won't. It fucking won't. It fucking won't. It
fucking won't. It fucking won't. It fucking won't. It
fucking won't. It fucking won't. It fucking won't. It
fucking won't. It fucking won't. It fucking won't. It
fucking won't. It fucking won't. It fucking won't. It
fucking won't. It fucking won't. It fucking won't. It
fucking won't. It fucking won't. It fucking won't. It
fucking won't. It fucking won't. It fucking won't. It

fucking won't. It fucking won't. It fucking won't. It
fucking won't. It fucking won't. It fucking won't. It
fucking won't. It fucking won't. It fucking won't. It
fucking won't. It fucking won't. It fucking won't. It
fucking won't. It fucking won't. It fucking won't. It
fucking won't. It fucking won't. It fucking won't. It
fucking won't. It fucking won't. It fucking won't. It
fucking won't. It fucking won't. It fucking won't. It
fucking won't. It fucking won't. It fucking won't. It
fucking won't. It fucking won't. It fucking won't. It
fucking won't. It fucking won't. It fucking won't. It
fucking won't. It fucking won't. It fucking won't. It
fucking won't. It fucking won't. It fucking won't. It
fucking won't. It fucking won't. It fucking won't. It
fucking won't. It fucking won't. It fucking won't. It
fucking won't. It fucking won't. It fucking won't. It
fucking won't. It fucking won't. It fucking won't. It
fucking won't. It fucking won't. It fucking won't. It
fucking won't. It fucking won't. It fucking won't. It
fucking won't. It fucking won't. It fucking won't. It
fucking won't. It fucking won't. It fucking won't. It
fucking won't. It fucking won't. It fucking won't. It
fucking won't. It fucking won't. It fucking won't. It
fucking won't. It fucking won't. It fucking won't. It
fucking won't. It fucking won't. It fucking won't. It
fucking won't. It fucking won't. It fucking won't. It
fucking won't. It fucking won't. It fucking won't. It
fucking won't. It fucking won't. It fucking won't. It
fucking won't. It fucking won't. It fucking won't. It
fucking won't. It fucking won't. It fucking won't. It

fucking won't. It fucking won't. It fucking won't. It
fucking won't. It fucking won't. It fucking won't. It
fucking won't. It fucking won't. It fucking won't. It
fucking won't. It fucking won't. It fucking won't. It
fucking won't. It fucking won't. It fucking won't. It
fucking won't. It fucking won't. It fucking won't. It
fucking won't. It fucking won't. It fucking won't. It
fucking won't. It fucking won't. It fucking won't. It
fucking won't. It fucking won't. It fucking won't. It
fucking won't. It fucking won't. It fucking won't. It
fucking won't. It fucking won't. It fucking won't. It
fucking won't. It fucking won't. It fucking won't. It
fucking won't. It fucking won't. It fucking won't. It
fucking won't. It fucking won't. It fucking won't. It
fucking won't. It fucking won't. It fucking won't. It
fucking won't. It fucking won't. It fucking won't. It
fucking won't. It fucking won't. It fucking won't. It
fucking won't. It fucking won't. It fucking won't. It
fucking won't. It fucking won't. It fucking won't. It
fucking won't. It fucking won't. It fucking won't. It
fucking won't. It fucking won't. It fucking won't. It
fucking won't. It fucking won't. It fucking won't. It
fucking won't. It fucking won't. It fucking won't. It
fucking won't. It fucking won't. It fucking won't. It
fucking won't. It fucking won't. It fucking won't. It
fucking won't. It fucking won't. It fucking won't. It
fucking won't. It fucking won't. It fucking won't. It
fucking won't. It fucking won't. It fucking won't. It
fucking won't. It fucking won't. It fucking won't. It

fucking won't. It fucking won't. It fucking won't. It
fucking won't. It fucking won't. It fucking won't. It
fucking won't. It fucking won't. It fucking won't. It
fucking won't. It fucking won't. It fucking won't. It
fucking won't. It fucking won't. It fucking won't. It
fucking won't. It fucking won't. It fucking won't. It
fucking won't. It fucking won't. It fucking won't. It
fucking won't. It fucking won't. It fucking won't. It
fucking won't. It fucking won't. It fucking won't. It
fucking won't. It fucking won't. It fucking won't. It
fucking won't. It fucking won't. It fucking won't. It
fucking won't. It fucking won't. It fucking won't. It
fucking won't. It fucking won't. It fucking won't. It
fucking won't. It fucking won't. It fucking won't. It
fucking won't. It fucking won't. It fucking won't. It
fucking won't. It fucking won't. It fucking won't. It
fucking won't. It fucking won't. It fucking won't. It
fucking won't. It fucking won't. It fucking won't. It
fucking won't. It fucking won't. It fucking won't. It
fucking won't. It fucking won't. It fucking won't. It
fucking won't. It fucking won't. It fucking won't. It
fucking won't. It fucking won't. It fucking won't. It
fucking won't. It fucking won't. It fucking won't. It
fucking won't. It fucking won't. It fucking won't. It
fucking won't. It fucking won't. It fucking won't. It
fucking won't. It fucking won't. It fucking won't. It
fucking won't. It fucking won't. It fucking won't. It
fucking won't. It fucking won't. It fucking won't. It
fucking won't. It fucking won't. It fucking won't. It
fucking won't. It fucking won't. It fucking won't. It
fucking won't. It fucking won't. It fucking won't. It

fucking won't. It fucking won't. It fucking won't. It
fucking won't. It fucking won't. It fucking won't. It
fucking won't. It fucking won't. It fucking won't. It
fucking won't. It fucking won't. It fucking won't. It
fucking won't. It fucking won't. It fucking won't. It
fucking won't. It fucking won't. It fucking won't. It
fucking won't. It fucking won't. It fucking won't. It
fucking won't. It fucking won't. It fucking won't. It
fucking won't. It fucking won't. It fucking won't. It
fucking won't. It fucking won't. It fucking won't. It
fucking won't. It fucking won't. It fucking won't. It
fucking won't. It fucking won't. It fucking won't. It
fucking won't. It fucking won't. It fucking won't. It
fucking won't. It fucking won't. It fucking won't. It
fucking won't. It fucking won't. It fucking won't. It
fucking won't. It fucking won't. It fucking won't. It
fucking won't. It fucking won't. It fucking won't. It
fucking won't. It fucking won't. It fucking won't. It
fucking won't. It fucking won't. It fucking won't. It
fucking won't. It fucking won't. It fucking won't. It
fucking won't. It fucking won't. It fucking won't. It
fucking won't. It fucking won't. It fucking won't. It
fucking won't. It fucking won't. It fucking won't. It
fucking won't. It fucking won't. It fucking won't. It
fucking won't. It fucking won't. It fucking won't. It
fucking won't. It fucking won't. It fucking won't. It
fucking won't. It fucking won't. It fucking won't. It
fucking won't. It fucking won't. It fucking won't. It
fucking won't. It fucking won't. It fucking won't. It
fucking won't. It fucking won't. It fucking won't. It

fucking won't. It fucking won't. It fucking won't. It
fucking won't. It fucking won't. It fucking won't. It
fucking won't. It fucking won't. It fucking won't. It
fucking won't. It fucking won't. It fucking won't. It
fucking won't. It fucking won't. It fucking won't. It
fucking won't. It fucking won't. It fucking won't. It
fucking won't. It fucking won't. It fucking won't. It
fucking won't. It fucking won't. It fucking won't. It
fucking won't. It fucking won't. It fucking won't. It
fucking won't. It fucking won't. It fucking won't. It
fucking won't. It fucking won't. It fucking won't. It
fucking won't. It fucking won't. It fucking won't. It
fucking won't. It fucking won't. It fucking won't. It
fucking won't. It fucking won't. It fucking won't. It
fucking won't. It fucking won't. It fucking won't. It
fucking won't. It fucking won't. It fucking won't. It
fucking won't. It fucking won't. It fucking won't. It
fucking won't. It fucking won't. It fucking won't. It
fucking won't. It fucking won't. It fucking won't. It
fucking won't. It fucking won't. It fucking won't. It
fucking won't. It fucking won't. It fucking won't. It
fucking won't. It fucking won't. It fucking won't. It
fucking won't. It fucking won't. It fucking won't. It
fucking won't. It fucking won't. It fucking won't. It
fucking won't. It fucking won't. It fucking won't. It
fucking won't. It fucking won't. It fucking won't. It
fucking won't. It fucking won't. It fucking won't. It
fucking won't. It fucking won't. It fucking won't. It
fucking won't. It fucking won't. It fucking won't. It
fucking won't. It fucking won't. It fucking won't.

It fucking won't. It

fucking won't. It fucking won't. It fucking won't. It
fucking won't. It fucking won't. It fucking won't. It
fucking won't. It fucking won't. It fucking won't. It
fucking won't. It fucking won't. It fucking won't. It
fucking won't. It fucking won't. It fucking won't. It
fucking won't. It fucking won't. It fucking won't. It
fucking won't. It fucking won't. It fucking won't. It
fucking won't. It fucking won't. It fucking won't. It
fucking won't. It fucking won't. It fucking won't. It
fucking won't. It fucking won't. It fucking won't. It
fucking won't. It fucking won't. It fucking won't. It
fucking won't. It fucking won't. It fucking won't. It
fucking won't. It fucking won't. It fucking won't. It
fucking won't. It fucking won't. It fucking won't. It
fucking won't. It fucking won't. It fucking won't. It
fucking won't. It fucking won't. It fucking won't. It
fucking won't. It fucking won't. It fucking won't. It
fucking won't. It fucking won't. It fucking won't. It
fucking won't. It fucking won't. It fucking won't. It
fucking won't. It fucking won't. It fucking won't. It
fucking won't. It fucking won't. It fucking won't. It
fucking won't. It fucking won't. It fucking won't. It
fucking won't. It fucking won't. It fucking won't. It
fucking won't. It fucking won't. It fucking won't. It
fucking won't. It fucking won't. It fucking won't. It
fucking won't. It fucking won't. It fucking won't. It
fucking won't. It fucking won't. It fucking won't. It
fucking won't. It fucking won't. It fucking won't. It
fucking won't. It fucking won't. It fucking won't. It
fucking won't. It fucking won't. It fucking won't. It

fucking won't. It fucking won't. It fucking won't. It
fucking won't. It fucking won't. It fucking won't. It
fucking won't. It fucking won't. It fucking won't. It
fucking won't. It fucking won't. It fucking won't. It
fucking won't. It fucking won't. It fucking won't. It
fucking won't. It fucking won't. It fucking won't. It
fucking won't. It fucking won't. It fucking won't. It
fucking won't. It fucking won't. It fucking won't. It
fucking won't. It fucking won't. It fucking won't. It
fucking won't. It fucking won't. It fucking won't. It
fucking won't. It fucking won't. It fucking won't. It
fucking won't. It fucking won't. It fucking won't. It
fucking won't. It fucking won't. It fucking won't. It
fucking won't. It fucking won't. It fucking won't. It
fucking won't. It fucking won't. It fucking won't. It
fucking won't. It fucking won't. It fucking won't. It
fucking won't. It fucking won't. It fucking won't. It
fucking won't. It fucking won't. It fucking won't. It
fucking won't. It fucking won't. It fucking won't. It
fucking won't. It fucking won't. It fucking won't. It
fucking won't. It fucking won't. It fucking won't. It
fucking won't. It fucking won't. It fucking won't. It
fucking won't. It fucking won't. It fucking won't. It
fucking won't. It fucking won't. It fucking won't. It
fucking won't. It fucking won't. It fucking won't. It
fucking won't. It fucking won't. It fucking won't. It
fucking won't. It fucking won't. It fucking won't. It
fucking won't. It fucking won't. It fucking won't. It
fucking won't. It fucking won't. It fucking won't. It
fucking won't. It fucking won't. It fucking won't. It

fucking won't. It fucking won't. It fucking won't. It
fucking won't. It fucking won't. It fucking won't. It
fucking won't. It fucking won't. It fucking won't. It
fucking won't. It fucking won't. It fucking won't. It
fucking won't. It fucking won't. It fucking won't. It
fucking won't. It fucking won't. It fucking won't. It
fucking won't. It fucking won't. It fucking won't. It
fucking won't. It fucking won't. It fucking won't. It
fucking won't. It fucking won't. It fucking won't. It
fucking won't. It fucking won't. It fucking won't. It
fucking won't. It fucking won't. It fucking won't. It
fucking won't. It fucking won't. It fucking won't. It
fucking won't. It fucking won't. It fucking won't. It
fucking won't. It fucking won't. It fucking won't. It
fucking won't. It fucking won't. It fucking won't. It
fucking won't. It fucking won't. It fucking won't. It
fucking won't. It fucking won't. It fucking won't. It
fucking won't. It fucking won't. It fucking won't. It
fucking won't. It fucking won't. It fucking won't. It
fucking won't. It fucking won't. It fucking won't. It
fucking won't. It fucking won't. It fucking won't. It
fucking won't. It fucking won't. It fucking won't. It
fucking won't. It fucking won't. It fucking won't. It
fucking won't. It fucking won't. It fucking won't. It
fucking won't. It fucking won't. It fucking won't. It
fucking won't. It fucking won't. It fucking won't. It
fucking won't. It fucking won't. It fucking won't. It
fucking won't. It fucking won't. It fucking won't. It
fucking won't. It fucking won't. It fucking won't. It
fucking won't. It fucking won't. It fucking won't. It

fucking won't. It fucking won't. It fucking won't. It
fucking won't. It fucking won't. It fucking won't. It
fucking won't. It fucking won't. It fucking won't. It
fucking won't. It fucking won't. It fucking won't. It
fucking won't. It fucking won't. It fucking won't. It
fucking won't. It fucking won't. It fucking won't. It
fucking won't. It fucking won't. It fucking won't. It
fucking won't. It fucking won't. It fucking won't. It
fucking won't. It fucking won't. It fucking won't. It
fucking won't. It fucking won't. It fucking won't. It
fucking won't. It fucking won't. It fucking won't. It
fucking won't. It fucking won't. It fucking won't. It
fucking won't. It fucking won't. It fucking won't. It
fucking won't. It fucking won't. It fucking won't. It
fucking won't. It fucking won't. It fucking won't. It
fucking won't. It fucking won't. It fucking won't. It
fucking won't. It fucking won't. It fucking won't. It
fucking won't. It fucking won't. It fucking won't. It
fucking won't. It fucking won't. It fucking won't. It
fucking won't. It fucking won't. It fucking won't. It
fucking won't. It fucking won't. It fucking won't. It
fucking won't. It fucking won't. It fucking won't. It
fucking won't. It fucking won't. It fucking won't. It
fucking won't. It fucking won't. It fucking won't. It
fucking won't. It fucking won't. It fucking won't. It
fucking won't. It fucking won't. It fucking won't. It
fucking won't. It fucking won't. It fucking won't. It
fucking won't. It fucking won't. It fucking won't. It
fucking won't. It fucking won't. It fucking won't. It
fucking won't. It fucking won't. It fucking won't. It

fucking won't. It fucking won't. It fucking won't. It
fucking won't. It fucking won't. It fucking won't. It
fucking won't. It fucking won't. It fucking won't. It
fucking won't. It fucking won't. It fucking won't. It
fucking won't. It fucking won't. It fucking won't. It
fucking won't. It fucking won't. It fucking won't. It
fucking won't. It fucking won't. It fucking won't. It
fucking won't. It fucking won't. It fucking won't. It
fucking won't. It fucking won't. It fucking won't. It
fucking won't. It fucking won't. It fucking won't. It
fucking won't. It fucking won't. It fucking won't. It
fucking won't. It fucking won't. It fucking won't. It
fucking won't. It fucking won't. It fucking won't. It
fucking won't. It fucking won't. It fucking won't. It
fucking won't. It fucking won't. It fucking won't. It
fucking won't. It fucking won't. It fucking won't. It
fucking won't. It fucking won't. It fucking won't. It
fucking won't. It fucking won't. It fucking won't. It
fucking won't. It fucking won't. It fucking won't. It
fucking won't. It fucking won't. It fucking won't. It
fucking won't. It fucking won't. It fucking won't. It
fucking won't. It fucking won't. It fucking won't. It
fucking won't. It fucking won't. It fucking won't. It
fucking won't. It fucking won't. It fucking won't. It
fucking won't. It fucking won't. It fucking won't. It
fucking won't. It fucking won't. It fucking won't. It
fucking won't. It fucking won't. It fucking won't. It
fucking won't. It fucking won't. It fucking won't. It
fucking won't. It fucking won't. It fucking won't. It
fucking won't. It fucking won't. It fucking won't. It

fucking won't. It fucking won't. It fucking won't. It
fucking won't. It fucking won't. It fucking won't. It
fucking won't. It fucking won't. It fucking won't. It
fucking won't. It fucking won't. It fucking won't. It
fucking won't. It fucking won't. It fucking won't. It
fucking won't. It fucking won't. It fucking won't. It
fucking won't. It fucking won't. It fucking won't. It
fucking won't. It fucking won't. It fucking won't. It
fucking won't. It fucking won't. It fucking won't. It
fucking won't. It fucking won't. It fucking won't. It
fucking won't. It fucking won't. It fucking won't. It
fucking won't. It fucking won't. It fucking won't. It
fucking won't. It fucking won't. It fucking won't. It
fucking won't. It fucking won't. It fucking won't. It
fucking won't. It fucking won't. It fucking won't. It
fucking won't. It fucking won't. It fucking won't. It
fucking won't. It fucking won't. It fucking won't. It
fucking won't. It fucking won't. It fucking won't. It
fucking won't. It fucking won't. It fucking won't. It
fucking won't. It fucking won't. It fucking won't. It
fucking won't. It fucking won't. It fucking won't. It
fucking won't. It fucking won't. It fucking won't. It
fucking won't. It fucking won't. It fucking won't. It
fucking won't. It fucking won't. It fucking won't. It
fucking won't. It fucking won't. It fucking won't. It
fucking won't. It fucking won't. It fucking won't. It
fucking won't. It fucking won't. It fucking won't. It
fucking won't. It fucking won't. It fucking won't. It
fucking won't. It fucking won't. It fucking won't. It
fucking won't. It fucking won't. It fucking won't. It

fucking won't. It fucking won't. It fucking won't. It
fucking won't. It fucking won't. It fucking won't. It
fucking won't. It fucking won't. It fucking won't. It
fucking won't. It fucking won't. It fucking won't. It
fucking won't. It fucking won't. It fucking won't. It
fucking won't. It fucking won't. It fucking won't. It
fucking won't. It fucking won't. It fucking won't. It
fucking won't. It fucking won't. It fucking won't. It
fucking won't. It fucking won't. It fucking won't. It
fucking won't. It fucking won't. It fucking won't. It
fucking won't. It fucking won't. It fucking won't. It
fucking won't. It fucking won't. It fucking won't. It
fucking won't. It fucking won't. It fucking won't. It
fucking won't. It fucking won't. It fucking won't. It
fucking won't. It fucking won't. It fucking won't. It
fucking won't. It fucking won't. It fucking won't. It
fucking won't. It fucking won't. It fucking won't. It
fucking won't. It fucking won't. It fucking won't. It
fucking won't. It fucking won't. It fucking won't. It
fucking won't. It fucking won't. It fucking won't. It
fucking won't. It fucking won't. It fucking won't. It
fucking won't. It fucking won't. It fucking won't. It
fucking won't. It fucking won't. It fucking won't. It
fucking won't. It fucking won't. It fucking won't. It
fucking won't. It fucking won't. It fucking won't. It
fucking won't. It fucking won't. It fucking won't. It
fucking won't. It fucking won't. It fucking won't. It
fucking won't. It fucking won't. It fucking won't. It
fucking won't. It fucking won't. It fucking won't. It

fucking won't. It fucking won't. It fucking won't. It
fucking won't. It fucking won't. It fucking won't. It
fucking won't. It fucking won't. It fucking won't. It
fucking won't. It fucking won't. It fucking won't. It
fucking won't. It fucking won't. It fucking won't. It
fucking won't. It fucking won't. It fucking won't. It
fucking won't. It fucking won't. It fucking won't. It
fucking won't. It fucking won't. It fucking won't. It
fucking won't. It fucking won't. It fucking won't. It
fucking won't. It fucking won't. It fucking won't. It
fucking won't. It fucking won't. It fucking won't. It
fucking won't. It fucking won't. It fucking won't. It
fucking won't. It fucking won't. It fucking won't. It
fucking won't. It fucking won't. It fucking won't. It
fucking won't. It fucking won't. It fucking won't. It
fucking won't. It fucking won't. It fucking won't. It
fucking won't. It fucking won't. It fucking won't. It
fucking won't. It fucking won't. It fucking won't. It
fucking won't. It fucking won't. It fucking won't. It
fucking won't. It fucking won't. It fucking won't. It
fucking won't. It fucking won't. It fucking won't. It
fucking won't. It fucking won't. It fucking won't. It
fucking won't. It fucking won't. It fucking won't. It
fucking won't. It fucking won't. It fucking won't. It
fucking won't. It fucking won't. It fucking won't. It
fucking won't. It fucking won't. It fucking won't. It
fucking won't. It fucking won't. It fucking won't. It
fucking won't. It fucking won't. It fucking won't. It
fucking won't. It fucking won't. It fucking won't. It
fucking won't. It fucking won't. It fucking won't. It

fucking won't. It fucking won't. It fucking won't. It
fucking won't. It fucking won't. It fucking won't. It
fucking won't. It fucking won't. It fucking won't. It
fucking won't. It fucking won't. It fucking won't. It
fucking won't. It fucking won't. It fucking won't. It
fucking won't. It fucking won't. It fucking won't. It
fucking won't. It fucking won't. It fucking won't. It
fucking won't. It fucking won't. It fucking won't. It
fucking won't. It fucking won't. It fucking won't. It
fucking won't. It fucking won't. It fucking won't. It
fucking won't. It fucking won't. It fucking won't. It
fucking won't. It fucking won't. It fucking won't. It
fucking won't. It fucking won't. It fucking won't. It
fucking won't. It fucking won't. It fucking won't. It
fucking won't. It fucking won't. It fucking won't. It
fucking won't. It fucking won't. It fucking won't. It
fucking won't. It fucking won't. It fucking won't. It
fucking won't. It fucking won't. It fucking won't. It
fucking won't. It fucking won't. It fucking won't. It
fucking won't. It fucking won't. It fucking won't. It
fucking won't. It fucking won't. It fucking won't. It
fucking won't. It fucking won't. It fucking won't. It
fucking won't. It fucking won't. It fucking won't. It
fucking won't. It fucking won't. It fucking won't. It
fucking won't. It fucking won't. It fucking won't. It
fucking won't. It fucking won't. It fucking won't. It
fucking won't. It fucking won't. It fucking won't. It
fucking won't. It fucking won't. It fucking won't. It
fucking won't. It fucking won't. It fucking won't. It
fucking won't. It fucking won't. It fucking won't. It
fucking won't. It fucking won't. It fucking won't. It

fucking won't. It fucking won't. It fucking won't. It
fucking won't. It fucking won't. It fucking won't. It
fucking won't. It fucking won't. It fucking won't. It
fucking won't. It fucking won't. It fucking won't. It
fucking won't. It fucking won't. It fucking won't. It
fucking won't. It fucking won't. It fucking won't. It
fucking won't. It fucking won't. It fucking won't. It
fucking won't. It fucking won't. It fucking won't. It
fucking won't. It fucking won't. It fucking won't. It
fucking won't. It fucking won't. It fucking won't. It
fucking won't. It fucking won't. It fucking won't. It
fucking won't. It fucking won't. It fucking won't. It
fucking won't. It fucking won't. It fucking won't. It
fucking won't. It fucking won't. It fucking won't. It
fucking won't. It fucking won't. It fucking won't. It
fucking won't. It fucking won't. It fucking won't. It
fucking won't. It fucking won't. It fucking won't. It
fucking won't. It fucking won't. It fucking won't. It
fucking won't. It fucking won't. It fucking won't. It
fucking won't. It fucking won't. It fucking won't. It
fucking won't. It fucking won't. It fucking won't. It
fucking won't. It fucking won't. It fucking won't. It
fucking won't. It fucking won't. It fucking won't. It
fucking won't. It fucking won't. It fucking won't. It
fucking won't. It fucking won't. It fucking won't. It
fucking won't. It fucking won't. It fucking won't. It
fucking won't. It fucking won't. It fucking won't. It
fucking won't. It fucking won't. It fucking won't. It
fucking won't. It fucking won't. It fucking won't. It
fucking won't. It fucking won't. It fucking won't. It

fucking won't. It fucking won't. It fucking won't. It
fucking won't. It fucking won't. It fucking won't. It
fucking won't. It fucking won't. It fucking won't. It
fucking won't. It fucking won't. It fucking won't. It
fucking won't. It fucking won't. It fucking won't. It
fucking won't. It fucking won't. It fucking won't. It
fucking won't. It fucking won't. It fucking won't. It
fucking won't. It fucking won't. It fucking won't. It
fucking won't. It fucking won't. It fucking won't. It
fucking won't. It fucking won't. It fucking won't. It
fucking won't. It fucking won't. It fucking won't. It
fucking won't. It fucking won't. It fucking won't. It
fucking won't. It fucking won't. It fucking won't. It
fucking won't. It fucking won't. It fucking won't. It
fucking won't. It fucking won't. It fucking won't. It
fucking won't. It fucking won't. It fucking won't. It
fucking won't. It fucking won't. It fucking won't. It
fucking won't. It fucking won't. It fucking won't. It
fucking won't. It fucking won't. It fucking won't. It
fucking won't. It fucking won't. It fucking won't. It
fucking won't. It fucking won't. It fucking won't. It
fucking won't. It fucking won't. It fucking won't. It
fucking won't. It fucking won't. It fucking won't. It
fucking won't. It fucking won't. It fucking won't. It
fucking won't. It fucking won't. It fucking won't. It
fucking won't. It fucking won't. It fucking won't. It
fucking won't. It fucking won't. It fucking won't. It
fucking won't. It fucking won't. It fucking won't. It
fucking won't. It fucking won't. It fucking won't. It
fucking won't. It fucking won't. It fucking won't. It

fucking won't. It fucking won't. It fucking won't. It
fucking won't. It fucking won't. It fucking won't. It
fucking won't. It fucking won't. It fucking won't. It
fucking won't. It fucking won't. It fucking won't. It
fucking won't. It fucking won't. It fucking won't. It
fucking won't. It fucking won't. It fucking won't. It
fucking won't. It fucking won't. It fucking won't. It
fucking won't. It fucking won't. It fucking won't. It
fucking won't. It fucking won't. It fucking won't. It
fucking won't. It fucking won't. It fucking won't. It
fucking won't. It fucking won't. It fucking won't. It
fucking won't. It fucking won't. It fucking won't. It
fucking won't. It fucking won't. It fucking won't. It
fucking won't. It fucking won't. It fucking won't. It
fucking won't. It fucking won't. It fucking won't. It
fucking won't. It fucking won't. It fucking won't. It
fucking won't. It fucking won't. It fucking won't. It
fucking won't. It fucking won't. It fucking won't. It
fucking won't. It fucking won't. It fucking won't. It
fucking won't. It fucking won't. It fucking won't. It
fucking won't. It fucking won't. It fucking won't. It
fucking won't. It fucking won't. It fucking won't. It
fucking won't. It fucking won't. It fucking won't. It
fucking won't. It fucking won't. It fucking won't. It
fucking won't. It fucking won't. It fucking won't. It
fucking won't. It fucking won't. It fucking won't. It
fucking won't. It fucking won't. It fucking won't. It
fucking won't. It fucking won't.

It fucking won't. It fucking won't. It fucking won't. It
fucking won't. It fucking won't. It fucking won't. It

235

fucking won't. It fucking won't. It fucking won't. It
fucking won't. It fucking won't. It fucking won't. It
fucking won't. It fucking won't. It fucking won't. It
fucking won't. It fucking won't. It fucking won't. It
fucking won't. It fucking won't. It fucking won't. It
fucking won't. It fucking won't. It fucking won't. It
fucking won't. It fucking won't. It fucking won't. It
fucking won't. It fucking won't. It fucking won't. It
fucking won't. It fucking won't. It fucking won't. It
fucking won't. It fucking won't. It fucking won't. It
fucking won't. It fucking won't. It fucking won't. It
fucking won't. It fucking won't. It fucking won't. It
fucking won't. It fucking won't. It fucking won't. It
fucking won't. It fucking won't. It fucking won't. It
fucking won't. It fucking won't. It fucking won't. It
fucking won't. It fucking won't. It fucking won't. It
fucking won't. It fucking won't. It fucking won't. It
fucking won't. It fucking won't. It fucking won't. It
fucking won't. It fucking won't. It fucking won't. It
fucking won't. It fucking won't. It fucking won't. It
fucking won't. It fucking won't. It fucking won't. It
fucking won't. It fucking won't. It fucking won't. It
fucking won't. It fucking won't. It fucking won't. It
fucking won't. It fucking won't. It fucking won't. It
fucking won't. It fucking won't. It fucking won't. It
fucking won't. It fucking won't. It fucking won't. It
fucking won't. It fucking won't. It fucking won't. It
fucking won't. It fucking won't. It fucking won't. It
fucking won't. It fucking won't. It fucking won't. It
fucking won't. It fucking won't. It fucking won't. It

fucking won't. It fucking won't. It fucking won't. It
fucking won't. It fucking won't. It fucking won't. It
fucking won't. It fucking won't. It fucking won't. It
fucking won't. It fucking won't. It fucking won't. It
fucking won't. It fucking won't. It fucking won't. It
fucking won't. It fucking won't. It fucking won't. It
fucking won't. It fucking won't. It fucking won't. It
fucking won't. It fucking won't. It fucking won't. It
fucking won't. It fucking won't. It fucking won't. It
fucking won't. It fucking won't. It fucking won't. It
fucking won't. It fucking won't. It fucking won't. It
fucking won't. It fucking won't. It fucking won't. It
fucking won't. It fucking won't. It fucking won't. It
fucking won't. It fucking won't. It fucking won't. It
fucking won't. It fucking won't. It fucking won't. It
fucking won't. It fucking won't. It fucking won't. It
fucking won't. It fucking won't. It fucking won't. It
fucking won't. It fucking won't. It fucking won't. It
fucking won't. It fucking won't. It fucking won't. It
fucking won't. It fucking won't. It fucking won't. It
fucking won't. It fucking won't. It fucking won't. It
fucking won't. It fucking won't. It fucking won't. It
fucking won't. It fucking won't. It fucking won't. It
fucking won't. It fucking won't. It fucking won't. It
fucking won't. It fucking won't. It fucking won't. It
fucking won't. It fucking won't. It fucking won't. It
fucking won't. It fucking won't. It fucking won't. It
fucking won't. It fucking won't. It fucking won't. It
fucking won't. It fucking won't. It fucking won't. It
fucking won't. It fucking won't. It fucking won't. It

fucking won't. It fucking won't. It fucking won't. It
fucking won't. It fucking won't. It fucking won't. It
fucking won't. It fucking won't. It fucking won't. It
fucking won't. It fucking won't. It fucking won't. It
fucking won't. It fucking won't. It fucking won't. It
fucking won't. It fucking won't. It fucking won't. It
fucking won't. It fucking won't. It fucking won't. It
fucking won't. It fucking won't. It fucking won't. It
fucking won't. It fucking won't. It fucking won't. It
fucking won't. It fucking won't. It fucking won't. It
fucking won't. It fucking won't. It fucking won't. It
fucking won't. It fucking won't. It fucking won't. It
fucking won't. It fucking won't. It fucking won't. It
fucking won't. It fucking won't. It fucking won't. It
fucking won't. It fucking won't. It fucking won't. It
fucking won't. It fucking won't. It fucking won't. It
fucking won't. It fucking won't. It fucking won't. It
fucking won't. It fucking won't. It fucking won't. It
fucking won't. It fucking won't. It fucking won't. It
fucking won't. It fucking won't. It fucking won't. It
fucking won't. It fucking won't. It fucking won't. It
fucking won't. It fucking won't. It fucking won't. It
fucking won't. It fucking won't. It fucking won't. It
fucking won't. It fucking won't. It fucking won't. It
fucking won't. It fucking won't. It fucking won't. It
fucking won't. It fucking won't. It fucking won't. It
fucking won't. It fucking won't. It fucking won't. It
fucking won't. It fucking won't. It fucking won't. It
fucking won't. It fucking won't. It fucking won't. It
fucking won't. It fucking won't. It fucking won't. It

fucking won't. It fucking won't. It fucking won't. It
fucking won't. It fucking won't. It fucking won't. It
fucking won't. It fucking won't. It fucking won't. It
fucking won't. It fucking won't. It fucking won't. It
fucking won't. It fucking won't. It fucking won't. It
fucking won't. It fucking won't. It fucking won't. It
fucking won't. It fucking won't. It fucking won't. It
fucking won't. It fucking won't. It fucking won't. It
fucking won't. It fucking won't. It fucking won't. It
fucking won't. It fucking won't. It fucking won't. It
fucking won't. It fucking won't. It fucking won't. It
fucking won't. It fucking won't. It fucking won't. It
fucking won't. It fucking won't. It fucking won't. It
fucking won't. It fucking won't. It fucking won't. It
fucking won't. It fucking won't. It fucking won't. It
fucking won't. It fucking won't. It fucking won't. It
fucking won't. It fucking won't. It fucking won't. It
fucking won't. It fucking won't. It fucking won't. It
fucking won't. It fucking won't. It fucking won't. It
fucking won't. It fucking won't. It fucking won't. It
fucking won't. It fucking won't. It fucking won't. It
fucking won't. It fucking won't. It fucking won't. It
fucking won't. It fucking won't. It fucking won't. It
fucking won't. It fucking won't. It fucking won't. It
fucking won't. It fucking won't. It fucking won't. It
fucking won't. It fucking won't. It fucking won't. It
fucking won't. It fucking won't. It fucking won't. It
fucking won't. It fucking won't. It fucking won't. It
fucking won't. It fucking won't. It fucking won't. It
fucking won't. It fucking won't. It fucking won't. It

fucking won't. It fucking won't. It fucking won't. It
fucking won't. It fucking won't. It fucking won't. It
fucking won't. It fucking won't. It fucking won't. It
fucking won't. It fucking won't. It fucking won't. It
fucking won't. It fucking won't. It fucking won't. It
fucking won't. It fucking won't. It fucking won't. It
fucking won't. It fucking won't. It fucking won't. It
fucking won't. It fucking won't. It fucking won't. It
fucking won't. It fucking won't. It fucking won't. It
fucking won't. It fucking won't. It fucking won't. It
fucking won't. It fucking won't. It fucking won't. It
fucking won't. It fucking won't. It fucking won't. It
fucking won't. It fucking won't. It fucking won't. It
fucking won't. It fucking won't. It fucking won't. It
fucking won't. It fucking won't. It fucking won't. It
fucking won't. It fucking won't. It fucking won't. It
fucking won't. It fucking won't. It fucking won't. It
fucking won't. It fucking won't. It fucking won't. It
fucking won't. It fucking won't. It fucking won't. It
fucking won't. It fucking won't. It fucking won't. It
fucking won't. It fucking won't. It fucking won't. It
fucking won't. It fucking won't. It fucking won't. It
fucking won't. It fucking won't. It fucking won't. It
fucking won't. It fucking won't. It fucking won't. It
fucking won't. It fucking won't. It fucking won't. It
fucking won't. It fucking won't. It fucking won't. It
fucking won't. It fucking won't. It fucking won't. It
fucking won't. It fucking won't. It fucking won't. It
fucking won't. It fucking won't. It fucking won't. It
fucking won't. It fucking won't. It fucking won't. It

fucking won't. It fucking won't. It fucking won't. It
fucking won't. It fucking won't. It fucking won't. It
fucking won't. It fucking won't. It fucking won't. It
fucking won't. It fucking won't. It fucking won't. It
fucking won't. It fucking won't. It fucking won't. It
fucking won't. It fucking won't. It fucking won't. It
fucking won't. It fucking won't. It fucking won't. It
fucking won't. It fucking won't. It fucking won't. It
fucking won't. It fucking won't. It fucking won't. It
fucking won't. It fucking won't. It fucking won't. It
fucking won't. It fucking won't. It fucking won't. It
fucking won't. It fucking won't. It fucking won't. It
fucking won't. It fucking won't. It fucking won't. It
fucking won't. It fucking won't. It fucking won't. It
fucking won't. It fucking won't. It fucking won't. It
fucking won't. It fucking won't. It fucking won't. It
fucking won't. It fucking won't. It fucking won't. It
fucking won't. It fucking won't. It fucking won't. It
fucking won't. It fucking won't. It fucking won't. It
fucking won't. It fucking won't. It fucking won't. It
fucking won't. It fucking won't. It fucking won't. It
fucking won't. It fucking won't. It fucking won't. It
fucking won't. It fucking won't. It fucking won't. It
fucking won't. It fucking won't. It fucking won't. It
fucking won't. It fucking won't. It fucking won't. It
fucking won't. It fucking won't. It fucking won't. It
fucking won't. It fucking won't. It fucking won't. It
fucking won't. It fucking won't. It fucking won't. It
fucking won't. It fucking won't. It fucking won't. It
fucking won't. It fucking won't. It fucking won't. It

fucking won't. It fucking won't. It fucking won't. It
fucking won't. It fucking won't. It fucking won't. It
fucking won't. It fucking won't. It fucking won't. It
fucking won't. It fucking won't. It fucking won't. It
fucking won't. It fucking won't. It fucking won't. It
fucking won't. It fucking won't. It fucking won't. It
fucking won't. It fucking won't. It fucking won't. It
fucking won't. It fucking won't. It fucking won't. It
fucking won't. It fucking won't. It fucking won't. It
fucking won't. It fucking won't. It fucking won't. It
fucking won't. It fucking won't. It fucking won't. It
fucking won't. It fucking won't. It fucking won't. It
fucking won't. It fucking won't. It fucking won't. It
fucking won't. It fucking won't. It fucking won't. It
fucking won't. It fucking won't. It fucking won't. It
fucking won't. It fucking won't. It fucking won't. It
fucking won't. It fucking won't. It fucking won't. It
fucking won't. It fucking won't. It fucking won't. It
fucking won't. It fucking won't. It fucking won't. It
fucking won't. It fucking won't. It fucking won't. It
fucking won't. It fucking won't. It fucking won't. It
fucking won't. It fucking won't. It fucking won't. It
fucking won't. It fucking won't. It fucking won't. It
fucking won't. It fucking won't. It fucking won't. It
fucking won't. It fucking won't. It fucking won't. It
fucking won't. It fucking won't. It fucking won't. It
fucking won't. It fucking won't. It fucking won't. It
fucking won't. It fucking won't. It fucking won't. It
fucking won't. It fucking won't. It fucking won't. It
fucking won't. It fucking won't. It fucking won't. It

fucking won't. It fucking won't. It fucking won't. It
fucking won't. It fucking won't. It fucking won't. It
fucking won't. It fucking won't. It fucking won't. It
fucking won't. It fucking won't. It fucking won't. It
fucking won't. It fucking won't. It fucking won't. It
fucking won't. It fucking won't. It fucking won't. It
fucking won't. It fucking won't. It fucking won't. It
fucking won't. It fucking won't. It fucking won't. It
fucking won't. It fucking won't. It fucking won't. It
fucking won't. It fucking won't. It fucking won't. It
fucking won't. It fucking won't. It fucking won't. It
fucking won't. It fucking won't. It fucking won't. It
fucking won't. It fucking won't. It fucking won't. It
fucking won't. It fucking won't. It fucking won't. It
fucking won't. It fucking won't. It fucking won't. It
fucking won't. It fucking won't. It fucking won't. It
fucking won't. It fucking won't. It fucking won't. It
fucking won't. It fucking won't. It fucking won't. It
fucking won't. It fucking won't. It fucking won't. It
fucking won't. It fucking won't. It fucking won't. It
fucking won't. It fucking won't. It fucking won't. It
fucking won't. It fucking won't. It fucking won't. It
fucking won't. It fucking won't. It fucking won't. It
fucking won't. It fucking won't. It fucking won't. It
fucking won't. It fucking won't. It fucking won't. It
fucking won't. It fucking won't. It fucking won't. It
fucking won't. It fucking won't. It fucking won't. It
fucking won't. It fucking won't. It fucking won't. It
fucking won't. It fucking won't. It fucking won't. It
fucking won't. It fucking won't. It fucking won't. It

fucking won't. It fucking won't. It fucking won't. It
fucking won't. It fucking won't. It fucking won't. It
fucking won't. It fucking won't. It fucking won't. It
fucking won't. It fucking won't. It fucking won't. It
fucking won't. It fucking won't. It fucking won't. It
fucking won't. It fucking won't. It fucking won't. It
fucking won't. It fucking won't. It fucking won't. It
fucking won't. It fucking won't. It fucking won't. It
fucking won't. It fucking won't. It fucking won't. It
fucking won't. It fucking won't. It fucking won't. It
fucking won't. It fucking won't. It fucking won't. It
fucking won't. It fucking won't. It fucking won't. It
fucking won't. It fucking won't. It fucking won't. It
fucking won't. It fucking won't. It fucking won't. It
fucking won't. It fucking won't. It fucking won't. It
fucking won't. It fucking won't. It fucking won't. It
fucking won't. It fucking won't. It fucking won't. It
fucking won't. It fucking won't. It fucking won't. It
fucking won't. It fucking won't. It fucking won't. It
fucking won't. It fucking won't. It fucking won't. It
fucking won't. It fucking won't. It fucking won't. It
fucking won't. It fucking won't. It fucking won't. It
fucking won't. It fucking won't. It fucking won't. It
fucking won't. It fucking won't. It fucking won't. It
fucking won't. It fucking won't. It fucking won't. It
fucking won't. It fucking won't. It fucking won't. It
fucking won't. It fucking won't. It fucking won't. It
fucking won't. It fucking won't. It fucking won't. It
fucking won't. It fucking won't. It fucking won't. It
fucking won't. It fucking won't. It fucking won't. It
fucking won't. It fucking won't. It fucking won't. It

fucking won't. It fucking won't. It fucking won't. It
fucking won't. It fucking won't. It fucking won't. It
fucking won't. It fucking won't. It fucking won't. It
fucking won't. It fucking won't. It fucking won't. It
fucking won't. It fucking won't. It fucking won't. It
fucking won't. It fucking won't. It fucking won't. It
fucking won't. It fucking won't. It fucking won't. It
fucking won't. It fucking won't. It fucking won't. It
fucking won't. It fucking won't. It fucking won't. It
fucking won't. It fucking won't. It fucking won't. It
fucking won't. It fucking won't. It fucking won't. It
fucking won't. It fucking won't. It fucking won't. It
fucking won't. It fucking won't. It fucking won't. It
fucking won't. It fucking won't. It fucking won't. It
fucking won't. It fucking won't. It fucking won't. It
fucking won't. It fucking won't. It fucking won't. It
fucking won't. It fucking won't. It fucking won't. It
fucking won't. It fucking won't. It fucking won't. It
fucking won't. It fucking won't. It fucking won't. It
fucking won't. It fucking won't. It fucking won't. It
fucking won't. It fucking won't. It fucking won't. It
fucking won't. It fucking won't. It fucking won't. It
fucking won't. It fucking won't. It fucking won't. It
fucking won't. It fucking won't. It fucking won't. It
fucking won't. It fucking won't. It fucking won't. It
fucking won't. It fucking won't. It fucking won't. It
fucking won't. It fucking won't. It fucking won't. It
fucking won't. It fucking won't. It fucking won't. It
fucking won't. It fucking won't. It fucking won't. It
fucking won't. It fucking won't. It fucking won't. It

fucking won't. It fucking won't. It fucking won't. It
fucking won't. It fucking won't. It fucking won't. It
fucking won't. It fucking won't. It fucking won't. It
fucking won't. It fucking won't. It fucking won't. It
fucking won't. It fucking won't. It fucking won't. It
fucking won't. It fucking won't. It fucking won't. It
fucking won't. It fucking won't. It fucking won't. It
fucking won't. It fucking won't. It fucking won't. It
fucking won't. It fucking won't. It fucking won't. It
fucking won't. It fucking won't. It fucking won't. It
fucking won't. It fucking won't. It fucking won't. It
fucking won't. It fucking won't. It fucking won't. It
fucking won't. It fucking won't. It fucking won't. It
fucking won't. It fucking won't. It fucking won't. It
fucking won't. It fucking won't. It fucking won't. It
fucking won't. It fucking won't. It fucking won't. It
fucking won't. It fucking won't. It fucking won't. It
fucking won't. It fucking won't. It fucking won't. It
fucking won't. It fucking won't. It fucking won't. It
fucking won't. It fucking won't. It fucking won't. It
fucking won't. It fucking won't. It fucking won't. It
fucking won't. It fucking won't. It fucking won't. It
fucking won't. It fucking won't. It fucking won't. It
fucking won't. It fucking won't. It fucking won't. It
fucking won't. It fucking won't. It fucking won't. It
fucking won't. It fucking won't. It fucking won't. It
fucking won't. It fucking won't. It fucking won't. It
fucking won't. It fucking won't. It fucking won't. It
fucking won't. It fucking won't. It fucking won't. It

Made in the USA
Middletown, DE
30 July 2021

44627060R00149